TOEFLテスト大戦略シリーズ Ⅳ

TOEFL ITP® テスト リーディング 問題攻略

旺文社 編

TOEFL and TOEFL ITP are registered trademarks of Educational Testing Service (ETS).
This publication is not endorsed or approved by ETS.

はじめに

TOEFL (Test of English as a Foreign Language) テストは，主にアメリカなど英語圏へ留学する際に必要とされる試験です。アメリカのテスト開発機関ETS (Educational Testing Service) によって制作されています。本書で扱うTOEFL ITP (Institutional Testing Program) テストは，ETSが提供する団体向けのテストです。ETSによると，TOEFL ITPテストは，世界50か国，2,500以上の団体で実施され，受験者数は80万人を超えています。日本においても，高等学校，専門学校，短期大学，大学，企業など500以上の団体で，英語力の測定，大学のクラス分け，大学院入試，成績評価，単位認定，海外留学の選考試験などとして利用されています。

本書はTOEFL ITPテストのリーディングセクションに特化した問題集です。「攻略ポイント＋練習問題」「Practice Tests」「重要語彙リスト」の3つのCHAPTERで構成されています。

●CHAPTER 1「攻略ポイント＋練習問題」
ETS公認トレーナーである五十峰聖先生が，よく出題される10の問題パターンとポイントを解説しています。

●CHAPTER 2「Practice Tests」
模擬試験を3回分収録しています。TOEFLテストに精通した河野太一先生が，問題を吟味しています。

●CHAPTER3「重要語彙リスト」
本書に掲載されているパッセージの中で，特に覚えておきたい単語をまとめています。

読者の皆さんにとって，本書がTOEFL ITPテストのリーディング力強化にお役に立てることを願っています。最後に，本書を刊行するにあたり多大なご尽力をいただきました五十峰聖先生(CHAPTER 1「攻略ポイント」ご執筆)と河野太一先生(問題校閲，CHAPTER 3ご執筆)に，深く感謝申し上げます。

旺文社

もくじ

はじめに
本書の利用法 ……………………………………………… 6
TOEFL ITP テスト Information ………………………… 8

CHAPTER 1　攻略ポイント＋練習問題

Lesson 1　Factual Questions ……………………………… 14
Lesson 2　Negative Factual Questions ………………… 24
Lesson 3　Vocabulary Questions ………………………… 34
Lesson 4　Reference Questions ………………………… 44
Lesson 5　Inference Questions …………………………… 54
Lesson 6　Purpose Questions …………………………… 64
Lesson 7　Main Idea Questions ………………………… 74
Lesson 8　Where Questions ……………………………… 84
Lesson 9　Conclusion Questions ………………………… 94
Lesson 10　Other Questions ……………………………… 104

CHAPTER 2　Practice Tests

Practice Test 1　問題　解答・解説 …… 116

Practice Test 2　問題　解答・解説 …… 158

Practice Test 3　問題　解答・解説 …… 197

CHAPTER 3　重要語彙リスト

重要語彙リスト …………………………………… 238

Practice Tests 解答用紙 …………………………… 255

攻略ポイント執筆●五十峰　聖
桜美林大学芸術文化学群特任講師。ウエストバージニア大学より高等教育経営学修士号を取得。ETS TOEFL ITP® Teacher Development Workshop Facilitator（公認 TOEFL トレーナー）として日本各地の大学・高校、自治体、政府機関、企業などを対象に TOEFL ワークショップを行う。

問題校閲・重要語彙リスト執筆●河野太一
河野塾塾長。早稲田大学政治経済学部中退。テンプル大学ジャパンキャンパス卒業（心理学専攻）。テンプル大学ジャパンキャンパス大学院卒業（英語教授法専攻）。大手留学準備校にて教務主任を務めたのち、独立。河野塾にて幅広い層の生徒に TOEFL/IELTS/GMAT/GRE 対策を指導している。TOEFL iBT 116 点。英語発音指導士®。

編集協力●株式会社シー・レップス、Nadia McKechnie、合同会社ミノス・イングリッシュ、田中晶子、
　　　　　株式会社 CPI Japan
装丁デザイン●内津　剛（及川真咲デザイン事務所）
本文デザイン●尾引美代

本書の利用法

本書は,「攻略ポイント+練習問題」「Practice Tests」「重要語彙リスト」から構成されています。

『攻略ポイント+練習問題』

●例題を通して,10の出題パターンの「解き方」と「ポイント」を確認しましょう。また,普段の学習に生かせる「学習アドバイス」もぜひ参考にしてください。

●次に練習問題に挑戦してみましょう。

『Practice Tests』

本番と同じ形式の模擬試験を3回分収録しています。解答用紙は巻末にあります。学習したことが身についているか，苦手な問題はないか，確認しましょう。

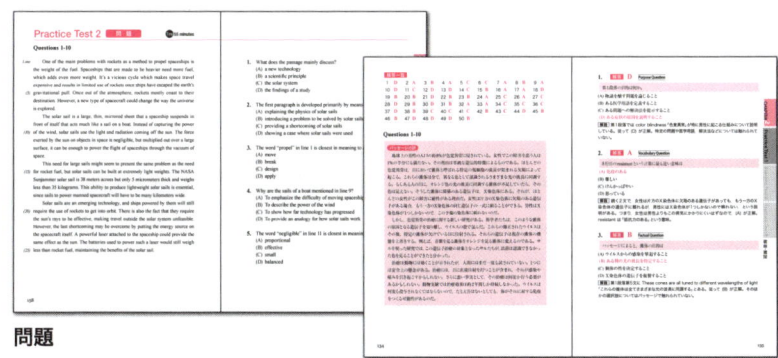

問題

解答・解説

※Directionは，Practice Test 1にのみ収録しています。

『重要語彙リスト』

本書のパッセージで学習した，ぜひ覚えておきたい単語をまとめています。

7

TOEFL ITPテスト Information

TOEFL ITPテストとは

　TOEFLテストは，Test of English as a Foreign Languageの略で，主に北米の大学や大学院で学ぶことを志願する際に，英語を母語としない人の英語能力を測定するテストです。アメリカの教育研究機関ETS (Educational Testing Service) によって制作されています。TOEFL ITPとは，ETSが提供する団体向けテストプログラムです。テストは過去のTOEFL PBTテスト（ペーパー形式）の問題を利用しており，Level 1とLevel 2 の2つのレベルが設けられています。日本においても，大学，高等学校，企業など，全国500以上のさまざまな団体に利用されています。本書はスコアがTOEFLテストと高い相関関係にある一般的なLevel 1のテストに対応しています。

※2024年8月現在の情報です。受験の際はETS Japanホームページで最新情報をご確認ください。

ITP (Level1) の構成

テストの各セクションの構成です。解答方法は，4つの選択肢の中から1つを選び，マークシートをぬりつぶします。

セクション	パート	設問数	内容	解答時間
1 Listening Comprehension（リスニング）	Part A	30	短い会話を聞き，質問に答える	約35分
	Part B	8	2つの長い会話を聞き，それぞれいくつかの質問に答える	
	Part C	12	3つの長いトークや講義の一部を聞き，それぞれいくつかの質問に答える	
2 Structure and Written Expression（文法）	Structure	15	空所のある短い文章を読み，空所に入る語句を選ぶ	25分
	Written Expression	25	短い文章の4箇所の下線部のうち，誤りのあるものを選ぶ	
3 Reading Comprehension（リーディング）	Reading	50	5つのパッセージを読み，それぞれいくつかの質問に答える	55分

合計　約115分

ITPのスコア

スコアは，各セクションごとに以下のスコア範囲で算出されます。全体スコアは最低310点〜最高677点になります。結果は実施団体宛に送付されます。

セクション		スコアの範囲
1	Listening Comprehension	31〜68
2	Structure and Written Expression	31〜68
3	Reading Comprehension	31〜67
	全体	310〜677

TOEFL ITPテスト Information

iBTとの違い

TOEFLテストには，ITPとiBTという2つのタイプがあります。特に用途，試験形式や出題されるセクションが大きく異なりますので，それぞれの違いを理解しておきましょう。

	ITP	iBT
用途	通常，留学で求められる公式なスコアとしては使えないが，大学のクラス分け，大学院入試，交換留学の学内選抜，iBT受験の準備などに広く使われる	主に北米を中心とした英語圏への留学に必要な公式スコアとして使われる
個人・団体	団体受験のみ （個人では申し込めない）	個人で受験 （受験者が自分で申し込む）
形式	ペーパー版／デジタル版	PC
問題作成	かつて使われたPBTの問題を利用	新たに作成
セクション	リスニング／文法／リーディング	リーディング／リスニング／スピーキング／ライティング ＊リーディング・リスニングは内容や形式がITPとは異なる
時間	約2時間	約2時間
スコア	310〜677 （各セクション31〜67または68）	0〜120 （各セクション0〜30）

問い合わせ先

英語教育関係者，高等学校・大学教職員，国際交流団体・企業関係者など，ご自身の学生・生徒・社員などに対してTOEFL ITP実施をご検討の方は，下記よりお問い合わせください。個人でのお申し込みはできませんのでご注意ください。

ETS Japan合同会社
TOEFL® テスト日本事務局
ホームページ：https://www.etsjapan.jp/

CHAPTER 1
攻略のポイント＋練習問題

- **Lesson 1** Factual Questions ⋯⋯⋯⋯ 14
- **Lesson 2** Negative Factual Questions ⋯ 24
- **Lesson 3** Vocabulary Questions ⋯⋯⋯ 34
- **Lesson 4** Reference Questions ⋯⋯⋯⋯ 44
- **Lesson 5** Inference Questions ⋯⋯⋯⋯ 54
- **Lesson 6** Purpose Questions ⋯⋯⋯⋯⋯ 64
- **Lesson 7** Main Idea Questions ⋯⋯⋯⋯ 74
- **Lesson 8** Where Questions ⋯⋯⋯⋯⋯ 84
- **Lesson 9** Conclusion Questions ⋯⋯⋯ 94
- **Lesson 10** Other Questions ⋯⋯⋯⋯⋯ 104

Lesson 1　Factual Questions
事実を問う問題

例題

Line　　Plasma is one of the four states of matter along with liquid, solid, and gas. It forms when gasses are exposed to either extreme heat or a strong electrical charge. The electrons in atoms separate from their nuclei and float freely between them. This makes plasma react to electric and magnetic forces, unlike
(5)　gas. Stars are made of plasma, making it the most common form of matter in the universe. On earth, we see plasma in forms such as lightning, aurora, and sparks from static electricity. Plasma is useful in industry as it can produce temperatures far higher than fire.

① Plasma
② forms

According to the passage, plasma can be created by
(A)　separating the electrons found in a solid
(B)　running an electrical current through a liquid
(C)　heating a gas to an extremely high temperature
(D)　halting evaporation between a liquid and a gas

全訳

　プラズマは液体，固体，気体とともに物質の4つの状態の1つである。それは，気体が高熱もしくは高電荷にさらされたときにつくられる。原子の中の電子が核から分離して，それらの間を自由に浮遊する。これによって，プラズマは気体とは違い，電力や磁力に反応する。星はプラズマでできていて，そのためにプラズマは宇宙で最も一般的な物質の形態になっている。地上では，われわれは稲妻やオーロラ，それに静電気が起こす火花の形でプラズマを目にする。プラズマは火よりもはるかに高い温度をつくり出すことができるので，産業の役に立つ。

　パッセージによると，プラズマをつくることができるのは
　(A)　固体の中に見つけられる電子を分離させることによって
　(B)　液体に電流を流すことによって
　(C)　気体を熱して極端に高い温度にすることによって
　(D)　液体と気体との間で蒸発を止めることによって

①設問文の plasma に相当するキーワード　②設問文の created に相当するキーワード

> [解き方]

パッセージで述べられる事実についての問題です。まず，設問文の中からキーワードを設定するところから始めます。トピックでもある plasma，そしてより細かく正解の根拠を特定する2つ目のキーワード，created に注目します。そこでパッセージの中で「プラズマがつくられること」に関する記述を探しながら読み進めます。すると第2文に It (= plasma) forms とあるので，ここが該当する箇所です。あとは文のそれ以降の内容で「気体が高熱もしくは高電荷にさらされたとき」と説明があるので，それに内容が一番近い(C)を選びます。

ここがポイント
1. まず設問文から読む。
2. 設問文内のキーワードを決める。
3. より細かい情報を探せるように，必要であればキーワードを2つ以上設定する。
4. パッセージからキーワードに該当する箇所を探す。
5. パッセージの情報に一番近い選択肢を選ぶ。

学習アドバイス

事実を問う問題は，パッセージの一部に記述されている情報を探し読む問題です。あてもなく読み始めるのではなく，「何を探すべきか」をきちんと意識してから読み始めるようにしましょう。そのためには日ごろから「設問文から読む」「必要な情報を探す」ことを心がけましょう。

Passage 1

Line   In the mid-19th century, the United States experienced its first immigration boom. This caused a backlash across the country and many were fearful that the nation would be overrun with European immigrants. This led to the formation of the American Party, which ran on a nativist platform.
(5) The party was against immigration in general but more specifically against Catholic immigration. Many of the immigrants were Irish Catholics, and the American Party was worried they would vote as a single, large entity. The party was very secretive, which earned them the nickname the Know-Nothing Party. The American Party was popular enough to win a state in the 1856
(10) presidential election, but dissolved shortly after that. Besides anti-immigration, its members didn't have much in common and disagreed over multiple issues, most notably slavery.

The passage states that the American Party was against Catholic immigrants because they thought Catholics would
(A) all vote the same way
(B) set up churches in cities
(C) vote against slavery
(D) try to install a monarchy

全訳

　19世紀半ばに，アメリカは最初の移民ブームを経験した。このため，国中で反発が生じ，国がヨーロッパからの移民で溢れかえるのではないかと多くの人が恐れた。その結果，移民排斥の綱領を進めるアメリカ党が誕生した。この党は移民全般に反対だったが，特にカトリックの移民に反対だった。移民の多くはアイルランド出身のカトリック教徒で，アメリカ党は彼らが1つの大きな集合体として投票するのではないかと心配した。この党は大変な秘密主義だったため，ノウ・ナッシング（何も知らない）党とあだ名がついたほどだった。アメリカ党は1856年の大統領選挙において，1つの州で勝利を得るほどの人気はあったが，そのすぐ後に解党した。党員たちには移民反対以外に共通点があまりなく，複数の問題，とりわけ奴隷制度において意見が分かれていた。

　パッセージが述べるには，アメリカ党がカトリックの移民に反対していた理由は，彼らはカトリック教徒たちが

(A) 全員が同じように投票すると思ったから
(B) 町々に教会を設立すると思ったから
(C) 奴隷制度に反対の投票をすると思ったから
(D) 君主制を敷こうとすると思ったから

解説

　第4文にアメリカ党が特にカトリックの移民に反対していたとある。その理由は続く第5文で述べられており，the American Party was worried they would vote as a single, large entity「アメリカ党は彼らが1つの大きな集合体として投票するのではないかと心配した」とある。従って (A) が正解。a single, large entity は直訳すると，「1つの大きな本体，実体」という意味で，「1つの大きな集団として投票する」，つまり「同じように投票する」ということ。

Passage 2

Line   Motor racing is popular all over the world, but the most popular form in North America is stock car racing. Stock car racing uses generally-sold models that have been heavily modified. The origins of stock car racing are actually a product of the legal history of the United States. In the early 20th century
(5) there was a huge market for illegally produced liquor. Taxes were so high on regulated spirits that many people bought cheaper illegal liquor. Bootleg liquor manufacturers modified their cars to carry more of their product for deliveries and to outrun and outmaneuver law enforcement vehicles. The early days of stock car racing included multiple drivers, mechanics, and team owners who
(10) made most of their money from the illegal liquor trade. Eventually liquor laws were relaxed and legal distilling became more lucrative. Still, the popular sport of stock car racing remains as a testament to this bygone era.

Why was illegal liquor so popular in the early 20th century?
(A) It was of better quality than legal liquor.
(B) It was endorsed by popular race car drivers.
(C) It was less expensive than legal liquor.
(D) It was illegal to make liquor at the time.

> **全訳**

　自動車レースは世界中で人気があるが，北米で最も人気のある形態はストックカーレースである。ストックカーレースは，大幅に改造された，一般に売られている車種を使う。ストックカーレースの発祥は，実はアメリカの法律史の産物である。20世紀初期には違法に製造した酒類の巨大な市場があった。規制された蒸留酒の税金があまりに高かったので，多くの人がより安い違法な酒類を買った。密造酒の生産者は自分たちの車を改造して，より多くの製品を配達でき，また取り締まりの車を振り切って出し抜けるようにした。初期のストックカーレースには，ドライバー，自動車修理工，それに自分たちの富のほとんどを違法の酒類の取引で築いたチームオーナーたちが何人もかかわっていた。やがて酒に関する法律は緩められ，合法的な蒸留の方がもうかるようになった。それでも，人気の高いスポーツであるストックカーレースは，この過ぎ去った時代の証として残っているのである。

　違法な酒類はなぜ20世紀初期にそれほど人気があったのか。
　(A) 合法的な酒類よりも品質が高かったから。
　(B) 人気のあるレースドライバーたちが推奨していたから。
　(C) 合法的な酒類よりも値段が安かったから。
　(D) そのときには酒類を作るのが違法だったから。

> **解説**

　違法な酒類については第4文以降に言及がある。第5文には Taxes were so high on regulated spirits that many people bought cheaper illegal liquor.「規制された蒸留酒の税金があまりに高かったので，多くの人がより安い違法な酒類を買った」とあり，この内容に合う (C) が正解。パッセージの cheaper を選択肢では less expensive と言い換えている。

Passage 3

Line Patents are one of the ways governments promote innovation. If someone creates a new invention they can patent it and prevent others from copying their idea and making money off it. Ideally this provides incentive for companies and individuals to create new useful technologies since they are
(5) guaranteed the exclusive rights to exploit their inventions.

However, one quirk of patents is that they don't require the patent holder to actually make the invention. Patent holders can simply file a design with the Patent Office with no intention of following through on manufacturing it. They can then either sell the rights to a company to make the invention
(10) or sue a company that does so without their permission. Patent holders who engage in this type of activity are known as "patent trolls" and have become a large problem in recent years. The number of patents granted each year has nearly doubled since the year 2000, and some say many of these are vaguely worded attempts to patent something so broad that companies producing
(15) existing products could be sued for technically violating the new patents. Such actions actually stifle innovation by letting unscrupulous patents holders hold companies hostage.

1. Patents encourage innovation by
   (A) giving money to people who create new inventions
   (B) providing education to engineers trying to invent things
   (C) cataloging and displaying the designs for new inventions
   (D) stopping others from profiting on someone's invention

2. Patent trolls make money off other companies making their inventions because
   (A) patent holders aren't required to produce their inventions themselves
   (B) patents do not apply to companies that are in different countries
   (C) companies have to pay extra to file patents similar to previous ones
   (D) inventors receive a tax break for each patent that they hold

CHAPTER 1 Lesson 1 Factual Questions

全訳

　特許は政府が革新を促進する方法の1つである。誰かが新しい発明品を作り出すと，彼らはそれを特許にして，ほかの人がそのアイディアをまねしてそれで金もうけをするのを防ぐことができる。理想を言えば，企業や個人は，自分たちの発明を利用する独占的な権利を保障されるのだから，これによって彼らは新しくて有益な技術を作り出そうというやる気を出すはずである。

　しかし，特許の皮肉な点の1つは，特許権者は実際にその発明品を作る必要がないということだ。特許権者は，それを製造までやり通すつもりがなくても，特許局に考案を届け出ることができるのである。そうすれば彼らは，発明品を作る権利をある会社に売ったり，彼らの許可なしにそのようなことをする会社を訴えたりできるのだ。こういった種類の活動に従事する特許権者たちは「特許荒らし」として知られ，近年大きな問題になっている。毎年与えられる特許権の数は2000年以降ほぼ倍になっていて，これらの多くはあまりに広範囲な特許を取るための漠然とした表現による試みだと言われている。これにより既存の製品を作る会社が，新しい特許を技術的に侵害したとして訴えられる可能性さえあるのである。このような行動は，不謹慎な特許権者たちが会社を人質に取るのを許すことによって，実際に革新の息の根を止めてしまうのだ。

1. 特許が革新を促進する方法は
   (A) 新しい発明品を作り出す人々に金を与えること
   (B) ものを発明しようとしている技術者たちに教育を施すこと
   (C) 新しい発明品の考案の目録を作ったり展示したりすること
   (D) ほかの人々が誰かの発明品でもうけることを防ぐこと

2. 特許荒らしたちが自分たちの発明品を作るほかの会社から金をもうけられる理由は
   (A) 特許権者は自分たち自身で発明品を製造することを要求されないから
   (B) 特許は他国にある会社には適用されないから
   (C) 会社が以前の特許に似たものを申請する場合には余分に払わなければならないから
   (D) 発明者たちは彼らが持っているそれぞれの特許に対して税金控除を受けるから

解説

1. 第1段落第1文が Patents are one of the ways governments promote innovation.「特許は政府が革新を促進する方法の1つである」で始まっているので，その内容を詳しく見ていくと，特許を取得することで prevent others from copying their idea and making money off it「ほかの人がそのアイディアをまねしてそれで金もうけをするのを防ぐ」（第2文）とあり，これが provides incentive「やる気を与える」（第3文）ことにつながることがわかる。従って (D) が正解。

2. patent trolls については第2段落第1〜3文に説明がある。特許権者は「実際にその発明品を作る必要がない」（第1文）が，「特許局に考案を届け出る」ことが可能で（第2文），それにより，「発明品を作る権利をある会社に売ったり，彼らの許可なしにそのようなことをする会社を訴えたりできる」（第3文）とある。この内容に合う (A) が正解。

Passage 4

Line   The Earth's magnetic field is a result of electrically charged metals inside the earth's molten core. This field is useful in many ways to humans, most obviously in the realm of navigation. The positive and negative axis of the magnetic field line up nearly with the true north and south poles. This is what
(5) allows compasses to work: The magnetically charged point of a compass lines up with the north magnetic pole.

Though this magnetic field has remained constant throughout human history, it has not always been this way. Metallic rocks millions of years old have crystalline structures that point toward either the south pole or the north
(10) pole. By amassing and comparing them, scientists have found that the polarity of the Earth's magnetic field has changed hundreds of times over its history. Each period between switches is known as a chron and can last anywhere between 10,000,000 years and 100,000 years.

No one has figured out if there is any sort of pattern to how long chrons
(15) last, or in fact what causes these switches in the first place. The current chron has lasted 780,000 years, but there is no way to determine if the earth is soon due for another reversal. Even if it is, the flip can take up to 10,000 years to carry out, making it difficult to tell when it has started.

1. According to the passage, the earth's magnetic field is caused by
(A) metals deep inside the Earth
(B) the Earth's rotation
(C) lava flows under the ocean bed
(D) large ore deposits near the poles

2. According to the passage, what is a chron?
(A) A unit of measurement for the strength of a magnetic field
(B) The period the magnetic pole stays oriented in one direction
(C) The method of using a compass for navigation
(D) The amount of time it takes for a magnetic field to reverse

全訳

　地球の磁場は，地球の溶融中心核の中にある帯電した金属によるものである。この磁場は人間にとっていろいろな場面で有用で，特にナビゲーションの分野において最も明らかである。磁場の正と負の軸は，実際の北極と南極とほぼ並んでいる。このおかげで，方位磁針が使えるのだ。方位磁針の磁気を帯びた針の先が北磁極と並ぶからである。

　この磁場は人類の歴史を通して一定であったが，常にそうであったわけではない。何百年もの時を経た金属を含む岩石は，南極か北極のどちらかを指す結晶質の構造体を持っている。それらを収集して比較することによって，科学者たちは，地球の磁場の極性はその歴史において何百回も変化してきたことを発見した。変化の間の期間はクロンとして知られていて，その長さは10万年から1,000万年の間である。

　クロンが続く長さにパターンのようなものはあるのか，また実は，何がそもそもこれらの変化を起こしているのかは，分かっていない。現在のクロンは78万年続いているが，地球がまもなく再び逆転する予定であるかどうかを決める方法はない。もしそうだとしても，逆転が起こるには最長で1万年かかるので，それがいつ始まったのかを判断するのは難しい。

1. パッセージによると，地球の磁場の原因は
   (A) 地球の地下深くにある金属である
   (B) 地球の自転である
   (C) 海底の下を流れる溶岩である
   (D) 極地近くにある大きな鉱床である

2. パッセージによると，クロンとは何か。
   (A) 地場の強さのための測定単位
   (B) 磁極が1つの方向に向いたままでいる期間
   (C) ナビゲーションのために方位磁針を使う方法
   (D) 磁場が逆転するのにかかる時間の量

解説

1. 第1段落第1文に The Earth's magnetic field is a result of electrically charged metals inside the earth's molten core.「地球の磁場は，地球の溶融中心核の中にある帯電した金属によるものである」とあるので，(A) が正解。パッセージの a result of が問題文では caused by に，inside the earth's molten core が (A) では deep inside the Earth に言い換えられている。

2. 第2段落最終文に Each period between switches is known as a chron「変化の間の期間はクロンとして知られている」とあるので，その前の内容を詳しく見ていくと，第2文に金属を含む岩石が point toward either the south pole or the north pole「南極か北極のどちらかを指す」とある。switches とはこの指す方向の変化を指し，period between switches とは「変化と変化の間の期間」，つまりどちらか一方の方向に向かっている期間だと考えられる。(B) が正解。

Lesson 2 Negative Factual Questions
事実と異なるものを問う問題

例題

Line
　　Around the 1950's, a style of modern architecture known as Googie gained traction in the United States, particularly in Los Angeles. Googie architecture was modern, but instead of taking cues from contemporary art and design, it looked to the future①. Visual motifs such as space ships, atomic models and
(5) starbursts② were used, and made Googie buildings look like they were out of science fiction③. The style was mostly used for "low class" buildings such as car washes and fast food restaurants, buildings that tend to be demolished after a couple of decades. Still, there are a few remaining specimens of the style to be found in Southern California.

　According to the passage, all of the following are characteristics of Googie architecture EXCEPT
　(A) that it used starbursts as one of its visual motifs
　(B) that its design was rather futuristic
　(C) that its buildings resembled ones from science fiction
　(D) that it was influenced by contemporary art

全訳

　1950年代ごろ，「グーギー」として知られる近代建築スタイルが，アメリカ，特にロサンゼルスで勢いを増した。グーギー建築は近代的であったが，現代芸術や現代デザインからヒントを得る代わりに，未来を見据えていた。宇宙船，原子モデル，星形などの視覚的なモチーフが使われ，グーギーの建物を空想科学小説から出てきたかのように見せていた。このスタイルはほとんどの場合，洗車場やファストフードレストランなどの「低級」建造物，20〜30年で取り壊されるような建造物に使われた。それでも，南カリフォルニアにはこのスタイルの残留する見本がいくつか残っている。

　パッセージによると，次のうちグーギー建築の特徴でないものは
　(A) 星形を視覚的なモチーフの1つとして使ったこと
　(B) そのデザインがやや未来的であったこと
　(C) その建物は空想科学小説のものに似ていたこと
　(D) 現代美術から影響を受けたこと

①選択肢 (B) の根拠　②選択肢 (A) の根拠　③選択肢 (C) の根拠

解き方

パッセージでは述べられていないものを答える問題です。まず設問文のキーワードであるcharacteristics of Googie architecture「グーギー建築の特徴」に着眼し，選択肢とパッセージの内容を比較してから，合致していれば消去します。

(A) starbursts「星形」⇒ 4～5行目にVisual motifs such as ... starburstsとあるので消去。
(B) futuristic「未来的な」⇒ 4行目にit looked to the futureとあるので消去。
(C) science fiction「空想科学小説」⇒ 5～6行目にGoogie buildings look like ... science fictionとあるので消去。
(D) contemporary art「現代美術」⇒ 3行目にcontemporary artの記述はあるが，instead of taking cues「ヒントを得る代わりに」とあるので，グーギー建築の特徴としては不適切。よってこれが正解。

ここがポイント

Lesson 1で習った「事実を問う問題」とは逆の発想で，「書かれていない」または「本文の内容に合っていない」選択肢が正解になることを忘れないでください。以下のことを覚えておきましょう。

- 設問文を分析し，キーワードを設定する。
- キーワードに該当する部分のパッセージを読む。
- 多少時間をかけてでも，パッセージと合っている選択肢を1つずつ消去する。

学習アドバイス

TOEFLでは，「言い換え (paraphrase)」の特定が非常に重要です。つまり，パッセージや会話文で使われている言葉・表現がそのまま正解の選択肢になるということは少なく，同じアイディアを別の表現で言い換えているものが正解になりやすいのです。ですから「パッセージと同じ単語だから」と安易に選択肢を選ぶのではなく，多少表現が違っても，その裏にあるアイディアと同じかどうかで判断するように癖をつけましょう。

Passage 1

Line   Although most of the world's countries have used Daylight Saving Time at some point, today it is mostly regulated to Europe and North America. Even in territories where it is still used, there are arguments on what benefits, if any, it provides. Some say moving summer daylight hours later on the clock
(5) promotes exercise by giving people more time after work to go outside, though this benefit is hard to prove. Another proposed benefit is that it decreases energy consumption by reducing the number of dark hours before midnight, but studies have shown a miniscule effect or none at all. There is also a claim that it improves working conditions by matching people's work schedules with
(10) the sun, though opponents say the same effect could be achieved by changing work hours based on the season.

Which of the following is NOT mentioned in the passage as a benefit of Daylight Saving Time?
(A) It encourages people to exercise.
(B) It is more convenient for farmers.
(C) It lines up with people's work habits.
(D) It reduces electricity usage.

> **全訳**
>
> 世界中のほとんどの国がどこかの時点で夏時間を使用してきたが，今日では主にヨーロッパと北アメリカに限られている。いまだに使われている地域においても，もしあるとするならば，どのような利点があるかについて議論がなされている。夏の日中時間を時計上で後ろにずらすことによって，仕事の後で外へ出かける時間が増え，運動を促進できると言う人もいるが，この利点を証明するのは困難だ。ほかに提案された利点は，夜中になるまでの暗い時間を減らすことによって，エネルギー消費を減らせるということだ。しかし研究では，効果はほとんどまたは全く示されていない。人々の労働スケジュールを太陽と合わせることによって，労働状況が改善されるという主張もある。だが反対意見の人たちは，季節に応じて労働時間を変えることで同じ効果が得られると言っている。
>
> 次のうちパッセージの中で夏時間の利点として述べられていないものはどれか。
> (A) 人々に運動を促す。
> **(B) 農家にとってより便利である。**
> (C) 人々の労働習慣に合う。
> (D) 電気の使用を減らすことができる。

> **解説**
>
> (A) については第3文に「仕事の後で外へ出かける時間が増え，運動を促進できる」とある。(C) については，最終文の前半に「人々の労働スケジュールを太陽と合わせることによって，労働状況が改善される」とある。(D) については第4文に「夜中になるまでの暗い時間を減らすことによって，エネルギー消費を減らせる」とある。(B) については述べられていないので，これが正解。

Passage 2

Line When appraising the quality of a diamond there are four attributes to consider. First is the carat, or weight. Diamonds and other gemstones are measured in carats. A carat is equal to 200 milligrams. The next is color. Diamonds usually range from yellow to perfectly clear, the latter of which
(5) receives the highest rating. Very rarely there are other colors, such as blue and pink. These diamonds are very valuable, but since they are so rare there is no standardized grading system for them. Another rated attribute is clarity. The fewer cloudy spots and cracks, the higher the value of the diamond. Only around 20% of diamonds are considered clear enough to use in jewelry instead
(10) of industrial purposes. The last attribute is cut. This is the only attribute that is not an innate quality of the raw diamond, and refers to how well the diamond is cut and polished. All together these rubrics for grading diamonds make up the Four Cs.

According to the passage, all of the following are attributes diamonds are graded on EXCEPT
(A) cut
(B) clarity
(C) carat
(D) consistency

> 📘 **全訳**

　ダイヤモンドの品質を評価する際には，考慮すべき性質が4つある。まずはカラット，すなわち重量である。ダイヤモンドやそのほかの宝石用原石は，カラットで測られる。1カラットは200ミリグラムに相当する。次は色である。ダイヤモンドは通常，黄色から完全な透明までの幅があり，後者が最も高い評価を得る。非常にまれに，ブルーやピンクなどのほかの色もある。これらのダイヤモンドは非常に価値があるが，あまりにもまれなため，基準とされる評価の方式が存在しない。評価されるもう1つの性質は透明度だ。曇りやひびが少ないほど，ダイヤモンドの価値は高い。ダイヤモンドのうち，工業目的ではなく宝飾品として使えるほど透明だと見なされるものはおよそ20％しかない。最後の性質はカットである。この性質だけがダイヤモンドの原石にももともと備わっていないもので，ダイヤモンドがどれだけうまくカットされ，磨かれているかを表す。ダイヤモンドを評価するこれらの項目全てから，4つのCというものができるのだ。

パッセージによると，次のうちダイヤモンドが評価される性質でないものは
(A) カット
(B) 透明度
(C) カラット
(D) 密度

> 📝 **解説**

　ダイヤモンドの品質については第1文に「考慮すべき性質が4つある」とあり，具体的には「カラット」（第2文），「色」（第5文），「透明度」（第9文），「カット」（第12文）の4つだとわかる。(D) については言及されていないので，これが正解。consistency には「（言動などの）一貫性」という意味のほか，「（液体・溶液の）濃度，密度」という意味がある。

Passage 3

Line Pasta is perhaps the best known food that has been exported from Italy. Spaghetti is the most well-known variety of pasta with Italian restaurants all over the world serving the ubiquitous dish. While it's the most common form of pasta, there are dozens of varieties in all different shapes and sizes.
(5) Some people might assume that these different types are simply for personal preference, but different pasta shapes are used for different purposes.

The most important reason for different pasta shapes is what kind of sauce they are paired with. Smooth pastas like spaghetti and vermicelli are best paired with thin sauces, while textured pastas with ridges such as penne
(10) and fusilli are best used with thicker, chunkier sauces. There is also what kind of dish the pasta is being used for. Soups might require small pastas like orzo or ditalini, while baked dishes use large hollow pastas like manicotti that are stuffed with ingredients. There is even a geographic consideration on what pasta to use. Regional dishes might use a certain pasta because it's made with
(15) local wheat or its shape is based on some aspect of that region's history.

1. Which of the following is NOT mentioned in the passage as a type of pasta?
   (A) Ravioli
   (B) Penne
   (C) Manicotti
   (D) Orzo

2. The passage states that all of the following are reasons to use a certain type of pasta EXCEPT
   (A) what kind of dish is being made
   (B) what region a dish is from
   (C) what kind of sauce is used
   (D) what wine a pasta is paired with

> **全訳**

　パスタはイタリアから輸出されている食品のうちで，おそらく最もよく知られたものである。スパゲティは最もよく知られているパスタの種類で，世界中のイタリアンレストランが，このどこにでもある料理を提供している。これが最も一般的な形式のパスタではあるが，形や大きさの違うものが何十種類もある。これらのタイプの違いは単に個人の好みのためだという人もいるかもしれないが，形の違うパスタは違った目的に使われるのだ。

　さまざまなパスタの形の最も重要な理由は，それらが組み合わされるソースの種類だ。スパゲティやヴェルミチェッリのようななめらかなパスタは，薄いソースと組み合わせるのが最もよく，ペンネやフジッリのように溝のあるパスタは，濃くて具の多いソースと使うのが最もよい。またそのパスタがどのような料理に使われるかということもある。スープにはオルゾやディタリーニのような小さなパスタが必要だろうし，オーブンで焼く料理にはマニコッティのように，中に材料を詰められる大きくて空洞になったパスタが使われる。さらには，どんなパスタを使うかには地理的な考慮すらある。地方の料理ではその土地の小麦が使われていたり，形がその地域の歴史のなんらかの特徴に基づいて作られたりするため，特定のパスタを使うこともあるだろう。

1. 次のうちパッセージの中で言及されていないパスタの種類はどれか。
   - (A) ラビオリ
   - (B) ペンネ
   - (C) マニコッティ
   - (D) オルゾ

2. 次のうち特定の種類のパスタを使う理由としてパッセージで述べられていないものは
   - (A) どのような種類の料理が作られているか
   - (B) どの地域に料理が由来しているか
   - (C) どのような種類のソースが使われているか
   - (D) どのワインとパスタが組み合わされているか

> **解説**

1. 第2段落でさまざまなパスタが紹介されており，具体的には「スパゲティやヴェルミチェッリ」と「ペンネやフジッリ」（第2文），「オルゾやディタリーニ」と「マニコッティ」（第4文）の7つの名前が挙がっている。(A)「ラビオリ」はパッセージ中に出てこないので，これが正解。

2. パスタを選ぶ理由も第2段落で説明されている。(A) について第3文，(B) については最終文，(C) については第1文で，それぞれに合うパスタが選ばれるという説明がある。(D) の「ワイン」との組み合わせについてはパッセージに言及がないので，これが正解。

Passage 4

Line In almost all democracies around the world, citizens vote for who to represent them based on region. Urban citizens and rural citizens, for example, have different needs to be addressed. However, the question of how to draw these regions can lead to gerrymandering. Gerrymandering is the practice
(5) of drawing the boundaries of electoral districts in order to create a certain outcome.

Gerrymandering often does this by grouping people together — usually based on demographics such as religion, ethnicity, or income range — in the same district, even if they live in far-away locations. Another method weakens
(10) a group's voting power by splitting them up. If people in cities vote for the orange party and people in the country vote for the purple party, the city can be broken up into little wedges connected to large areas of rural territory. Even though the city has a large population, its citizens are all in different districts where they are outnumbered by rural voters. Gerrymandering can also be
(15) used to get rid of specific politicians by redrawing their districts to feature more voters of a different party.

Gerrymandering can be avoided by making sure all parties are present in the redistricting process. Unfortunately, this can lead to all parties making districts safe for their own party. Other options are to give the responsibility to
(20) an independent committee or to use a computer algorithm to create districts.

1. According to the passage, all of the following are tactics used in gerrymandering EXCEPT
   (A) packing a district full of one demographic
   (B) making districts as small as possible
   (C) changing districts to remove a particular person
   (D) dividing cities into separate districts

2. According to the passage, all of the following are methods for preventing gerrymandering EXCEPT
   (A) ensuring all parties are involved
   (B) letting voters determine boundaries
   (C) using an independent council to redistrict areas
   (D) using computer models to draw boundaries

> **全訳**

　世界中のほとんどの民主主義国家において，国民は地域に基づいて彼らを代表する人に投票する。例えば，都市の住民と農村地域の住民は，対処してほしい要求が違う。しかし，どのようにこれらの地域を線引きするかという問題は，ゲリマンダーにつながる可能性がある。ゲリマンダーとは，一定の結果を生み出すために選挙区の境界線を引く行為である。

　ゲリマンダーはしばしば人々を，遠く離れた場所に住んでいたとしても，同じ選挙区のグループにまとめることで行われる。それはたいてい，宗教，民族，または収入の幅などの人口統計に基づいている。また別の方法として，グループを分割してしまうことによって彼らの投票力を弱めるというものがある。もし都市の人々がオレンジ党に投票し，地方の人々がパープル党に投票すると，都市は地方地域の広い地帯につながった，小さいくさび状の区域に分割されることがある。都市の人口が多いとしても，その住民たちは全員さまざまな選挙区に入れられ，そこで地方の投票者たちに数で負けてしまうのである。ゲリマンダーはまた，違う政党の投票者たちを中心にするように選挙区を線引きし直すことによって，特定の政治家たちを追い払うためにも使われる。

　ゲリマンダーは，再区割りの過程に必ず全ての党が参加するようにすることで，避けることができる。残念ながら，これは全ての党が自分たちの党に安全な選挙区をつくる可能性につながる。ほかの選択肢としては，独立した委員会に責任を任せるか，選挙区をつくるのにコンピューターのアルゴリズムを使うというものがある。

1. パッセージによると，次のうちゲリマンダーに使われない手法は
　(A) 1つの人口統計で選挙区を埋め尽くす
　(B) 選挙区をできるだけ小さくする
　(C) 特定の人を排除するために選挙区を変える
　(D) 都市を別々の選挙区に分ける

2. パッセージによると，次のうちゲリマンダーを避けるための方法でないものは
　(A) 必ず全ての党が関わるようにする
　(B) 投票者たちに境界線を決めさせる
　(C) 独立した評議会を使って地域を再区割りする
　(D) コンピューターモデルを使って境界線を引く

解説

1. gerrymandering とは第1段落最終文に説明があるように，「一定の結果を生み出すために選挙区の境界線を引く行為」のこと。その具体的な内容は第2段落で，(A) については第1文，(C) については最終文，(D) については第3文に説明がある。(B) についてはパッセージに言及がないので，これが正解。

2. Gerrymandering can be avoided ... で始まる第3段落で，その防止策が説明されている。具体的には，「全ての党が参加するようにする」（第1文），「独立した委員会に責任を任せる」（最終文），「コンピューターのアルゴリズムを使う」（最終文）の3点である。(B) の「投票者たちに境界線を決めさせる」ことは防止策に含まれていないので，これが正解。

Lesson 3 Vocabulary Questions
語彙問題

例題

Line

An ultra-long-haul non-stop flight is a flight that not only goes long distances across oceans and continents but also does so without stopping to refuel. The first regularly scheduled ultra-long-haul non-stop flight service was between Western Australia and present-day Sri Lanka, and ran from 1943 to
(5) 1945. The grueling 27-hour 5,650 km service had multiple crews and was called the Double Sunrise, because the sun rose twice during the flight. Today, the record for longest non-stop flight is the Singapore to Newark 16,600 km service operated by Singapore Airlines from 2004 until 2013. This service flew over Alaska and Asia and took over 18 hours to complete.

The word "grueling" in line 5 is closest in meaning to

(A) adventurous

(B) exhausting

(C) technical

(D) deadly

全訳

超長距離直航便は，大洋や大陸を越えて長距離を飛行するだけでなく，給油のために停まることもせずにこれを行う。最初の定期超長距離直航便サービスは，西オーストラリア州と現在のスリランカの間で，1943年から1945年まで運航していた。へとへとに疲れる27時間5,650キロの飛行は，多数の乗務員を要し，飛行の間に2度日が昇るため，ダブルサンライズと呼ばれた。今日，長距離直航便の最長記録は，2004年から2013年までシンガポール航空が運航していた，シンガポールからニューアークに至る1万6,600キロの便である。この便はアラスカとアジア上空を飛び，到着までに18時間以上を要した。

5行目の grueling という言葉に最も近い意味は
(A) 大胆な
(B) 疲労困憊させる
(C) 技術的な
(D) 致命的な

①ヒントとなる情報1　②ヒントとなる情報2

> 解き方

単語の意味が問われる問題です。gruelingは「疲れさせる，厳しい」という意味の形容詞です。特につらいことが長く続く様子を描写する際に使われます。1行目にultra-long-haul non-stop，2～3行目にwithout stopping to refuelと記述があるので，それらをヒントにして選択肢からイメージできるものを選びます。(A)はポジティブな意味，(C)では関連がなく，(D)では誇張され過ぎています。

gruelはイギリス英語ではもともとa thin watery porridge「薄くて水っぽい粥」を意味し，貧困にあえぐ人々に与えられたことから「つらい」という意味を含むようになったと言われています。gruesome「身の毛もよだつほど恐ろしい」，grotesque「グロテスクな，醜い」なども併せて覚えておくとよいでしょう。

> **ここがポイント**
>
> 語彙問題の解き方には，大きく分けて2パターンがあります。
> 1. 単語の意味をすでに知っている場合
>   ⇒自分が知っている意味を当てはめ，文脈に適切かどうかを確認してから，それに一番近い意味を持つ選択肢を選ぶ。
> 2. 単語の意味が分からない場合
>   ⇒単語の周辺にあるヒントとなる内容や，話の流れからポジティブまたはネガティブな意味かなどを読み取り，消去法で選ぶ。

> **学習アドバイス**
>
> 知っている語彙を増やすことはもちろん必要ですが，それでも自分の知らない単語に遭遇することは避けられません。その際に，文脈に基づいて意味を推測するのも重要なスキルです。単語を学習する際には，
> ・単語単体だけではなく，例文やパッセージとともに覚える
> ・英文を読んで分からない単語があるとき，どのような意味なら適切にフィットするかを推測する
>
> ことを心がけてください。また類義語辞典 (thesaurus) を使い，1つの単語を調べたら同時に類義語も加えて覚えるよう習慣づけましょう。

Passage 1

Line   Mount Everest, the tallest and arguably most famous peak in the world, is definitely one of the most perilous mountains to climb. The top of Everest has been reached over 5,000 times but has resulted in over 200 deaths. The world also has plenty of other mountains that are just as challenging or even more so.
(5) K2, the world's second highest peak, has been summited just over 300 times but has resulted in 80 deaths. It is so treacherous to climb that unlike Everest, it has never been successfully climbed in the winter. However, the prize of most lethal mountain to climb goes to the tenth highest mountain in the world, Annapurna I. This beast of a peak has so far claimed 61 lives with less than
(10) 200 successful ascents.

    The word "treacherous" in line 6 is closest in meaning to
    (A) difficult
    (B) long
    (C) exciting
    (D) dangerous

> **全訳**
>
> 　世界で最も高く，おそらく最も有名な山エベレストは，間違いなく登るのに最も危険な山の1つである。エベレストの頂上は5,000回登頂されたが，その結果，200人以上が死亡している。世界にはほかにも同じくらい，あるいはより困難な山がたくさんある。世界第2位の高さのK2は300回以上登頂されたが，80人が亡くなっている。登るのが非常に危険なので，エベレストと違って冬には1度も登頂が成功していない。しかし，登るのが最も致命的な山の称号が与えられるのは，世界で10番目に高いアンナプルナⅠ峰だ。このけだもののような頂は，これまで61人の命を奪い，成功した登頂は200回以下である。
>
> 6行目の treacherous という言葉に最も近い意味は
> (A) 難しい
> (B) 長い
> (C) わくわくする
> **(D) 危険な**

> **解説**
>
> 　エベレストと同じくらい危険な山として K2 の名前を挙げた後に，「登るのが非常に treacherous なので，エベレストと違って冬には1度も登頂が成功していない」と続いているので，treacherous の意味は (A) か (D) に絞ることができる。正解は (D) で，treacherous は「危険な，油断できない」という意味。

Passage 2

Line   The earliest watches go back to 16th century Europe but were not popular until the 17th century. These watches were mechanical, which meant they were powered and moved by springs and gears. They were mostly pocket-watches. Wristwatches also existed but were mostly worn by women. Until the
(5) early 20th century, men mostly wore pocket-watches. Wristwatches really took off when they were worn by soldiers in World War I. Warfare brought about a number of advances including shatter resistant glass and glowing hands and numbers that could be seen in the dark.
       One of the most significant changes in watches would come in 1969 with
(10) the first mass-produced quartz watch. Quartz watches use an electric signal to tell time up to 10 times more accurately than mechanical watches. They are also much cheaper to produce. Today, most watches use a quartz mechanism to tell time. However, the latest development in watches is the smartwatch. Though still new, smartwatches are bringing features such as fitness tracking
(15) and notifications to the wrist.

   The word "advances" in line 7 is closest in meaning to
   (A) increases
   (B) finances
   (C) improvements
   (D) accuracies

38

CHAPTER 1 Lesson3 Vocabulary Questions

> 全訳

　最も初期の携帯用の時計は16世紀ヨーロッパにさかのぼるが，17世紀までは一般的ではなかった。これらの時計は機械仕掛けで，これはつまり，ばねや歯車で動いていたということだ。それらの大部分が懐中時計だった。腕時計もあったが，身に着けていたのはほとんどが女性だった。20世紀初期までは，大部分の男性は懐中時計を持っていた。腕時計が本当によく使われ始めたのは，第一次世界大戦で兵士が身に着けたときだ。戦争は，粉砕防止のガラスや，暗闇でも見えるように光る針や数字などを含む数多くの進歩をもたらした。

　時計における最も重要な変化の1つは，初めて大量生産されたクォーツ時計によって，1969年に起こった。クォーツ時計は電気信号を使い，機械式時計よりも10倍正確に時を告げる。それらはまた，ずっと安い値段で製造できる。今日では，ほとんどの時計が時刻を計るのにクォーツ装置を使用している。しかし，時計における最新の発展はスマートウォッチである。まだ新しいが，スマートウォッチは健康状態を記録したり，手首へ通知したりする機能を備えている。

7行目の advances という言葉に最も近い意味は
(A) 増加
(B) 財源
(C) 進歩
(D) 正確さ

> 解説

　advances は戦争が brought about「もたらした」もので，その具体例は直後の including 以降にある「粉砕防止のガラス」や「暗闇でも見えるように光る針や数字」である。従って advances は「メリット，進歩」といった意味だと推測できる。正解は (C) で，advance は「進歩，向上」という意味。

Passage 3

Line   Have you heard of the phrases "early bird" and "night owl"? They are used to describe people who naturally go to bed and wake up early versus those who go to bed and wake up late. In our society, there is an image of early birds as productive and socially active go-getters. Meanwhile, night owls are
(5) viewed as less productive people who stay up late drinking or binge-watching TV. These stereotypes may have some truth to them, but not everything is positive for early birds or negative for night owls.

Early birds have the advantage in many of our social activities such as work and school because these take place in the daytime. Night owls may
(10) suffer social jet lag, whereby they constantly feel sleepy during society's most active hours. Also, early birds are less likely to have issues with over eating or smoking. However, early birds tend to run out of steam toward the end of the day, while night owls often gain a burst of energy in the evening. Studies also show that night owls are more creative and are more likely to take chances that
(15) may lead to more financial or professional success.

1. The word "productive" in line 4 is closest in meaning to
   (A) positive
   (B) important
   (C) effective
   (D) essential

2. The word "constantly" in line 10 is closest in meaning to
   (A) always
   (B) abundantly
   (C) occasionally
   (D) intermittently

全訳

early bird（早起きの人）や night owl（夜更かしの人）という言い回しを聞いたことはあるだろうか。生来早寝早起きの人々と、彼らに対し、遅く寝て遅く起きる人々を言い表すのにかつて使われた言葉だ。われわれの社会では、早起きの人は生産的で社会的に活発なやり手だという印象がある。一方、夜更かしの人はそれほど生産的ではなく、遅くまで起きていて酒を飲み、テレビばかり見ている人として見なされる。そうした固定観念にはいくらか真実が含まれているかもしれないが、早起きの人にとって全てが肯定的ではないし、夜更かしの人にとって全てが否定的というわけでもない。

　早起きの人は、仕事や学校など社会活動の多くにおいて有利である。それらは日中に行われるからだ。夜更かしの人は、社会の最も活動的な時間帯にいつも眠気を感じるなど、社会的な時差ぼけに苦しむかもしれない。さらに、早起きの人は過食や喫煙などの問題を抱えにくい。しかし、早起きの人は1日の終わりごろに失速する傾向があるが、夜更かしの人は夜になるとしばしば活力がみなぎる。また研究では、夜更かしの人の方が創造的で、より経済的、職業的な成功につながるかもしれない機会をつかむ可能性が高いということも示されている。

1. 4行目の productive という言葉に最も近い意味は
   (A) 肯定的な
   (B) 重要な
   (C) 効果的な
   (D) 必要不可欠な

2. 10行目の constantly という言葉に最も近い意味は
   (A) 常に
   (B) 豊富に
   (C) たまに
   (D) 断続的に

解説

1. productive を含む部分は an image of early birds as productive and socially active go-getters「早起きの人は productive で社会的に活発なやり手だという印象」という内容。また productive は product に -ive が付いた形なので、生産物について表す形容詞だと推測できる。正解は (C)。productive は「生産的な」という意味。

2. constantly を含む文は Night owls may suffer social jet lag, whereby they constantly feel sleepy during society's most active hours.「夜更かしの人は、社会の最も活動的な時間帯に constantly に眠気を感じるなど、社会的な時差ぼけに苦しむかもしれない」という内容。また、constantly は constant「絶え間ない」に -ly が付いた形の副詞なので、(A) が正解だと推測できる。(D) の intermittently は「断続的に（＝途切れたり続いたり）」という意味。

41

Passage 4

Line   The Underground Railroad may sound like an early version of a subway system, but in fact, it was not underground and had nothing to do with trains. It was a network of secret paths and safe houses in the United States used to help enslaved African-Americans escape north to the free states or even
(5)   Canada. It was called the Underground Railroad because it was underground in the sense that it was secret. And it was a railroad because railway terms were used to describe the network. For example, the people guiding the slaves to freedom were called conductors and the safe houses in which they stopped to hide and rest were called stations. From the early 1800's when the Railroad
(10) was founded until 1850, more than 100,000 African-American slaves escaped to freedom.

   One of the most famous conductors on this Underground Railroad was Harriet Tubman. She was an African-American woman born into slavery in 1822. After a hard life in which she was whipped and injured by a metal
(15) object thrown at her head, she escaped to Philadelphia in 1849. However, she returned to Maryland to save her family from slavery. This was the start of her eight-year career as a conductor on the Railroad. In total, she would lead 13 missions, freeing over 70 slaves. She once described her success with a train metaphor saying, "I never ran my train off the track and I never lost a
(20) passenger."

1. The word "enslaved" in line 4 is closest in meaning to
   (A) held captive
   (B) given opportunity
   (C) provided housing
   (D) offered support

2. The word "metaphor" in line 19 is closest in meaning to
   (A) comparison
   (B) vocabulary
   (C) term
   (D) dictionary

> **全訳**

　The Underground Railroad（地下鉄道）は，昔の地下鉄網のように聞こえるかもしれないが，実は地下にあったものではなく，鉄道とも関係がなかった。これは，奴隷にされたアフリカ系アメリカ人が，自由州やカナダにまで北方へと逃げるのを助けるために使われた，アメリカにおける秘密の通り道と隠れ家のネットワークだったのだ。秘密だったという意味での地下組織だったため，地下鉄道と呼ばれていた。そして，ネットワークを表すのに鉄道用語が使われたので，鉄道だったのだ。例えば，奴隷たちを自由へと案内する人々は車掌と呼ばれ，隠れたり休んだりするために立ち寄る隠れ家は駅と呼ばれた。鉄道が立ち上げられた1800年代初期から1850年までに，10万人以上のアフリカ系アメリカ人奴隷が自由を求めて逃亡した。

　この地下鉄道で最も有名な車掌の1人が，ハリエット・タブマンであった。彼女は1822年に奴隷として生まれたアフリカ系アメリカ人女性だ。むち打たれ，頭に金属の物を投げつけられてけがをするなど，苦難の生活を経験した後，彼女は1849年にフィラデルフィアに逃げ出した。しかし，家族を奴隷制度から救うために，彼女はメリーランドに戻って来た。これが，鉄道の車掌としての8年にわたる彼女の経歴の始まりだった。彼女は全部で13の任務を指揮し，70人以上の奴隷を自由にした。彼女はあるとき自分の成功を鉄道に例えて，「私は列車を脱線させたことは1度もないし，乗客を1人も死なせませんでした」と言った。

1. 4行目の enslaved という言葉の意味に最も近い意味は
   (A) 捕らえられた
   (B) 機会を与えられた
   (C) 家を用意された
   (D) 支えを提供された

2. 19行目の metaphor という言葉に最も近い意味は
   (A) たとえ
   (B) 語彙
   (C) 用語
   (D) 辞書

> **解説**

1. enslaved は slave「奴隷」に名詞を動詞化する接頭辞 en- が付いた形。ここでは -ed で終わり，名詞の前に置かれているので，「奴隷にさせられた」といった意味の過去分詞だと推測できる。(A) が正解。hold ～ captive で「～を捕える」という意味。

2. 最終文の "I never ran my train off the track and I never lost a passenger."「私は列車を脱線させたことは1度もないし，乗客を1人も死なせませんでした」が彼女の成功を言い表す a train metaphor「鉄道の metaphor」の具体的な内容。つまり metaphor は「比喩，たとえ」といった意味だと推測できる。(A) が正解。

Lesson 4 Reference Questions
指示内容を問う問題

> 例題

Line
　In many countries, new doctors swear to keep a series of ethical standards called the Hippocratic Oath. The original oath① was written between the 5th and 3rd century BC by Greek physician Hippocrates or by his disciples. In its original form, it② was a promise made by doctors to the healing gods to uphold
(5)　certain moral responsibilities in the practice of medicine. In modern times, the oath has been updated but still encourages doctors to show empathy toward patients, to choose prevention over cure when possible, and to remember that they are treating humans and not an abstract illness among other things.

　　The word "it" in line 4 refers to
　　(A) the 3rd century BC
　　(B) the original oath written in ancient Greece
　　(C) the practice of medicine
　　(D) the updated oath in modern times

> 全訳

　多くの国では，新たに医師になる者は，ヒポクラテスの誓いと呼ばれる一連の倫理規範を守ると誓いを立てる。最初の誓いは，紀元前5世紀から3世紀の間に，ギリシャの医師ヒポクラテス，または彼の弟子たちによって書かれたものだ。もともとは，医療行為において，癒しの神々に対し一定の倫理的責任を守るという，医師たちがする約束だった。現代では，誓いは改訂されているが，それでも患者たちに対して共感を示すこと，できれば治療よりは予防を選ぶこと，そして何よりも，抽象的な病ではなく，人間を治療しているのだということを忘れないよう，医師に促している。

　　4行目の it という言葉が指すのは
　　(A) 紀元前3世紀
　　(B) 古代ギリシャで書かれた最初の誓い
　　(C) 医療行為
　　(D) 現代の改訂された誓い

①代名詞と同じ役割をする，前のセンテンスの主語　②問われている代名詞

> 解き方

パッセージにあるitやtheyなどの言葉が何を指すか答える問題です。ここでのitは主語ですので，まず，同じ役割である前のセンテンスもしくは節の主語を検討します。それが当てはまらない場合は，直前にある単数名詞の可能性もあります。前のセンテンスの主語はThe original oath「最初の誓い」なので，it wasに続くa promiseと意味が通じます。

(A)「紀元前3世紀」は時代なので，「医師によって約束される」は不適当です。
(C) もしこれがitの内容だとすると，the practice of medicine ... in the practice of medicineという文になってしまうので，おかしくなります。
(D) itの前にoriginalとあるので，modern times「現代」では不適当です。

ここがポイント

指示内容を問う問題では，itやtheyなどの代名詞の場合と，文中の語句が示す内容を問われる場合の2パターンがあります。いずれの場合も，以下を覚えておきましょう。

- 単数か複数かをチェックする。
- 先行するセンテンスまたは節の中にある，同じ役割（主語・目的語）の名詞を検討する。
- 選択肢の語句を，問われている代名詞や単語に当てはめて，意味が通るかを確認する。

学習アドバイス

ReadingはListeningとは違い，何度でも戻って読むことができます。文章を読んでいるときに代名詞が出てきたら，すぐに前のセンテンスに戻り，どの内容を示すのかをチェックする癖をつけましょう。またTOEFLのReference問題としては出題されませんが，カンマを伴うwhichの場合（..., which）は，1語ではなく前の節全体の内容を示す場合もありますので，常に文脈と意味を意識しながら読むようにしましょう。

Passage 1

Line It's probably no surprise to most people that hummingbirds are the world's smallest birds. The smallest hummingbird, the appropriately named bee hummingbird, is just 5 centimeters long and weighs less than a small coin. Hummingbirds in general get their name from the noise their wings make
(5) when flapping rapidly. This enables hummingbirds to hover in mid-air and fly left, right, up, down, back, forth, and even upside down. In addition to rapidly beating their wings, their heart rate can reach an astounding 1,260 per minute. They have long bills and tongues, which they use to lick the nectar from the flowers that are their source of food.

The word "This" in line 5 refers to
(A) humming
(B) naming
(C) flapping
(D) hovering

46

> **全訳**
>
> 　ハチドリが世界最小の鳥だということは，ほとんどの人にとってはおそらく驚くことではないだろう。最も小さいハチドリは，いみじくもマメハチドリという名で，体長はたったの5センチ，体重も小さな硬貨ほどもない。一般的なハチドリは，高速で羽ばたくときに翼がたてる音から名前が付いている。このおかげで，ハチドリは空中に浮かび，左右，上下，前後，そして逆さまでさえも飛べるのだ。翼を素早く羽ばたかせることに加えて，彼らの心拍は毎分1,260という驚異的な数字にまで達することがある。彼らは長いくちばしと舌を持ち，それを使って彼らの食料源である花の蜜をなめるのだ。
>
> 5行目のThisという言葉が指すのは
> (A)　ブンブン音をたてること
> (B)　名前を付けること
> **(C)　羽ばたくこと**
> (D)　浮かんでいること

解説

This enables hummingbirds to hover in mid-air and fly left, right, up, down, back, forth, and even upside down.「このおかげで，ハチドリは空中に浮かび，左右，上下，前後，そして逆さまでさえも飛べるのだ」とある。どうすれば自在に飛ぶことができるのかを考えながら前の文の内容を確認すると，This は flapping (rapidly) を指していると分かる。(C) が正解。

Passage 2

Line   The streaks of light we see in the night sky are meteors or what are also commonly called shooting stars. Meteors start out as meteoroids — space-traveling rocks usually ranging in size from a few centimeters to up to a meter wide. When a meteoroid enters the Earth's atmosphere, it becomes a meteor,
(5) and friction from the air causes it to burn and appear as a streak in the night sky. An especially bright meteor is called a fireball. When a bunch of meteors fall to the Earth together, this is called a meteor shower. Meteor showers are made up of left-over comet debris that the Earth passes through during its orbit. One of the most famous and brilliant of these showers occurs every
(10) August and is called the Perseids. Any meteor that makes it to the Earth's surface without completely burning up is called a meteorite. The largest known meteorite was found in 1920 in Namibia, Africa and is about 3 meters by 3 meters in size.

The word "its" in line 8 refers to
(A) comet's
(B) meteor's
(C) Earth's
(D) meteor shower's

> **全訳**

夜空に私たちが見る光の筋は，流星か，いわゆる一般的に流れ星と呼ばれるものだ。流星は流星物質として始まる。流星物質とは，幅が数センチから最大1メートルの大きさの，宇宙を旅する岩である。流星物質が地球の大気圏に入ると，流星となり，空気との摩擦で燃えて，夜空の筋となって現れるのだ。特に明るい流星は火球と呼ばれる。流星の群れが一緒に地球に降ってくるとき，これは流星群と呼ばれる。流星群は，地球が軌道を回る間に通りすぎる彗星の残骸の残りでできている。そうした流星群の最も有名で明るいものは，毎年8月に起こり，ペルセウス座流星群と呼ばれる。完全に燃え尽きることなく地球の表面に達する流星が，隕石と呼ばれる。知られている最大の隕石は，1920年にアフリカのナミビアで発見された，約3メートルかける3メートルの大きさのものである。

8行目の its という言葉が指すのは
(A) 彗星の
(B) 流星の
(C) 地球の
(D) 流星群の

> **解説**

left-over comet debris that the Earth passes through during its orbit「地球がその(its)軌道を回る間に通りすぎる彗星の残骸の残り」という内容で，its は前述の単数形の名詞を受けることから，この「軌道」は地球自体の「軌道」だと考えられる。(C) が正解。

Passage 3

Line　　James Watson, Francis Crick, and Maurice Wilkins are known as the discoverers of the DNA double helix and were famously awarded the 1962 Nobel Prize in Physiology or Medicine for this discovery. However, this accomplishment may not have been possible without the contribution of a
(5) female scientist named Rosalind Franklin.

　　Franklin was born in London, England in 1920. Her specialties were chemistry and x-ray photography. One of her most important contributions concerning DNA was her discovery that its structure depends on the level of hydration, or amount of water it contains. She was able to come to this
(10) conclusion because of her background in chemistry. Her other contribution was photograph 51 taken in 1953. It was actually taken by Raymond Gosling, a Ph.D. student under her supervision. Photograph 51 is the first photo to show the double helix structure of DNA that would later be confirmed after further research.

(15)　　Sadly, Franklin died in 1958 at the age of 37 from ovarian cancer. She was never nominated for the Nobel Prize and for many years her role in the discovery of DNA was downplayed. This was due to a number of factors including gender discrimination against women in science at the time.

1. The phrase "this accomplishment" in lines 3-4 refers to
 (A) discovering X-rays
 (B) finding the DNA double helix
 (C) awarding scientists a Nobel Prize
 (D) Rosalind Franklin's contribution

2. The word "This" in line 17 refers to
 (A) supervising Ph.D. students
 (B) confirming the structure of DNA
 (C) failing to appreciate Rosalind Franklin's role
 (D) discriminating against women

> **全訳**

　ジェームズ・ワトソン，フランシス・クリック，モーリス・ウィルキンスは，DNAの二重らせんの発見者として知られており，周知のとおり，この発見で1962年にノーベル生理学・医学賞を受賞した。しかし，この業績は，ロザリンド・フランクリンという名の女性科学者の貢献なくしては可能ではなかったかもしれない。

　フランクリンは1920年，イギリスのロンドンに生まれた。彼女の専門は科学とX線撮影だった。DNAに関する彼女の最も重要な貢献の1つは，その構造が水和の程度，つまり水分含量によって決まるという発見だった。彼女には化学の分野の経歴があったため，この結論に達することができたのだ。彼女のもう1つの貢献は，1953年に撮影されたフォトグラフ51であった。それは彼女の監督の下で，実際は博士課程の学生レイモンド・ゴスリングによって撮影された。フォトグラフ51はDNAの二重らせん構造を示した最初の写真で，それは後にさらなる研究で裏付けられた。

　悲しいことに，フランクリンは1958年に37歳の若さで卵巣がんによって亡くなった。ノーベル賞の候補になったこともなく，DNAの発見における彼女の役割は長い間軽く扱われた。これは当時の科学界における女性に対する性差別を含む，数々の要因によるものだった。

1. 3～4行目の this accomplishment という言い回しが指すのは
   (A) X線の発見
   (B) DNAの二重らせんの発見
   (C) 科学者へのノーベル賞の授与
   (D) ロザリンド・フランクリンの貢献

2. 17行目の This という言葉が指すのは
   (A) 博士課程の学生を監督すること
   (B) DNAの構造を裏付けること
   (C) ロザリンド・フランクリンの役割を正しく評価できないこと
   (D) 女性を差別していること

> **解説**

1. ある事柄に関する説明をした上で，this accomplishment「この業績」と続いているはずだと考えられるので，直前の内容を詳しく読むと，the discoverers of the DNA double helix「DNAの二重らせんの発見者」とある。つまり，DNAの二重らせんを見つけたことが「この業績」だと考えられる。(B) が正解。

2. This は直前の文の内容を受けていると考えられるが，前文中の表現をそのまま使っている選択肢がないので，正しく言い換えられているものを選ぶ。「ノーベル賞の候補になったこともなく，DNAの発見における彼女の役割は長い間軽く扱われた」とは，実績を正しく評価されることがなく，不当に扱われたということ。正解は (C)。

Passage 4

Line   President of the United States may not be the riskiest job in the world but it has had its moments of danger and even fatality. Sadly, four US presidents have been killed while holding their country's highest office, including Abraham Lincoln and John F. Kennedy. However, did you know there have
(5) been at least 20 attempts to kill a president? While many of these have been for political reasons, a surprising number of these attempts have been by people suffering from mental illness.

The first attempt on a president's life was against Andrew Jackson in 1835. An unemployed man named Richard Lawrence shot at Jackson with two
(10) guns but both misfired. Jackson fought back with his walking cane. Lawrence was eventually restrained by Jackson's political rival David Crockett who strongly disliked Jackson. Apparently, Lawrence thought he was the long-dead King Richard III of England and was found insane and institutionalized.

One of the most dramatic attempts was against Harry Truman in 1950.
(15) Two gunmen in support of independence from the United States for Puerto Rico tried to enter Blair House where Truman was staying since the White House was in its renovation. However, they were stopped by guards, including the Secret Service. Truman, on the second floor, was unhurt but one of the gunmen and a White House police officer were killed by gunfire.

1. The word "these" in line 5 refers to
(A) moments
(B) states
(C) reasons
(D) attempts

2. The word "its" in line 17 refers to
(A) Blair House's
(B) the White House's
(C) the Secret Service's
(D) Puerto Rico's

> **全訳**
>
> アメリカの大統領は世界で最も危険な仕事ではないかもしれないが，危険で，致命的な瞬間さえあった。悲しいことに，エイブラハム・リンカーンとジョン・F・ケネディを含む4人のアメリカ大統領が，国家の最高職に就いている間に殺されている。しかし，大統領を暗殺する試みが，少なくとも20回はあったことを知っていただろうか。その多くは政治的理由からだが，それらのうち驚くべき数の試みが，精神的疾患を抱える人々によるものである。
>
> 大統領の命を狙った最初の企ては，1835年のアンドリュー・ジャクソンに対するものだ。リチャード・ローレンスという無職の男が2丁の銃でジャクソンを撃ったが，どちらも不発に終わった。ジャクソンは杖で反撃した。ローレンスは，やがてジャクソンの政敵でジャクソンを非常に嫌っていたデヴィッド・クロケットによって捕えられた。どうやらローレンスは，自分はずっと前に死んだ英国王リチャード三世だと思い込んでいたらしく，心神喪失だと判定し，施設に収監された。
>
> 最も劇的だったのは，1950年のハリー・トルーマンに対する企てだ。ホワイトハウスが改修中だったことから，トルーマンが滞在していたブレアハウスに，プエルトリコのアメリカからの独立を支持する2人の殺し屋が入ろうとした。しかし，彼らはシークレットサービスを含む護衛に阻止された。トルーマンは2階にいて無傷だったが，殺し屋の1人とホワイトハウスの警官が，発砲で亡くなった。

1. 5行目の these という言葉が指すのは
   (A) 瞬間
   (B) 州
   (C) 理由
   (D) 企て

2. 17行目の its という言葉が指すのは
   (A) ブレアハウスの
   (B) ホワイトハウスの
   (C) シークレットサービスの
   (D) プエルトリコの

解説

1. these は通例，既出の複数名詞を指す。ここでは直前の文の 20 attempts を指しており，many of these attempts と読みかえても意味がとおる。(D) が正解。these を含む文の後半に these attempts とあるのも参考になる。
2. Blair House where Truman was staying since the White House was in its renovation から，Blair House はトルーマンがホワイトハウスの代わりに滞在していた場所で，その理由は the White House が改修中だったからだと考えられる。(B) が正解。

Lesson 5 Inference Questions
推論する問題

例題

Line
　　Though the principles of hot air balloons have been known for almost two thousand years, it wasn't until 1783 that the French brothers Joseph-Michel Montgolfier and Jacques-Étienne Montgolfier built the first balloon meant to carry humans. One of the reasons this hadn't been attempted before is people
(5) weren't certain there was breathable atmosphere that high in the air. The first untethered, manned flight was initially planned to involve condemned criminals before two noblemen volunteered to pilot it. The flight was completed successfully and safely, though one of the noblemen, Jean-François Pilâtre de Rozier, later died in a separate attempt to cross the English Channel.

　　It can be inferred that the first balloon flight was intended to be piloted by condemned criminals because
　　(A) the Montgolfier brothers were in prison at the time
　　(B) the criminals had experience with aviation
　　(C) it was thought the pilots might die in the attempt
　　(D) they asked for the honor of being the first pilots

全訳

　熱気球の原理は2,000年近い間知られているにもかかわらず、フランス人の兄弟ジョゼフ＝ミシェル・モンゴルフィエとジャック＝エティエンヌ・モンゴルフィエが人間を運ぶための初めての気球を組み立てたのは1783年になってからであった。これがそれ以前に試みられなかった理由の1つは、人々は、それほど空高くに呼吸ができる大気があるかどうか不確かだったからだ。最初の命綱なしの人間を乗せた飛行は、2人の貴族がそれを操縦しようと申し出る前、もともとは死刑囚を乗せる計画だった。飛行は成功し、かつ安全に達成されたが、そのうちの貴族の1人、ジャン＝フランソワ・ピラートル・ド・ロジェは、後にこれとは別の英仏海峡を渡る試みで死亡した。

　最初の気球飛行を、死刑囚に操縦させるつもりであった理由として推測されることは
　(A) そのときモンゴルフィエ兄弟は刑務所に入っていた
　(B) 囚人たちは飛行の経験があった
　(C) その試みではパイロットが死亡するかもしれないと考えられていた
　(D) 彼らは最初のパイロットになる名誉を求めた

①最初の有人熱気球　②それまでに人を乗せなかった理由　③死刑囚を乗せる予定

> 解き方

パッセージの内容から推論する問題です。設問文にあるthe first balloon flightとcondemned criminalsに着眼し，なぜ死刑囚が乗る予定だったかを読み取ります。4～5行目のpeople weren't ... airの部分で「呼吸ができる大気があるかどうか不確かだった」と記述されていることから，危険な目に遭う，つまり死ぬ可能性もあったことが推測できます。だから死刑囚の利用が計画された，と考えるのが一番論理的な推考です。
(A) モンゴルフィエ兄弟が刑務所にいたことは，この内容からは推測できません。
(B) 囚人たちにaviation「飛行」の経験があることも，ここからは推測できません。
(D) 彼ら（死刑囚）が名誉を求めた，ということを示唆する記述はありません。

> ここがポイント

推論する場合，あくまでもそれなりのヒントがパッセージにあることが前提です。根拠のない，飛躍しすぎる推論は正解になりません。以下を復習してください。
- 事実を問う問題同様，設題文にキーワードを設定する。
- パッセージからキーワードを見つけ，質問が要求している情報を探す。
- It can be inferred from the passage thatのように設問文にヒントがない場合
  ⇒各選択肢を分析，キーワードを設定してそれぞれをパッセージの内容と照合する。

> 学習アドバイス

普段から論理的思考を磨くことが大事です。ちょっと難しく聞こえるかもしれませんが，最近ではロジカルシンキングというカタカナ語も浸透しつつあります。話やアイディアが「何を根拠に」「どのように展開して」「その結果どうなったか」などと筋道を立てて考えることが必要です。また日ごろから何かの事象に対して，「それはなぜそうなったか」と推考する癖をつけるようにしましょう。

Passage 1

Line   Over the last 15 years, most countries in the world have switched over to electronic passports. These documents maintain all the printed identification found in traditional passports, but augment them with embedded chips that digitally store information about the passport holder. The information
(5) can simply be what's already printed in the passport or include biometric information such as fingerprints. These chips are read wirelessly at border crossings and airports by machines to speed up the customs process. This capability of being read via radio signals has led some to complain that the information could be collected by identity thieves. Governments issuing these
(10) passports have put in security features to prevent such crimes, but privacy advocates still say the new passports present unnecessary risks.

The passage implies that opponents think the security features of electronic passports are
(A) far too expensive to use
(B) still not strong enough
(C) only for biometric information
(D) based on outdated technology

全訳

　ここ15年の間に，世界のほとんどの国々は電子パスポートに切り替えた。これらの文書は，以前のパスポートに見られるすべての印刷された身分証明を保持しているが，パスポート所有者に関する情報をデジタル化して保存する内蔵チップでそれらを増強している。その情報は単にすでにパスポートに印刷されていることであったり，指紋などの生体情報を含んでいたりする。これらのチップは国境検問所や空港において，税関の手続きをスピードアップするために，無線で機械に読み込まれる。無線信号によって読み込むことができるので，この情報が個人情報窃盗犯に集められる可能性があると苦情を言う人もでてきた。これらのパスポートを発行する政府はそういった犯罪を防ぐために安全対策を設けているが，プライバシー擁護者たちは今でも新しいパスポートが不必要な危険を呈していると言っている。

　　パッセージが示唆するには，反対者たちは電子パスポートの安全対策を
　　(A) 用いるにはあまりにも費用がかかりすぎると思っている
　　(B) まだ十分に強くないと思っている
　　(C) 生体情報に対するものだけだと思っている
　　(D) 時代遅れの技術に基づいていると思っている

解説

　新しいパスポートの安全性についてはパッセージ後半で述べられている。最終文に but privacy advocates still say the new passports present unnecessary risks「しかし，プライバシー擁護者たちは今でも新しいパスポートが不必要な危険を呈していると言っている」とあり，(B) の内容と一致する。

Passage 2

Line   Stereotypes affect how people treat one another and color our expectations of each other, but studies show that stereotypes can also affect how we perceive ourselves. The concept of stereotype threat states that our behavior is shaped by stereotypes about the groups we belong to. Studies
(5) have demonstrated this by comparing performance in tasks by groups that are perceived to be adept or inept at that task. In one study, women were split into two groups and given identical math tests. One group of women was asked questions before the test that suggested their gender is inherently weak in math. These test-takers performed worse on the test than the other
(10) group of women. The opposite effect has been observed as well. When people are reminded that they are part of a demographic that stereotypically excel at a task, they will outperform others in the same demographic that are not similarly prompted.

Which of the following can be inferred about stereotypes?
(A) They can unconsciously change people's behavior.
(B) They affect men more than women.
(C) They can only make people perform worse in studies.
(D) They affect tests more than real-life scenarios.

58

> **全訳**
>
> 　固定観念は，人々がお互いをどう扱うかに影響を与え，お互いに対する期待をねじ曲げるが，研究は，固定観念はわれわれが自分自身をどう認識するかにも影響を与え得るということを示している。ステレオタイプ・スレット（固定観念に対する恐怖）という概念は，われわれの行動は，自分の属する集団に関する固定概念によって形作られると述べている。このことは，ある課題において有能だと考えられる集団と無能だと考えられる集団とによる，課題の成績を比較するという研究によって示された。ある研究で，女性を2つの集団に分け，同じ数学のテストを実施した。一方の女性の集団はテストの前に，彼女たちの性別は生まれつき数学が苦手だということをほのめかす質問をされた。これらのテストの受験者は，もう一方の女性の集団よりもテストの成績が悪かった。反対の効果も観測されている。人々が，ある課題において秀でているという固定観念を持たれる層に属していると意識させられた場合には，同様な意識づけをさせられていない同じ層のほかの人よりも，成績が良くなるのである。
>
> 　次のうち固定観念について推測できることはどれか。
> **(A)** それらは無意識に人の行動を変える。
> (B) それらは女性よりも男性に影響を与える。
> (C) それらは勉強において人々の成績を下げるだけである。
> (D) それらは実生活の場面よりもテストに影響を与える。

解説

　(B) と (D) はパッセージに言及がない。(C) はパッセージ後半で説明されている研究内容と異なる。正解は (A) で，数学が苦手だとほのめかされた集団の方がテストの成績が悪かった一方で，「人々が，ある課題において秀でているという固定観念を持たれる層に属していると意識させられた場合には，…成績が良くなるのである」（最終文）という研究結果に一致する。

Passage 3

Line   Cancer is usually not thought of as a transmissible disease; that is, a disease that can be transferred to one person or another. Usually cancers are caused by factors such as poor diet, exposure to radiation, and genetics; things that can't be passed from person to person. There are some viruses such
(5) as hepatitis virus and HPV that can cause cancers, but the cancerous cells themselves aren't transmitted between people; viruses are just the agents that cause them.

This remains true in human medicine, but among some animals, transmissible cancers do exist. One of the most devastating is Devil Facial
(10) Tumor Disease (DFTD) which affects the Tasmanian devil of Australia. DFTD causes lesions on the mouths of Tasmanian devils, eventually moving inside the throat and preventing them from eating. Usually such tumors wouldn't be transmissible between animals, but fighting is an integral part of devil behavior. When devils bite each other on their faces, they tear off sections of
(15) the tumor, ingest them, and infect themselves. The disease is endemic to the Tasmanian devil population with close to 80% of the population infected, and is a major cause of the species' endangered status.

1. What is suggested as a possible cause for cancer in humans?
   (A) Spending too much time in the cold
   (B) Getting a bacterial infection
   (C) Being next to a person with cancer
   (D) Eating too much unhealthy food

2. The passage implies that Tasmanian devils would be less susceptible to DFTD if they
   (A) were less violent
   (B) had better immunes systems
   (C) had fewer offspring
   (D) were herbivores

> **全訳**

　がんはたいていの場合，伝染する病気，すなわち，1人の人から別の人にうつる病気だとは考えられていない。たいていの場合，がんは粗末な食生活，放射線被ばく，遺伝など，人から人にうつせない要素によって引き起こされる。肝炎ウイルスやヒトパピローマウイルスなど，がんを引き起こすウイルスもあるが，がん細胞そのものは人から人に伝染しない。ウイルスはそれらを引き起こす媒体にすぎないのである。

　人間の医学においてこのことは真実であり続けているが，一部の動物の間では伝染性のがんが実際に存在する。最も衝撃的なものの1つはオーストラリアのタスマニアデビルに発生するデビル顔面腫瘍性疾患（DFTD）である。DFTD はタスマニアデビルの口に外傷を引き起こし，やがて喉の内側に移動して，食べられないようにしてしまう。そのような腫瘍は，普通は動物間で伝染しないのだが，戦いはデビルにはなくてはならない行動なのである。デビルが互いに顔にかみつき合うと，腫瘍の部分をかじり取り，それを体内に取り込み，そうして自分自身を感染させてしまう。この病気はタスマニアデビルの集団に特有のもので，個体数の80%近くが感染しており，この種の絶滅危惧状況の大きな原因となっている。

1. 人間のがんの原因になり得るものとして何が示唆されているか。
　(A) 寒さの中で長時間過ごし過ぎる
　(B) バクテリアに感染する
　(C) がん患者の隣にいる
　(D) 不健康な食べ物を食べ過ぎる

2. パッセージが示唆するには，タスマニアデビルが DFTD により感染しにくくなる可能性があるのは，もし彼らが
　(A) あまりどう猛でなかった場合
　(B) 免疫力がもっとあった場合
　(C) 子供の数がもっと少なかった場合
　(D) 草食性だった場合

> **解説**

1. がんの原因については第1段落第2文に Usually cancers are caused by factors such as poor diet, exposure to radiation, and genetics「たいていの場合，がんは粗末な食生活，放射線被ばく，遺伝などによって引き起こされる」とある。poor diet の言い換えになっている (D) が正解。(C) は第2段落に動物における伝染については説明があるが，人間間の伝染については第1段落および第2段落第1文で否定されている。

2. 第2段落第4～5文から，タスマニアデビルが互いの顔をかみつくときに伝染の可能性が高まることが分かる。つまり，(A) どう猛でなければ，互いにかみつくことは減り，伝染の可能性は低くなると考えられる。(B) については，確かに免疫があれば感染は防げそうだが，パッセージには「免疫」に関する説明はないので，不適切。

Passage 4

Line   A shibboleth is any word or phrase that is used to identify if a person belongs to a group. The word comes from a story in the Bible where a tribe called the Ephraimites were defeated by another tribe called the Gileadites. The surviving Ephraimites tried to escape, but were stopped by the Gileadites.
(5) When the Ephraimites tried to claim they belonged to a different tribe, the Gileadites asked them to pronounce the word "shibboleth" meaning an ear of grain. Ephraimites pronounced this word as "sibboleth" and the Gileadites killed those who pronounced it as such.

Shibboleths have been used in warfare and sectarian violence throughout
(10) history and across the world from France to India. Very often they are used by an ethnic majority to identify and single out minorities for persecution. They can even be used to determine political affiliation, such as with the Northern Irish city called either Derry or Londonderry. People who advocate Northern Ireland joining the rest of Ireland prefer Derry, while those who prefer
(15) Northern Ireland remaining in the United Kingdom say Londonderry.

More broadly and less contentiously, shibboleths can be used to differentiate between natives of a region and those outside it. A local neighborhood or landmark may have an unusual local pronunciation and people pronouncing it "incorrectly" can single out themselves as newcomers.

1. It can be inferred from the passage that the Gileadites
 (A) knew the Ephraimites pronounced "shibboleth" differently
 (B) didn't know the correct definition of the word "shibboleth"
 (C) were a much smaller tribe than the Ephraimites
 (D) did not have their own home land to go back to

2. The passage implies that people prefer pronunciations of landmarks in their hometowns that are
 (A) native to that region
 (B) from the dictionary
 (C) used by outsiders
 (D) easier to pronounce

> **全訳**

shibboleth（シボレス，合言葉）とは，ある人がある集団に属しているかどうかを判断するために使われる，言葉や言い回しである。この言葉は，エフライム族がギレアデ族と呼ばれるほかの部族に打ち負かされたという，聖書の中の物語に由来する。生き残ったエフライム族は逃げようとするが，ギレアデ族に止められる。エフライム族は自分たちが違う部族に属するのだと主張しようとするが，ギレアデ族は彼らに，穀物の粒という意味の shibboleth（シボレス）という言葉を発音するように求める。エフライム族はこの言葉を sibboleth（スィボレス）と発音するために，ギレアデ族はこれをそのように発音する者たちを殺したという。

合言葉は歴史を通して，フランスからインドまでの世界で，戦争や宗派間の争いに使われてきた。非常に多くの場合，それらは多数民族が迫害するために少数民族を見分けて選び出すのに使われる。それらはデリーまたはロンドンデリーと呼ばれる北アイルランドの都市の場合のように，政治的な所属を判断するのにさえ使われることがある。北アイルランドがアイルランドのほかの地域と合併することを支持する人たちは「デリー」の方を好み，北アイルランドが英国にとどまる方がよいと考える人たちは「ロンドンデリー」と言うのだ。

より広範で穏やかな意味では，合言葉はある地域にもともと住んでいる人たちと外部の人たちとを区別するのに使われる。ある地域の近辺や名所には，おそらくその土地特有の変わった発音があり，人々が「正しくなく」発音すると，新参者だということをばらしてしまうのだ。

1. パッセージから推測できるのは，ギレアデ族は
   (A) エフライム族が shibboleth という言葉を違うように発音することを知っていた
   (B) shibboleth という言葉の正しい定義を知らなかった
   (C) エフライム族よりもずっと小さい種族だった
   (D) 帰って行くべき自分たちのふるさとを持っていなかった

2. パッセージが示唆するには，人々が好む彼らの地元にある名所の発音は
   (A) その地域に特有のもの
   (B) 辞書に由来する
   (C) 外来者に使われる
   (D) 発音しやすい

> **解説**

1. 第1段落最終文 Ephraimites pronounced this word as "sibboleth" and the Gileadites killed those who pronounced it as such.「エフライム族はこの言葉を sibboleth（スィボレス）と発音するために，ギレアデ族はこれをそのように発音する者たちを殺した」から，ギレアデ族はエフライム族に特有の shibboleth の発音の仕方を知っていたことが分かる。(A) が正解。

2. 第3段落の，合言葉は地域のもともとの住民とそのほかの人たちとを区別するのに使われ，土地特有の発音をしないと新参者だということがばれてしまう，という内容から (A) が正解だと分かる。(B), (C), (D) についてパッセージに言及がない。

Lesson 6　Purpose Questions
目的を問う問題

> 例題

Line　　Cameo glass is the art form of layering different colors of glass and then carving away at the upper layers until a relief sculpture is formed. The glass is etched and carved either through drills and knives or by dipping in an acid solution. The technique goes back at least as far as ancient Rome, though due to
(5)　the fragility of the pieces, fewer than twenty are still intact. While the surviving artifacts are priceless and were owned by the elite at the time, they were actually a cheaper alternative to the art form of jewel inlaying, which cameo glass imitated in style.

　　Why does the author mention jewel inlaying?
　　(A)　To set the time period in which cameo glass was popular
　　(B)　To demonstrate techniques shared when making it and cameo glass
　　(C)　To mention the art that cameo glass was a less expensive derivative of
　　(D)　To show the art form that eventually replaced cameo glass

> 全訳

　カメオガラスはさまざまな色のガラスを層にして，浮き彫りの彫刻になるまで上層部を削る芸術形式である。ガラスはきりとナイフを使うか，酸性溶液に浸すことで刻み彫られる。その技術は少なくとも古代ローマまでさかのぼるが，作品のもろさのゆえに，損傷を受けていないものは20個に満たない。残っている芸術品は値段がつかないほど貴重で，当時の上流階級が所有していたが，それらは実のところ宝石の象眼細工という芸術形式の安価な代替品で，カメオガラスはその様式をまねていたのだ。

　著者はなぜ宝石の象眼細工に言及しているか。
　(A)　カメオガラスが人気のあった時期を設定するため
　(B)　それとカメオガラスの製造において共通する技法を説明するため
　(C)　カメオガラスがどんな芸術の安価な派生物であるかに言及するため
　(D)　後にカメオガラスに取って代わった芸術形式を示すため

64

① cameo glass の説明　②作成手法について
③ While による意味の反転で,「貴重だが…」という文になる。they 以降で jewel inlaying との価値の比較がある。

> [解き方]

特定の情報が述べられる目的を読み取ります。パッセージのトピックはcameo glassですが, ここではjewel inlayingがなぜ記述されているのかを考慮します。5行目のWhileで始まる文の後半を読み取ると,「それら (cameo glass) はjewel inlayingという芸術形式の安価な代替品であった」ことが分かります。つまりjewel inlayingは, cameo glassがもともとどのようなものであったかを示すために記述されているわけです。

(A) time periodの部分が誤り―時期の話ではない。
(B) techniques sharedの部分が誤り―共通の技法の話ではない。
(D) eventually replacedの部分が誤り―取って代わったとは書いていない。

ここがポイント
- 設問文にWhy ...? が含まれる場合は目的を問う問題。
- 疑問形でなくともThe passage discusses ... in order toと問われる場合もあるので注意。
- キーワードを設定し, なぜその情報が記述されているかをその前後から読み取る。
- 選択肢を分析し, 消去法で解く。

学習アドバイス

詳細な情報が含まれる文章を読む場合, それらが何のために記述されているのか, 普段から頭の中に「?」を浮かべながら読み進めましょう。特に人名・地名・出来事・年号などの詳細な情報は, 何かを伝えたいがための例示になっている場合がほとんどです。その背景にあるアイディアは何か, 1歩下がって, より広い視野で理解するように意識しましょう。

Passage 1

Line   Unlike cars which can occupy a range of wheel-to-wheel widths, trains must have a wheel-span that perfectly matches the rails they ride on. Differences of only a few millimeters can be dangerous, and rail widths are explicitly standardized. These widths are known as track gauges, the most
(5) prevalent of which is known as the standard gauge and is set at 1,435 mm. Some people have claimed that the gauge is based on the width between the wagons of Roman chariots and the ruts they left on stone roads, but this isn't necessarily true. Train cars across Europe varied, but all stayed within a general range that standard gauge occupies. The gauge was implemented
(10) by engineer George Stephenson for use on the world's first railway that ran between the English cities of Liverpool and Manchester. With its start as the foundational track gauge in England, it spread out to become the dominant standard across the world, accounting for over 60% of the world's railways.

What is the main purpose of the passage?
(A) To explain an aspect of rail transportation standardization
(B) To show how far transportation has progressed since ancient times
(C) To give details of the different gauges used by trains
(D) To compare methods of transportation between ancient and modern times

> 全訳

　さまざまなタイヤ間の幅を使用できる車と違い，電車の車輪間の幅は，それらが乗って走るレールに完璧に合うものでなければならない。ほんの数ミリの差が危険であり，レールの幅は明確に基準化されている。これらの幅は軌間として知られていて，最も多いものが基準軌間として知られ，1,435 ミリに定められている。軌間はローマの二輪馬車の車輪間の幅と，石畳の道路に残されたわだちに基づいていると主張する人もいるが，それは必ずしも真実ではない。ヨーロッパ中の鉄道車両はさまざまであったが，全て基準軌間が使用する一般的な幅に収まっていた。軌間は，イギリスの都市リヴァプールとマンチェスターの間を走った世界初の鉄道を使用するために，技術師のジョージ・スチーブンソンによって実用化された。イギリスにおける基礎的な軌間の始まりとともに，それは世界の鉄道の 60％以上を占める，世界中の主要な基準として普及していった。

　パッセージの主な目的は何か。
- **(A) 鉄道輸送の標準化のある側面を説明すること**
- (B) 古代と比べて乗り物がどれほど進歩したかを示すこと
- (C) 電車に用いられるいろいろな軌間の詳細を説明すること
- (D) 古代と現代の輸送方法を比較すること

> 解説

　第 2 文に rail widths are explicitly standardized「レールの幅は明確に基準化されている」とあり，以降で gauge「軌間（＝線路の幅）」がヨーロッパおよび世界で普及した経緯について説明している。正解は (A)。時代ごとの比較ではないので (B) と (D) は誤り。(C) の「いろいろな軌間」はパッセージ全体の内容に合わない。

Passage 2

Line   Afrobeat was a musical genre that was pioneered primarily by a single man, the Nigerian musician Fela Kuti. Kuti developed the style primarily in Ghana in the 1970's, and mixed influences from funk, jazz, and traditional West African music. Afrobeat music often used ensembles of two-dozen
(5) people or more playing a diverse selection of instruments, including both African and western. The organ was a particularly prevalent instrument, and is one that is often associated with music descended from Afrobeat. One of the elements that defines Afrobeat, and much of Sub-Saharan African music, is polyrhythms. Polyrhythms are two or more distinct beats that exist at the same
(10) time, and do not necessarily sync with each other. These complex rhythms are a signature feature of Afrobeat and give it a distinct character.

Why does the author mention polyrhythms?
(A) To demonstrate what kinds of techniques were allowed by new technology
(B) To show what kinds of musical standards that Afrobeat was rebelling against
(C) To give an example of a natively African musical element used in Afrobeat
(D) To reveal what types of rhythms the organ was most suited to play

> **全訳**
>
> アフロビートは，主にたった1人の男性，ナイジェリアのミュージシャンであるフェラ・クティが先駆者となった音楽ジャンルだった。クティは主に1970年代にガーナでこのスタイルを発展させ，それにファンク，ジャズ，西アフリカの伝統音楽の影響を混ぜ合わせた。アフロビート音楽は，アフリカと西洋の両方のものを含むさまざまな楽器の一揃いを演奏する，24人かそれ以上の人々の集団を用いていた。オルガンは特に中心的な楽器であり，アフロビートの流れをくむ音楽としばしば関連付けられる。アフロビートや多くのサハラ以南のアフリカ音楽を決定づける要素の1つは，ポリリズムである。ポリリズムとは，同時に存在する2つかそれ以上のはっきりしたビートで，必ずしもお互いと同調してはいない。これらの複雑なリズムはアフロビートの特徴的な性質であり，それに独特な個性を与えている。
>
> 著者はなぜポリリズムに言及しているか。
> (A) 新しい技術によってどのような種類の技法ができたかを示すため
> (B) アフロビートがどのような音楽の規範に反抗していたかを示すため
> (C) アフロビートに用いられるアフリカ土着の音楽要素の例を挙げるため
> (D) オルガンがどのような種類のリズムを弾くのに最も適していたかを明らかにするため

解説

ポリリズムについては，最後の3文で説明されている。特に第5文を注意して読むと，「アフロビートや多くのサハラ以南のアフリカ音楽を決定づける要素」であることが分かる。(C) が正解。(A) の技術や技法，(B) のアフロビートが反抗する音楽規範，(D) のオルガンに最適のリズムについては，ポリリズムとは関係がない。

Passage 3

Line   During the 18th and 19th centuries, almost all of the Indian Subcontinent was slowly taken over by first the British East India Company and eventually by the government of the United Kingdom. What followed was over a century of foreign rule over India that ended in 1947. However, India was, in one
(5) sense, trading one foreign ruler for another. Before the British, most of India was under control of the Mughal Empire, a ruling family that broke off from the Persian Empire. Culturally the Mughals were distinct from the people of the land they ruled over. The situation was much like the Qing Dynasty in China. When European powers came into contact with India and China, they
(10) were both under the control of dynasties that were different from their general populace.

The Mughals spoke Persian in court instead of any of the Indian languages and practiced Islam instead of Hinduism. Despite these differences, the Mughal Empire did not try to impose their own culture on the general
(15) populace. Over time, cultural differences softened and the Mughals became more culturally Indian. Mughal monuments such as the Taj Mahal, though built by an empire with roots outside India, are now an accepted part of India's cultural fabric.

What is the purpose of the second paragraph?
(A) To show how the Mughals integrated into Indian culture
(B) To point out the many famous monuments the Mughals built
(C) To explain how many languages were spoken in India
(D) To detail the ways the Mughals imposed their religion on others

> **全訳**
>
> 　18世紀と19世紀の間，インド亜大陸のほとんどはゆっくりと，まずイギリスの東インド会社，そして最終的にはイギリス政府に征服されていった。その後に続いたのは，1947年に終わった，1世紀以上続く外国によるインド支配であった。しかしインドはある意味，外国支配者をそのまた別の支配者と取り替えていたのである。イギリス人の前には，インドのほとんどは，ペルシア帝国から分離した支配一族であるムガル帝国の支配下にあった。文化的には，ムガルは彼らが支配した土地に住む人々とは異なっていた。その状況は中国の清王朝とよく似ていた。ヨーロッパ勢力がインドや中国と接触したときには，彼らはどちらも自国の一般人民とは違う王朝に支配されていたのである。
>
> 　ムガルの人々は，宮廷ではインドの言葉のどれでもないペルシア語を話し，ヒンズー教ではなくイスラム教を実践した。これらの違いにもかかわらず，ムガル帝国は自分たちの文化を一般人民に強要しようとはしなかった。時がたつにつれ，文化的な違いは和らぎ，ムガルの人々は文化的にはよりインド化した。タージ・マハルなどのムガルの記念建造物は，インドの外にルーツを持つ帝国によって建てられたが，今ではインドの文化的構造として受け入れられている。
>
> 　第2段落の目的は何か。
> **(A) ムガルの人々がどのようにしてインド文化に溶け込んだかを示すこと**
> (B) ムガルの人々が建てた多くの有名な記念建造物を指摘すること
> (C) インドではどれほど多くの言語が話されていたかを説明すること
> (D) ムガルの人々が自分たちの宗教をほかの人々に強要したやり方を詳しく説明すること

解説

第2段落第3文「時がたつにつれ，文化的な違いは和らぎ，ムガルの人々は文化的にはよりインド化した」や，最終文「ムガルの記念建造物は…今ではインドの文化的構造として受け入れられている」から，(A) が正解だと分かる。(B) についてはタージ・マハルに触れているだけ。(C) について言及がない。(D) は第2文の内容に合わない。

Passage 4

Line Self-driving cars are fast becoming one of the most promising developments in transportation technology. Sensors surveying a full 360-degree view of the car's surroundings allow self-driving cars to be much more responsive, which makes them safer than cars driven by humans.
(5) However, even if self-driving cars are indeed safer than the cars they replace, they still offer ethical quandaries about how to best program them to react in the case of emergencies where injuries may occur.

For example, a self-driving car would be programmed to swerve around a pedestrian in order to avoid hitting them. But suppose swerving around *(10)* the pedestrian meant hitting a bicyclist. The programming of the artificial intelligence must decide which of the two actions to take. If the pedestrian was jaywalking, which means crossing the street illegally, should that be taken into account? What if the only way to avoid hitting a pedestrian was to crash into a wall, thereby injuring the passenger of the self-driving car? There *(15)* is also the question of who is legally culpable if someone is injured. The car manufacturer is one likely answer, but the person riding in it might also be considered responsible since it is his property that caused the injury.

Why does the author mention jaywalking in line 12?
(A) To provide background on traffic laws that self-driving cars must follow
(B) To give an example of accidents that self-driving cars are meant to correct
(C) To explain the most common reason for automobile accidents
(D) To point out a factor that might complicate what action a self-driving car would take

> 全訳

　自動運転車は，輸送技術の中で最も有望な開発の1つに急速になりつつある。自動車の周囲全360度の視野を監視するセンサーのおかげで，自動運転車はずっと反応がよく，そのため人が運転する車よりも安全である。しかし，たとえ自動運転車が，それらが取って代わる車よりも確実に安全だとしても，けがにつながるような緊急事態に反応するために，いかに最善のプログラムをするかについて，それらは依然として倫理的な難局をもたらす。

　例えば，自動運転車は歩行者にぶつかるのを避けるために歩行者からそれるようにプログラムされているだろう。しかし，歩行者を避けることで，自転車に乗っている人にぶつかることになるとすればどうだろう。人工知能のプログラミングは，その2つのうちどちらの行動を取るべきかを判断しなければならない。もし歩行者がジェイウォーク，つまり法律違反をして道路を渡っているとすれば，それは考慮に入れるべきだろうか。歩行者にぶつかるのを避ける唯一の方法が壁にぶつかることで，その結果自動運転車に乗っている人にけがを負わせることになったらどうだろうか。また，もし誰かがけがをした場合には，誰に法的過失があるのかという問題もある。自動車の製造業者というのがありそうな答えの1つだが，けがの原因となったのはそれに乗っている人の所有物なのだから，その人にもまた責任があると考えられるかもしれない。

著者はなぜ12行目でジェイウォークに言及しているか。
(A) 自動運転車が従わなければならない道路交通法の背景を説明するため
(B) 自動運転車が修正すべきとされる事故の例を挙げるため
(C) 自動車事故の最も一般的な理由を説明するため
(D) 自動運転車がどのような行動を取るべきかを複雑にするかもしれない要素を示すため

> 解説

　jaywalking の意味は，その直後に crossing the street illegally「法律違反をして道路を渡る」ことだと説明されている。第1段落の最終文で，自動運転車には倫理的な難局があることが述べられ，続く第2段落では，さまざまな例がその理由として挙げられている。jaywalking をする歩行者も自動運転車に判断を迷わせる例の1つと考えられるので，(D)が正解。

Lesson 7 Main Idea Questions
主旨を問う問題

例題

Line
The early form of the necktie originated in the 17th century from Croatian soldiers hired to fight in France. The Croatian soldiers tied cloths around their necks to hold up their uniforms and as decoration. The king of France liked the style so much that he had his own guards wear the accessory and named the ties
(5) *cravat* from the French word for Croatian. To this day *cravat* is the French word for necktie. The tie as we know it today came in the 1920's when advances in materials and construction led to ties that returned to their original shape after being untied. This also allowed for a variety of ways for them to be tied such as the most common and simple four-in-hand knot or symmetrical and thick
(10) Windsor knot.

What does the passage mainly discuss?
(A) How to wear ties
(B) The materials used to make ties
(C) How the Croatian soldiers fought in France
(D) How ties originated in France

全訳

　ネクタイの初期の形態は，17世紀にフランスで戦うために雇われたクロアチア人兵士たちから始まった。クロアチア人兵士たちは軍服を支えるため，また装飾として，首の回りに布を巻きつけていた。フランス国王はそのスタイルを非常に気に入ったので，自分の護衛にその飾りをつけさせ，クロアチア人を意味するフランス語からそのひもをクラバットと命名した。今日に至るまで，クラバットがネクタイを意味するフランス語となっている。1920年代，素材と構造の進歩によって，ほどいた後に元の形に戻るようになる，今日われわれが知るネクタイができた。これによりネクタイは，最も一般的で簡単なフォア・イン・ハンド・ノットや，左右対称でずんぐりしたウィンザー・ノットなど，さまざまなやり方で結べるようになったのである。

　　パッセージは主に何について述べているか。
　　(A) ネクタイの着用方法
　　(B) ネクタイを作るのに使われる素材
　　(C) クロアチア人兵士たちはどのようにフランスで戦ったか
　　(D) ネクタイはどのようにフランスで発祥したか

①初期のネクタイについて　②クロアチア兵士の着用方法　③現代のネクタイへの発展

> **解き方**

パッセージの主要な話題を答える問題です。以下のように，まずトピックを判明させ，そしてそれがどのように展開するのかに注意しながら読み進めていきます。
第1文「初期のネクタイ」→第2文「クロアチア人兵士によるネクタイの着用方法」→第3文「フランス王がいかにネクタイを取り入れて，定着したか」→第5文「1920年代以降から今日までのネクタイの発展」
このように，ネクタイの起源と，現在のネクタイになるまでの変遷が述べられています。
(A)　How to wear「着用方法」の部分は最後に登場するだけ。
(B)　materials「素材」について具体的な説明はない。
(C)　How ... fought「どのように戦ったか」の部分が内容と合わない。

ここがポイント

主旨を問う問題は，たいてい各パッセージの1問目に出題されます。例題のように短いパッセージならその場で読み通すことができますが，実際の試験問題ではパッセージは長いので，以下を実践しましょう。
- 最初から全部読もうとしない。
- 保留にしておき，ほかの問題を解き終えてから最後に解答する。
- パッセージがどのような展開になっているかに留意しながら読み進める。

学習アドバイス

この問題タイプで正解率を上げるには，大きく分けて2つのスキルを身につけることが必要です。
1）パッセージ全体を見渡すスキル：詳細だけにとらわれず，広い視野をもって全体の構成・展開を見極める。
2）選択肢を分析して消去するスキル：本文を読むだけでは正解できません。選択肢を1つ1つ分析し，どの部分がメインアイディアとして不適切なのか考え，消去法を徹底する。

この2点を日ごろから心がけて学習するようにしましょう。

Passage 1

Line   One of the world's most prestigious and unique automotive racing events is the 24 Hours of Le Mans held on a track just outside the town of Le Mans, France. The Le Mans is, as the name makes clear, a 24-hour endurance race. The first race was in 1923, and considering the automotive technology of
(5) the time, it's easy to imagine that it was a grueling test of skill, technical expertise, and willpower. It differs from other races in that its objective is not to test pure speed but to see which car can go fast reliably over a long period of time. Rules unique to Le Mans include having to turn off the car while refueling, and mechanics not being allowed to work on the car while it is being
(10) refueled. The race used to allow one driver to complete the entire race, but this was disallowed for obvious safety reasons. Today, most cars have a team of three drivers, though some have two.

What does the passage mainly discuss?
(A) Why Le Mans is so popular
(B) The history and rules of an international event
(C) Past winning cars and drivers
(D) The best techniques for the race

> **全訳**
>
> 　世界で最も名高く独特な自動車レースは，フランスのル・マンという町のすぐ外の走路で行われるル・マン24時間レースである。ル・マンはその名前から明らかなとおり，24時間耐久レースだ。最初のレースは1923年に開かれたが，当時の自動車技術を考えれば，それが運転技術，技術的専門知識，そして意志の力を試す厳しい試練だったことは想像するに難くない。その目的が純粋なスピードをテストするものではなく，どの車が長時間確実に高速で走れるかを見るためのものだという点で，ル・マンはほかのレースとは異なる。ル・マン独特のルールには，給油中にはエンジンを切らなくてはならないこと，給油中にはメカニックは車の調整をしてはならないということも含まれる。このレースでは，かつてレースを完走するのに1人のドライバーしか許されなかったが，これは明白な安全上の理由から禁止された。今日では，ドライバーが2人の車もあるが，大部分の車は3人のドライバーでチームを組んでいる。
>
> 　パッセージは主に何について述べているか。
> (A) なぜル・マンはそれほど人気があるか
> **(B) 国際的イベントの歴史とルール**
> (C) 過去の優勝車とドライバーたち
> (D) レースのための最善のテクニック

解説

パッセージ全体が「ル・マン24時間レース」の説明になっており，第5文以降ではその独特なルールにも言及している。従って (B) が正解。(A) については，人気があることは想像できるが，実際にパッセージでその理由を説明しているわけではないので，不適切。歴史についての説明はあるが，具体的な優勝車やドライバーについて触れていないので，(C) も誤り。(D) についても説明はない。

Passage 2

Line   Stretching is the act of elongating the muscles in order to make them more flexible for exercise and to relieve tightness and sometimes pain. When done properly, stretching has the effect of increasing one's range of motion and reducing injury during sports activities. Broadly speaking, there are two
(5) types of stretches—static and dynamic. Static stretching is when a body part is put into a position that stretches the muscle and that position is held for a set amount of time. Dynamic stretching takes place when a body part is moved through a range of motion and the muscle is stretched during that movement.

What does the passage mainly discuss?
(A) Dynamic stretching
(B) The dangers of stretching
(C) How to stretch after playing sports
(D) Types of stretching

> **全訳**

　ストレッチ体操は筋肉を引き伸ばす行為で，運動に備えて筋肉をより柔軟にし，緊張やときには痛みも緩和するために行う。正しく行えば，ストレッチ体操は動きの幅を広げ，スポーツ中のけがを減らす効果がある。大まかに言えば，ストレッチは2種類ある。スタティック（静的）とダイナミック（動的）である。スタティックストレッチ体操は，体の一部を筋肉が伸びる位置にもっていき，その位置を一定の時間保つものだ。ダイナミックストレッチ体操は，体の一部が可動域の中で動かされるときに生じ，その動きの最中に筋肉が伸ばされる。

　パッセージは主に何について述べているか。
　(A)　ダイナミックストレッチ体操
　(B)　ストレッチ体操の危険性
　(C)　スポーツをした後のストレッチのやり方
　(D)　ストレッチ体操の種類

> **解説**

　第1文 Stretching is ... でストレッチ体操の概要を述べた後，第3文以下で static stretching と dynamic stretching という2種類のストレッチ体操について説明している。(D) が正解。2種類のストレッチ体操について述べているので (A) は誤り。(B) の危険性や (C) の具体的な方法についてパッセージに言及がない。

Passage 3

Line   Many people enjoy the taste of soft drinks but not how they contribute to weight gain or possibly even diabetes. Companies have responded by offering low-calorie soft drinks with artificial sweeteners in place of natural sweeteners such as brown sugar or corn syrup. The most popular of these artificial
(5) sweeteners are saccharin and aspartame. The benefit of these sweeteners is that they provide the sweet flavor everyone craves without the downsides. However, there are concerns that they have their own unhealthy side effects that may even include an increased risk of cancer.

   The earliest sugar substitute was sugar of lead, and as its name makes
(10) clear, it was made of lead. It was used by the ancient Romans to sweeten food, but was abandoned because using it regularly resulted in lead poisoning. Saccharin, discovered in the late 1800's, is the second-oldest artificial sweetener, and is still in use. In the 1960's, it was found to cause cancer in lab rats. However, this was in extremely high doses, and it was also found that the
(15) way saccharin causes cancer in rats does not relate to humans. Nonetheless, while it is used in many countries, it is banned in some.

   What does the second paragraph mainly discuss?
   (A) The means by which artificial sweeteners are produced
   (B) Alternatives to artificial sweeteners
   (C) The history of artificial sweeteners
   (D) The latest developments in artificial sweeteners

全訳

　多くの人はソフトドリンクの味は楽しむものの、それが体重増加や、あるいは糖尿病にさえ寄与するかもしれないことに対しては、そうではない。企業は、ブラウン・シュガーやコーンシロップといった自然甘味料の代わりに、人工甘味料を使った低カロリーのソフトドリンクを提供することで応えてきた。そうした人工甘味料の中でも最もよく使われるものが、サッカリンとアスパルテームである。これらの甘味料の利点は、みんなが大好きな甘い味をマイナス面なく提供できるということだ。しかし、人工甘味料にも健康によくない副作用があるという懸念も存在し、それにはがんのリスクが高まることすら含まれる。

　最も初期の砂糖の代用品は鉛糖で、名前から明白なとおり、鉛から作られていた。古代ローマ人によって食べ物を甘くするために使われたが、定期的に使うと鉛中毒を起こしたため、使われなくなった。1800年代後半に発明されたサッカリンが、2番目に古い人工甘味料で、今でも使われている。1960年代には、それは実験用ラットにがんを引き起こすことが発見された。しかし、これは極度に高用量を使っていたし、サッカリンがラットにがんを引き起こす過程は、人間には関係がないということも分かった。それにもかかわらず、サッカリンは多くの国で使われている一方、禁止されている国もある。

　第2段落は主に何について述べているか。
　(A) 人工甘味料が生産される方法
　(B) 人工甘味料に代わるもの
　(C) 人工甘味料の歴史
　(D) 人工甘味料における最新の開発

解説

　第2段落は The earliest sugar ... Saccharin, discovered in the late 1800's, is ... In the 1960's, it was found ...「最も初期の砂糖は…。1800年代後半に発明されたサッカリンは…。1960年代には…が発見された」と、人工甘味料について年代を追って説明している。従って、(C) が正解。(A)、(B)、(D) については本文に言及がない。

Passage 4

Line   When cars first appeared at the end of the 19th century, there were few laws or regulations concerning who could drive. In the US, the earliest driver's license was issued around 1903 in Massachusetts and Missouri, but it was really just an ID that could be obtained for a small fee. Chicago and New York
(5) were the first places to require that drivers had to be tested before they could be allowed to operate a motor vehicle. By the 1920's, cars were commonplace, and an increasing number of states issued driver's licenses. However, still not all states tested drivers. In fact, last state to require an exam to drive was South Dakota in 1959.

(10)   Today, every state issues driver's licenses and requires a test in order to obtain one. The age for getting a license is as young as 14 years of age in several states, and up to 17 years in New Jersey. Over half of US states require driver education before applying for a license. However, teenagers without a license may obtain a permit to drive before getting a license. A permit allows
(15) the holder to drive with a licensed person in the passenger seat, or to drive alone at certain designated hours.

    What does the first paragraph mainly discuss?
    (A) How to obtain a driver's license in the US
    (B) The beginnings of driver's license
    (C) The minimum requirements for obtaining a license
    (D) Which states require testing in order to drive

> **全訳**

19世紀末に自動車が最初に登場したとき，誰が運転できるかに関する法律や規則はほとんどなかった。アメリカにおける最も初期の運転免許証は，1903年ごろにマサチューセッツとミズーリで発行されたものだが，それは少額で獲得できるただの身分証明書にすぎなかった。シカゴとニューヨークは，自動車の運転を許可する前に，ドライバーに試験を受けることを義務づけた最初の場所であった。1920年代までに，自動車はどこにでもあるようになり，ますます多くの州が運転免許証を発行した。しかし，全ての州がドライバーに試験を課したわけではなかった。実際，最後に運転試験を義務づけたのはサウスダコタで，1959年のことだった。

今日では全ての州が運転免許証を発行し，それを取得するための試験を必須としている。免許を取得する年齢は，14歳と低年齢の州がいくつかあり，一番高いのはニュージャージーの17歳である。アメリカの半分以上の州が，免許を申請する前に運転教習を義務づけている。しかし，免許を持たない十代の若者たちは，免許を取得する前に運転許可証をもらえることがある。許可証があれば，免許取得者が助手席にいる場合か，あるいは指定された時間であれば，1人で運転することもできるのだ。

第1段落は主に何について述べているか。
(A) アメリカで運転免許証を取得する方法
(B) 運転免許証の始まり
(C) 免許証を取得するための最低限の必要条件
(D) どの州が運転するための試験を義務づけているか

> **解説**

第1段落では，一貫して自動車の運転免許および試験が導入されてきた経緯について説明している。(B) が正解。具体的な免許の取得方法の説明ではないので，(A) と (C) は誤り。最終文から，サウスダコタを最後に全ての州で運転試験が導入されたことが分かるので，(D) も不適切。

Lesson 8 Where Questions
記述箇所を探す問題

> 例題

Line
　　Candy are sweets made specifically from sugar. Early types of candy eaten by <u>ancient people</u>① were simply honey with fruits and nuts mixed in. <u>The earliest processing of sugar began in the Middle Ages in Europe, but sugar was so expensive that only the rich could enjoy it.</u>② Candy didn't come to the masses until
(5) the 19th century when the industrial revolution allowed for the mass production of candy in factories. It was at this time that candy went from <u>a luxury food for the wealthy</u>③ to <u>the favorite treat of children</u>④, especially in Europe and in the United States.

Where in the passage does the author mention the change in the main consumer of candy?
(A) Lines 1-2
(B) Lines 2-4
(C) Lines 4-6
(D) Lines 6-7

> 全訳

　キャンディーは特に砂糖でできているお菓子だ。古代の人々が食べていた初期のタイプのキャンディーは，単に蜂蜜に果物やナッツを混ぜこんだものだった。最古の砂糖加工は中世のヨーロッパで始まったが，砂糖はあまりに高価だったため，金持ちしか楽しめなかった。キャンディーが大衆の口に入るようになったのは，19世紀になり，産業革命によって工場でキャンディーが大量生産できるようになってからである。このとき初めて，特にヨーロッパとアメリカにおいて，キャンディーが金持ちのぜいたくな食べ物から子供たちに人気のおやつに移ったのだ。

　著者はパッセージのどこでキャンディーの主な消費者の変化に言及しているか。
(A) 1～2行目
(B) 2～4行目
(C) 4～6行目
(D) 6～7行目

84

①初期のキャンディーの消費者　②中世のキャンディーの説明　③移行前の消費者
④移行後の消費者

> [解き方]

特定の情報がパッセージのどこで述べられるかを問う問題です。本文中で「キャンディーの消費者の変化」に言及している箇所を探します。前半では中世から19世紀にかけてのキャンディーの歴史や特徴が説明されており，「消費者」にあたる言及は4行目のthe rich「金持ち」があります。しかし，それが「変化した」との記述はありません。その後6〜7行目にa luxury food for the wealthy「金持ちのぜいたくな食べ物」からthe favorite treat of children「子供たちに人気のおやつ」に移った（went）と記述があることから，正解は(D)のLines 6-7となります。go from A to Bで「AからBに移る」という意味です。

> **ここがポイント**
>
> まず設問文を読み，何を探すべきなのかを理解した上で読み進めましょう。主に問われる点としては，
> ● 語句の定義や説明
> ● ある事象が起きた原因や理由
> ● 例示や根拠
>
> などが挙げられます。これらの内容についてはパッセージの複数箇所で述べられることもありますが，あくまでも選択肢で指定された行数だけをチェックすればOKです。

> **学習アドバイス**
>
> Readingにおいて，「メンタルマッピング」は必要なスキルです。これは，頭の中で「どの辺に何の情報が位置しているか」をある程度把握しておくことです。普段から書くことに頼らず，文章の脈絡を頭の中だけで整理して，メンタルマッピングのスキルを鍛えるようにしておきましょう。

Passage 1

Line   The pencil comes from the Roman stylus, which was a thin metal tool used for making scratches on paper. The earliest pencils were made from lead, but the idea really took off with the discovery of graphite in the 1500's. Graphite was ideal because it was darker than lead, and a nice bonus was
(5) that unlike lead, it wasn't poisonous. Early pencils were thin strips of lead used naked or wrapped in string. However graphite was so soft and brittle that it had to be put in something to be practical. The wood-encased graphite pencils we still use today were invented in Germany in the late 1600's. The reason many pencils today are yellow is because in the late 1800's, the best
(10) graphite came from China. Yellow is a royal color in Chinese culture and manufacturers wanted to express this in their product.

Where in the passage does the author mention why graphite is a good material for pencils?
(A) Lines 2-3
(B) Lines 4-5
(C) Lines 5-6
(D) Lines 6-7

全訳

鉛筆はローマの尖筆に由来する。紙に引っかいた跡をつけるために使われた細い金属の道具だ。最古の鉛筆は鉛でできていたが，1500年代の黒鉛の発見によって，その着想が実際に進展した。黒鉛は鉛より色が濃かったので理想的だったし，おまけに鉛と違って有毒ではなかった。初期の鉛筆は，細長くした鉛をそのままの状態かひもで包んで使われた。しかし黒鉛はとても軟らかくてもろかったので，実際に使うには何かに入れなくてはならなかった。今日でもいまだに私たちが使っている木で包みこんだ黒鉛の鉛筆は，1600年末期にドイツで発明された。今日の鉛筆の多くが黄色い理由は，1800年代後期には最も良質な黒鉛が中国製だったからだ。黄色は中国文化では高貴な色であり，製造者たちはこれを自分たちの製品で表現したかったのである。

著者はパッセージのどこで黒鉛が鉛筆に適した材料だということの理由に言及しているか。

(A) 2〜3行目
(B) 4〜5行目
(C) 5〜6行目
(D) 6〜7行目

解説

graphite「黒鉛」の利点の説明にあたるのは，Graphite was ideal because it was darker than lead「黒鉛は鉛より色が濃かったので理想的だった」と it wasn't poisonous「有毒ではなかった」の部分。従って (B) が正解。

Passage 2

Line   We may have discovered that mice have a fear of men, and this could pose a problem for scientific experimentation. Lab mice are the most commonly used animals for the study of mammals in areas of research including cancer, psychology and others. However, if mice have a special fear of men but not of
(5) women, this may cast a shadow on much of the scientific research conducted until now. Recent research has found that mice can smell testosterone (the male hormone) and react to it with fear. This is a big deal because fear induces stress and stress affects not only behavior but also the growth of cancer cells. The research found that the mice could sense a man in the room even
(10) if a woman was conducting the experiment. Although this new discovery is problematic for research methodology and results, it may give us new insight on how testosterone and other hormones may affect humans.

Where in the passage does the author explain why rats' fear of men is problematic?
(A) Lines 2-4
(B) Lines 4-6
(C) Lines 9-10
(D) Lines 10-12

> **全訳**

　マウスは男性に対して恐れを抱いており，これが科学実験に問題を引き起こしかねないということが分かってきたようだ。研究所のマウスは，がん，心理学，またそのほかを含む研究分野で，哺乳類の研究に最も一般的に使われる動物だ。しかし，マウスに特に男性に対する恐怖心はあるが女性にはないとしたら，これまで行われてきた科学研究のほとんどに影を落とす可能性もある。最近の研究では，マウスはテストステロン（男性ホルモン）の匂いを嗅ぐことができ，それに恐怖の反応を示すことが分かった。これは一大事である。というのも，恐怖はストレスを増し，ストレスは行動だけでなく，がん細胞の増加にも影響を与えるからだ。女性が実験を行っているとしても，マウスは室内にいる男性を感じることができるということが研究で分かった。この新しい発見は，研究方法と結果にとっては問題があるとしても，テストステロンやそのほかのホルモンの人間への影響に関して，新たな洞察を与えるかもしれない。

著者はパッセージのどこでマウスの男性に対する恐怖が問題であることを説明しているか。
(A) 2〜4行目
(B) 4〜6行目
(C) 9〜10行目
(D) 10〜12行目

> **解説**

第3文に「マウスに特に男性に対する恐怖心はあるが女性にはないとしたら，これまで行われてきた科学研究のほとんどに影を落とす可能性もある」とあり，さらにその具体的な説明が第5文にある。(B) が正解。

Passage 3

Line　　George Washington Carver was an African-American scientist and inventor. He was born into slavery but went on to become an accomplished botanist and discover over 300 uses of the peanut. In his lifetime, he became so famous that *TIME* magazine called him a "black Leonardo" after the
(5) famous artist and inventor Leonardo da Vinci. Born around 1865 Carver was raised by his former slave owners as their own child. They encouraged Carver to study and even taught him how to read and write.

　　Carver had to overcome some obstacles on his way to becoming a scientist. He was rejected from the first college he was accepted into, when
(10) they found out he was black. However, he would eventually become the first black student to graduate from Iowa State University, eventually earning a master's degree. This accomplishment would help him to gain a research and teaching position at the prestigious African-American Tuskegee Institute, where Carver would head the agricultural department. While it is not true
(15) that he invented peanut butter, he did develop numerous uses for and products from the peanut plant including plastics and even fuel.

1. Where in the passage does the author mention who Carver was compared to?
　　(A) Line 2
　　(B) Line 3
　　(C) Line 4
　　(D) Line 5

2. Where in the passage does the author mention why Carver was first not accepted to college?
　　(A) Lines 8-9
　　(B) Lines 9-10
　　(C) Lines 10-11
　　(D) Lines 12-13

> **全訳**

　ジョージ・ワシントン・カーヴァーは，アフリカ系アメリカ人の科学者であり発明家である。彼は奴隷として生まれたが，優れた植物学者となり，ピーナツの300以上の使用法を発見した。生きている間に非常に有名になり，『タイム』誌は彼を有名な芸術家で発明家のレオナルド・ダ・ヴィンチにちなんで「ブラック・レオナルド」と呼んだ。1865年ごろ生まれたカーヴァーは，かつて彼を奴隷として所有していた人たちに，わが子として育てられた。彼らは勉強するようカーヴァーを励まし，読み書きを教えさえした。

　カーヴァーは科学者になるまでに，いくつかの障害を乗り越えなくてはならなかった。最初に受け入れてもらえた大学に，黒人だと分かると入学を拒否された。しかし，やがてアイオワ州立大学を卒業する最初の黒人学生となり，ついには修士学位を取得した。この業績で，彼は一流のアフリカ系アメリカ人のためのタスキーギ大学で研究と教職の地位を得て，農学部長となった。彼がピーナッツバターを発明したという話は真実ではないとしても，確かにプラスチックや燃料さえ含めて，ラッカセイの数多くの利用法や製品を開発した。

1. 著者はパッセージのどこでカーヴァーがなぞらえられた人物に言及しているか。
   (A) 2行目
   (B) 3行目
   (C) 4行目
   (D) 5行目

2. 著者はパッセージのどこでカーヴァーが当初大学に受け入れられなかった理由に言及しているか。
   (A) 8～9行目
   (B) 9～10行目
   (C) 10～11行目
   (D) 12～13行目

> 解説

1. カーヴァーを別の人物とたとえているのは第1段落第3文で，「『タイム』誌は彼を有名な芸術家で発明家のレオナルド・ダ・ヴィンチにちなんで『ブラック・レオナルド』と呼んだ」とある。(D) が正解。

2. 学校に受け入れられなかった経験については，第2段落第2文に「最初に受け入れてもらえた大学に，黒人だと分かると入学を拒否された」と説明がある。(B) が正解。

Passage 4

Line Combustion-powered vehicles have been the standard in automobiles for over 100 years. However, in recent years, automakers are making strides in offering vehicles powered by electric batteries and other technologies such as hydrogen fuel cells. Believe it or not, electric-powered vehicles have existed
(5) almost from the time cars came on the market. In fact, in the 1900's, electric-powered cars were more popular than gasoline-powered cars and second only to steam-powered cars. Gasoline-powered cars surpassed electric and other types only after internal combustion engine cars became easier to use, and could go much longer distances before refueling.
(10) Over the next few decades, no progress was made with electric battery-powered cars. One of the reasons is that improvements in battery technology were not keeping up with the needs of car owners. One way around this issue has been hybrid cars. Hybrid cars still run on an internal combustion engine but also have a battery for shorter distances and lower speeds. However,
(15) hybrid cars are most likely a temporary solution. Companies are aggressively moving towards full electric car with a range of almost 500 kilometers. Right now, electric cars are still out of the price range of most buyers and the infrastructure for refueling them is still underdeveloped. But this is likely to change rapidly over the next few years.

1. Where in the passage does the author mention a time when electric cars were common?
(A) Lines 1-2
(B) Lines 5-7
(C) Lines 10-11
(D) Lines 17-18

2. Which of the following words does the author give an explanation?
(A) hydrogen fuel cells
(B) internal combustion engine
(C) hybrid cars
(D) infrastructure

> **全訳**

　燃焼動力車は，100年以上にわたって自動車における標準だった。しかし，近年になって，自動車メーカーは電気や水素燃料電池などといったそのほかの技術から動力を得る自動車を提供して，大幅に前進している。驚くべきことに，電気自動車は自動車が売り出された時代からずっと存在していた。実は，1900年代では，電気自動車はガソリン自動車よりも人気があり，蒸気自動車に次ぐ人気だった。ガソリン車が電気自動車やほかの種類の車を上回ったのは，内燃エンジン車が使いやすくなり，燃料補給をしなくても長距離を走れるようになってからだった。

　続く数十年間，電気自動車における進歩は何もなかった。その理由の1つは，電池技術の進歩が，自動車の所有者たちのニーズに追いついていなかったことだ。この問題を回避する1つの方法が，ハイブリッド車であった。ハイブリッド車は依然として内燃エンジンで走るが，短い距離や低速走行のための電池も備えている。しかし，ハイブリッド車は一時的な解決に終わりそうだ。企業は，ほぼ500キロの距離を走る完全電気自動車に向かって，積極的に動いている。現在，電気自動車はほとんどの買い手にとってまだ手が届かない値段であり，燃料補給の基幹施設もいまだに開発が遅れている。しかし，これは今後数年間で急速に変わると見られる。

1. 著者はパッセージのどこで電気自動車が一般的だった時代に言及しているか。
　(A) 1〜2行目
　(B) 5〜7行目
　(C) 10〜11行目
　(D) 17〜18行目

2. 次の言葉のうち著者はどれを説明しているか。
　(A) 水素燃料電池
　(B) 内燃エンジン
　(C) ハイブリッド車
　(D) 基幹施設

> **解説**

1. かつての電気自動車の人気については，第1段落第4文に「実は，1900年代では，電気自動車はガソリン自動車よりも人気があり，蒸気自動車に次ぐ人気だった」と説明がある。(B) が正解。

2. これは通常のWhere問題の逆パターンで，どの言葉がパッセージ内で説明・定義されているかを問う問題。(A) は第1段落第2文に最近の技術の具体例の1つとして名前が挙がっているだけ。(B) については第1段落最終文と第2段落第4文に出てくるが，その具体的な説明はない。(D) は第2段落の最後から2番目の文に出てくるが，やはり具体的な説明はない。第2段落第4文に「内燃エンジンで走るが電池も備えている」と説明がある (C) が正解。

Lesson 9 Conclusion Questions
結論を問う問題

> 例題

Line
    Today hop flowers are the primary source for flavoring beer, but before the Middle Ages, beer was flavored with a mixture of herbs known as gruit. Catholic monasteries were the major brewers at the time, and governments and the church granted them the exclusive rights to produce gruit. This license was effectively
(5) the same as the sole right to brew beer. Brewers who did not hold this license experimented with other beer flavorings until they settled on hops. These beers lasted longer and could be produced more cheaply than those made with gruit and eventually became the predominant variety.

    Which of the following statements does the passage support?
(A) Hops weren't as popular as gruit because gruit beers could be preserved.
(B) Hops were promoted by the Catholic Church as a replacement for gruit.
(C) Hops did not become popular as a beer flavoring until the last century.
(D) Hops became popular because brewers used them to get around regulations.

> 全訳

    今日ではホップの毬花がビールの風味付けをする主な原料だが，中世以前，ビールはグルートとして知られる薬草を混ぜたもので味付けされていた。カトリックの修道院が当時の主な醸造元で，政府や教会はグルートを生産する独占権を彼らに認めていた。この許可は事実上，ビール醸造の独占権と同じだった。この許可を持たない醸造者たちがほかのビール香味料を試し，ようやくホップに決めたのだ。ホップを使ったビールは長持ちし，グルートを使うよりも安く製造できたので，やがて主要な種類となった。

    次の主張のうちパッセージが立証しているものはどれか。
(A) グルートビールは保存できたので，ホップはグルートほど一般的ではなかった。
(B) ホップはグルートの代用としてカトリック教会によって奨励された。
(C) ホップは前世紀になるまでビールの香味料として一般的にはならなかった。
(D) 醸造者たちが規制を回避するために使ったので，ホップは一般的になった。

①トピック：ホップ　②中世はホップではなくグルート　③修道院によるグルート独占
④ほかの香味料→ホップの台頭

> **解き方**

結論を導き出す問題です。1) パッセージ全体の主要なアイディア，2) 最後の1～2文の流れ，の2点に注目する必要があります。例題では，1～4行目前半までが「グルートの生産はカトリック修道院が独占していた」という内容，それ以降では「グルートを扱えない醸造者は，ほかの香味料を模索した」という内容で，最終文のeventually以降で「（ホップが）主流となった」とまとめています。

(A) 保存についての言及はありません。
(B) 修道院はグルートを独占的に扱っていたので，カトリック教会がホップの発展に貢献することはなかったでしょう。
(C) グルートの後にホップは主流になりましたが，the last centuryに関する記述はパッセージにはありません。

ここがポイント

パッセージ全体の主旨が問われると同時に，ある程度の推測（inference）も必要になります。たとえ直接記述がないとしても，結論として正しい選択肢を選べるように，以下に注意しましょう。
- 筆者のトーン（態度）と合うものを選ぶ。
- 全体的にプラスかマイナスか，褒めているのか問題視しているのか，などに注目。
- 最終文でまとめているのか，将来的な展望なのか，などに注目。

> **学習アドバイス**

TOEFLのReadingでは，問題を解きながらパッセージを読み進める，という方法が効果的です。しかし普段の練習では，英文を1度通して読んでみましょう。そして読み終えたときに，全体的に何について何が言いたいのか，主要なアイディアや例はいくつどこに散りばめられているのか，そして結論として言えることは何か，などをまとめてみましょう。また，そのまとめを口頭で話したり書いたりすることも効果的です。

Passage 1

Line Dogs have been bred to have certain characteristics as long as humans have kept dogs. Breeds have been developed for tasks such as hunting, herding, retrieving, and more. Traits were selected based on how well the dogs could perform their tasks and for health. This changed with the development
(5) of kennel clubs and dog shows. These institutions valued dogs conforming to an idealized model of what the breed should look like. This placed the primary focus on dogs' looks, and breeds with certain exaggerated characteristics were bred, so these traits were even more overblown. This preoccupation with aesthetics came at the expense of health, and many pure-bred dogs have
(10) chronic ailments. Many advocates say that it's time to do away with breeding that conforms to an arbitrary "ideal," and breed for health instead.

Which of the following statements does the passage support?
(A) Current dog breeding practices are bad for dogs' health.
(B) There's no longer a need to breed dogs for hunting.
(C) Kennel clubs did not have an effect on dog breeding.
(D) Modern dog shows prioritize how well a dog works.

> 全訳

　犬は人間が飼ってきた間ずっと，特定の特徴を持つよう品種改良されてきた。狩りをしたり，家畜を移動させたり，獲物を捜して持ってきたり，そのほかの多くの作業のために品種が開発された。特性は，犬たちが作業をどれだけうまくこなせるかに基づいて，また健康のために選別された。これは，ケネルクラブやドッグショーの発展とともに変化した。そうした団体は，その種の犬がどのような外見であるべきかという理想的な型に当てはめて，犬たちを評価した。このため，犬の見た目に主に焦点が置かれ，誇張された特性を持つ品種が交配させられたことから，それらの特性はさらに高められた。この美的感覚への没頭は健康を犠牲にすることとなり，多くの純血種の犬は慢性病を持っている。多くの擁護者たちは，勝手な「理想」に合わせる品種改良をやめて，その代わりに，健康のために品種改良するときが来たと言っている。

　次の主張のうちパッセージが立証しているものはどれか。
(A) 現在の犬の品種改良方法は犬の健康によくない。
(B) もはや狩りのための犬を品種改良する必要はない。
(C) ケネルクラブは犬の品種改良に対して影響力はなかった。
(D) 現代のドッグショーは犬がどれほどよく働くかを優先させる。

> 解説

　最後から2番目の文に This preoccupation with aesthetics came at the expense of health, and many pure-bred dogs have chronic ailments.「この美的感覚への没頭は健康を犠牲にすることとなり，多くの純血種の犬は慢性病を持っている」とあり，この内容に合う (A) が正解。(B) は言及がない。(C) は第4～5文に矛盾する。(D) は第5～6文に合わない。

Passage 2

Line   The chemical compound that gives peppers their distinctive spiciness is known as capsaicin, named after the genus capsicum which all peppers belong to. Using selective breeding, botanists and farmers have created extremely hot peppers with high concentrations of the capsaicin. Although peppers are
(5) now intentionally bred for their capsaicin content, the chemical was originally a defense mechanism to prevent humans and other mammals from eating the peppers.

Capsaicin can be perceived by all mammals, but is not perceived by any species of bird. Birds can eat as many peppers as they want without feeling a
(10) burning sensation. Peppers evolved capsaicin as a way to selectively choose who spread their seeds. Mammals chew fruit, grinding up the seeds of plants and rendering them inviable. Birds, on the other hand, have no teeth; seeds travel through their digestive tract unmolested. What's more, birds often travel farther before depositing the seeds, more effectively propagating the species.

Which of the following statements does the passage support?
(A) Humans have bred peppers to contain less capsaicin over time.
(B) The peppers with the most capsaicin are naturally occurring varieties.
(C) The deterrent provided by capsaicin was undermined by human taste.
(D) Peppers evolved to be eaten by mammals rather than by birds.

> **全訳**
>
> トウガラシに特徴的な辛さを与える化合物は，カプサイシンとして知られている。全てのトウガラシが属するカプシカム（トウガラシ）属から名付けられたものだ。特定の種類を選んだ品種改良によって，植物学者や農業従事者たちは，高濃度のカプサイシンを含む非常に辛いトウガラシをつくり出した。今日では，トウガラシはカプサイシンの含有量のために意図的に品種改良されるが，この化合物はもともと，人間やほかの哺乳動物に食べられまいとするトウガラシの防御機能だった。
>
> カプサイシンは全ての哺乳動物には気付かれるが，どの種の鳥にも気付かれない。鳥はトウガラシをどんなにたくさん食べても，焼けるような辛さを感じない。トウガラシは，自分たちの種子をまき散らしてもらう相手を厳選する手段としてカプサイシンを進化させたのだ。哺乳動物は実をかんで，植物の種子を砕いて発芽できないようにしてしまう。ところが，鳥には歯がない。種子は彼らの消化器官を無傷で通り抜けるのだ。さらに，鳥は種子を出すまでにしばしば遠くまで旅をし，より効果的に種を増殖させるのだ。
>
> 次の主張のうちパッセージが立証しているものはどれか。
> (A) 人間は時間をかけてカプサイシンの少ないトウガラシを品種改良してきた。
> (B) 最も多いカプサイシンを含むトウガラシは自然に発生した種類である。
> **(C) カプサイシンがもたらす抑止効果は人間の好みで台なしになった。**
> (D) トウガラシは鳥よりも哺乳動物に食べられるために進化した。

> **解説**

第1段落最終文に the chemical (= capsaicin) was originally a defense mechanism to prevent humans and other mammals from eating the peppers「この化合物（＝カプサイシン）はもともと，人間やほかの哺乳動物に食べられまいとするトウガラシの防御機能だった」とある。しかし，その前までの内容から，人間はその辛さを好んで品種改良しているので，(C) が正解。(A) と (B) はその部分に矛盾する。(D) は第2段落の内容に合わない。

Passage 3

Line   The Turing Test is a test of artificial intelligence proposed by English scientist Alan Turing in the 1950's to determine if a machine can think. The test involves a person sitting at a computer having two text conversations, one with a computer program, and the other, with another person. If the computer
(5) program can consistently be mistaken for a person, it passes the test and can be considered, in some sense, intelligent.

The Turing Test is one of the most famous rubrics for determining computer intelligence, but many people question its validity. For one, the methods some programmers have used to attempt to pass the Turing Test
(10) have more to do with compiling long lists of answers to possible questions than with producing a system that can think up responses on the fly. Others have questioned if programming machines to act as humans is an appropriate goal for artificial intelligence. There is a huge range of "intelligent" behavior that humans cannot do that computers might be better suited to. It might be
(15) a better use of resources to program computers to complete useful tasks that humans can't do, instead of having them replicate human behavior like casual conversation.

Which of the following statements does the passage support?
(A) Computers are incapable of passing the Turing Test.
(B) The Turing Test only tests a narrow range of intelligence.
(C) It is very unlikely that a computer will ever pass the Turing Test.
(D) Alan Turing was the first person to study artificial intelligence.

> **全訳**

　チューリング・テストは，機械が考えることができるかを決める人工知能のテストで，1950年代に英国人科学者アラン・チューリングによって提唱された。テストには，人間がコンピューターの前に座り，2つの文字会話をすることが含まれる。一方の会話はコンピュータープログラムと，もう一方の会話はほかの人間とで行われる。もしもコンピュータープログラムが常に人間だと間違われれば，テストに合格し，ある意味で知的だと見なされる。

　チューリング・テストはコンピューターの知性を決める最も有名な評価基準の1つだが，その有効性を疑問視する人も多い。1つには，チューリング・テストに合格するために，一部のプログラマーたちが使ってきた方法は，急いで答えを考え出せるシステムをつくり出すよりも，むしろあり得る質問に対する答えの長いリストを積み重ねることだったからだ。また，人間と同じように行動するよう機械をプログラムすることが，人工知能にふさわしい目標なのかどうかを疑問視する人もいる。人間にできなくて，コンピューターの方が適している「知的な」行動はたくさんある。気軽な会話のような人間の行動をまねさせるより，人間にできない役に立つ仕事をやり遂げるようコンピューターをプログラムすることの方が，資産の有効な活用法かもしれない。

　次の主張のうちパッセージが立証しているものはどれか。
　(A) 　コンピューターはチューリング・テストに合格することはできない。
　(B) 　チューリング・テストは狭い範囲の知性しかテストできない。
　(C) 　コンピューターがチューリング・テストに合格することはまずなさそうだ。
　(D) 　アラン・チューリングは人工知能を研究した最初の人物だ。

> **解説**

(A) と (C) は，第2段落第2文の内容から，コンピューターがチューリング・テストに合格した，あるいはするだろうと推測できる。従って不適切。(D) は，アラン・チューリングは人工知能を研究した最初の人物とは書かれていないので，不適切。第2段落第2文より，チューリング・テストに合格するために，プログラマーは質問の答えとなるリストを機械に覚えさせているだけの場合があることが分かる。従って，その内容を言い換えた (B) が正解。

Passage 4

Line   There is a plethora of superstitions in the western theatrical tradition. The most well-known of these is likely the rule to never wish someone "good luck," but instead, to tell them to "break a leg." The origin of this practice is unclear, but it might date back to Shakespearian times when "break" was a
(5) synonym for "bend" and would refer to bowing or curtseying at the end of a performance. Other superstitions might be less familiar to those outside the drama world; they include prohibitions against whistling and the practice of leaving a single light called a ghost light on the stage when the theater is unoccupied.
(10)   While these superstitions are still followed, they at one time served a more practical use. Crew members who change stage sets used to whistle to signal to each other, and someone idly whistling could confuse the members and cause an accident. The ghost light dates back to a time when gas lights were used in theaters. If a valve had a leak, gas would build up in a theater
(15) until there was the danger of an explosion. A single light kept burning would make sure the gas would burn off gradually.

Which of the following statements does the passage support?
(A) Telling actors to "break a leg" is the oldest known theatrical superstition.
(B) Crew members don't whistle because it distracts the actors.
(C) Theaters stopped using ghost lights when lighting became electric.
(D) Many theatrical superstitions are actually based on safety precautions.

> **全訳**

　西洋の劇場の伝統には多くの迷信が存在する。これらの中で最もよく知られるものは，人に対して「幸運を」と祈る代わりに，「脚を折れ」と言う習慣だろう。この習慣の起源ははっきりしないが，シェイクスピアの時代にさかのぼるかもしれない。当時は break（折る）が bend（曲げる）と同義だったので，演技の最後にお辞儀をしたり，膝を曲げて会釈をしたりすることを意味したのだろう。そのほかの迷信は，演劇界の外にいる人々にはあまり知られていないかもしれない。それには口笛の禁止や，劇場が使われていないときに，舞台にゴーストライトという1つの明かりをともしておく習慣が含まれる。

　これらの迷信は今でも守られているが，かつてはもっと実用的な役割を果たしていた。舞台装置を変える劇団員は，互いに合図するのに口笛を吹いていたので，誰かが何の気なしに口笛を吹いたら団員が混乱し，事故になる可能性があった。ゴーストライトは劇場でガス灯が使われていた時代にさかのぼる。もしバルブに漏れがあったら，ガスが劇場内にたまり，爆発してしまう危険性があった。明かりを1つともしておくことで，ガスが必ず徐々に燃え尽きるようにしたのだ。

　次の主張のうちパッセージが立証しているものはどれか。
(A) 俳優たちに「脚を折れ」と言うことは，知られているものの中では最古の劇場の迷信である。
(B) 俳優の気が散るので，劇団員は口笛を吹かない。
(C) 明かりが電気になったときに，劇場はゴーストライトをすることをやめた。
(D) 多くの劇場の迷信は，実際は安全上の用心に基づいている。

> **解説**

第1段落で superstitions「迷信」の例として口笛の禁止やゴーストライトの灯火を挙げ，第2段落からそれらの背景には安全上の理由があったことが分かる。従って (D) が正解。(A) は迷信ではあるが，the oldest「最古の」という説明はない。(B) は第2段落第1〜2文の内容に合わない。(C) については第1段落最終文と第2段落冒頭から現在もゴーストライトを点灯していることが分かるので，不適切。

Lesson 10 Other Questions そのほかの問題

例題

Line
　Anzac biscuits are a hard cookie-like sweet made of ingredients including rolled oats, coconut, butter and golden syrup. They are from Australia and New Zealand and have a special history because they are associated with ANZAC, the Australian and New Zealand Army Corps. ANZAC was the military force
(5) that famously fought at the Gallipoli Landing in Turkey during World War I. Anzac biscuits were baked at the time to raise money to support the war. Contrary to popular belief, they were not sent to the fighting soldiers. Now, they are eaten especially on Anzac Day to honor the service of all Australian and New Zealand men and women in the armed forces.

　　The passage will probably continue with a discussion of

(A) how people currently eat Anzac biscuits on Anzac Day

(B) the growing popularity of Anzac biscuits in other countries

(C) the best way to package Anzac biscuits for shipping

(D) why Australia and New Zealand participated in World War I

全訳

　アンザックビスケットは堅いクッキーのようなお菓子で，ロールドオーツ，ココナツ，バター，ゴールデンシロップなどの材料から作られる。それはオーストラリアおよびニュージーランドのお菓子で，特別な歴史を持つ。というのもANZAC，つまりオーストラリア・ニュージーランド軍団と関係があるからだ。ANZACは，第一次世界大戦中のトルコにおけるガリポリの戦いで有名になった軍隊だった。当時，戦争を支援する資金を集めるためにアンザックビスケットが焼かれた。一般的に信じられていることと違って，ビスケットは戦闘中の兵士には送られなかったのだ。今日，それは軍隊に服役する全てのオーストラリアとニュージーランドの男女をたたえるために，特にアンザック・デーに食される。

　　このパッセージがおそらく続ける議論は

(A) 現在人々はアンザック・デーにアンザックビスケットをどのように食べるかについて

(B) 他国で高まるアンザックビスケットの人気について

(C) アンザックビスケットを発送用に包装する最善の方法について

(D) なぜオーストラリアとニュージーランドが第一次世界大戦に参戦したかについて

①トピックであるビスケットの説明　②戦争との関係　③パッセージ直後に続くアイディアの紹介

> 解き方

これまでに紹介した出題パターンのほかにも，さまざまな問題があります。これは，パッセージの直後にどのような話が続くかを推測する「After問題」です。後ろに続くアイディアは，パッセージの後半で記述されているようになっています。特に最後の1〜2文に注目して，新しく触れられているアイディアがないかを確かめましょう。ここではAnzac Dayにビスケットが食べられる目的について説明されているので，食べ方についての話が続くことが予測されます。

(B) オーストラリアとニュージーランドの記述しかないので，in other countriesが不適切。
(C) shipping「発送」に関する記述はないので，不適切。
(D) armed forces「軍隊」の記述はありますが，あくまでもビスケットの話なので，World War Iが不適切。

ここがポイント

After問題は，通常最後に出題されます。よって，以下の手順を確認しましょう。
- 問題を解きつつパッセージを読み進め，全体の流れを確認する。
- 最後の1〜2文に注目し，それまでに扱われていないアイディアが紹介されていないかをチェック。
- 選択肢を分析して，パッセージの最後で記述されていないアイディアを含むものは消去する。

学習アドバイス

そのほかの問題においては，全体の構造やアイディアを読み取ったり，キーワードを設定して情報を探したり，直接記述がなくても本文の流れから推測したりなど，今まで学習してきたスキルの応用力が試されます。よって，まず基本的な出題パターンの解法をしっかりと身につけてからチャレンジするようにしましょう。出題数は多くありませんが，高得点取得のためにはぜひとも正解する必要があります。がんばりましょう！

Passage 1

Line A Renaissance fair is an outdoor festival popular in the United States. The overall theme is based on Medieval or Renaissance-period Europe. First started in the 1950's in the US, the aim of these fairs is to recreate a time period such as Elizabethan England with historically accurate food,
(5) costumes and activities such as jousting. Participants, or "cast" in costumes and in character, will speak and behave as if they are a king, queen, knight, or whatever character they happen to be. There is often a fantasy element with cast members appearing as wizards or even mythical creatures such as the half-man, half-horse centaur. There are various activities for guests to
(10) enjoy including plays, fight reenactments and dancing. Guests can also buy numerous, often handmade, historically appropriate goods for sale. Although these fairs are focused on European history and culture, their popularity is mostly limited to the United States. Interestingly, in recent years, they have been imported to Europe and are spreading in Germany, the UK, etc.

What would be the best title for the passage?
(A) The Recent Rebirth of Renaissance Fairs
(B) Renaissance Fairs in Europe
(C) The History and Background of Renaissance Fairs
(D) The World's Largest Renaissance Fair

> **全訳**

　ルネサンス祭りはアメリカで人気の屋外の祭りである。全体的なテーマは，中世またはルネサンス期のヨーロッパに基づいている。1950年代にアメリカで初めて行われたこれらの祭りの目的は，例えばエリザベス朝イングランド王国のような時代を，歴史的に的確な食べ物，衣装，そして馬上やり合戦のような活動で再現することである。衣装を着てキャラクターに扮した「キャスト」である参加者たちは，自分たちがなることになった王や女王，騎士，あるいはそのほかのキャラクターであるかのように話し，振る舞う。ファンタジー的な要素が見られることもしばしばで，キャストたちは魔法使いばかりか，半人半馬のケンタウルスのような架空の生き物として姿を現すこともある。見物客が楽しめる活動もさまざまあり，演劇や戦闘の再現，ダンスなどがある。見物客はまた，たくさんの，しばしば手作りで，歴史に合った品物を買うこともできる。これらの祭りはヨーロッパの歴史と文化に焦点を当てているが，人気はほぼアメリカに限定されている。興味深いことに，近年では，ヨーロッパに輸入され，ドイツやイギリスなどで広まっている。

　パッセージのタイトルとして最もよいものは何か。
　(A)　最近のルネサンス祭りの復興
　(B)　ヨーロッパにおけるルネサンス祭り
　(C)　ルネサンス祭りの歴史と背景
　(D)　世界最大のルネサンス祭り

> **解説**

最も適切なタイトルを答える「Title問題」である。パッセージではルネサンス祭りについて，歴史やそのほかの詳細を説明している。(C) が正解。ルネサンス祭りが復興したという歴史の流れはないので (A) は不適切。ヨーロッパにおけるルネサンス祭りについては最終文で簡単に触れられているだけなので (B) も不適切。パッセージは一般的なルネサンス祭りについてのもので，ある特定のルネサンス祭りについては述べていないので，(D) も不適切。

Passage 2

Line   Today, the Leaning Tower of Pisa is a symbol of the town of Pisa and one of the most famous landmarks in Italy. It wasn't always so. Built as a bell tower in the 12th century, it was originally meant to stand straight. However, five years into its construction, it began to lean. In the hope that the clay and
(5) soil foundation would settle, construction was halted for about 100 years. Still, even after measures were taken to stop it from leaning, the tower continued to lean. Over the years, several attempts have been made to stabilize the tower. Finally, in 2008, engineers were able to successfully add structural support that stopped the tower from leaning any further, for the first time in its history.
(10) The tower is now celebrated for its lean and the residents of Pisa wouldn't want it any other way.

According to the passage, what has become the people's attitude toward the tower?

(A) They have an affection for it.
(B) They are not particularly interested in it.
(C) They would like to see it restored to its proper form.
(D) They are ashamed of it.

> **全訳**
>
> 今日，ピサの斜塔はピサの町のシンボルであり，イタリアで最も有名なランドマークの1つである。それは常にそうだったわけではない。12世紀に鐘楼として建てられたとき，それはもともとまっすぐ建つように意図されていた。しかしながら，建設開始から5年がたつと，傾き始めた。粘土と土の基礎が安定することを期待して，建設は約100年間中断された。それでもなお，傾きを止める措置が取られた後でさえ，その塔は傾き続けた。何年にもわたって塔を安定させるための試みがいくつもなされてきた。ついに2008年，塔の歴史上初めて，技師たちは塔がそれ以上傾くのを食い止める支柱を付け足すことに成功した。今では塔はその傾きが賛美されており，ピサの住人たちは，それ以外の姿になることを望んでいない。
>
> パッセージによると，塔に対する人々の態度はどのようになったか。
> **(A) それに愛着を持っている。**
> (B) それに特に興味はない。
> (C) 正しい姿に修復されたところを見たいと思っている。
> (D) それを恥じている。

解説

著者や事柄がどのような態度を表しているかを問う「Attitude 問題」である。最終文の the residents of Pisa wouldn't want it (= the leaning Tower of Pisa) any other way「ピサの住人たちはそれ (=ピサの斜塔) がそれ以外の姿になることを望んでいない」に合う (A) が正解。(B) は同じ文に合わず，また傾斜を食い止めようとしてきた歴史とも矛盾する。(C) と (D) も最終文に合わない。

Passage 3

Line   The world's first high-speed train service, the Japanese shinkansen, was launched in 1964 in time for the Tokyo Olympics. Shinkansen refers to the high-speed train line and somewhat anticlimactically means main trunk line. The first type of this train was the 0 Series with a short round nose, which
(5) resembled a bullet. It had a top speed of 220 kilometers and ran for over 40 years until its retirement in 2008. Today, the fastest shinkansen has a top speed of 300 kilometers.

Other countries have also developed high-speed train services. The French TGV, which stands for Train a Grande Vitesse or high-speed train,
(10) regularly reaches speeds of 320 kilometers and holds the record for fastest conventional train at a test speed of 575 kilometers set in 2007. Spain started its high-speed rail service in 1992, but now has the longest distance service in Europe and is second in the world after China.

Recently, maglev trains are pushing the limits of high-speed trains in
(15) terms of speed and comfort. Maglev trains use magnets to lift the entire train off of the track, and propel it forward at high speeds. Currently, the fastest maglev train offering commercial services is the Shanghai Maglev Train. The service carries passengers the 30 kilometers from Shanghai to Shanghai Pudong International Airport at a top speed of 431 kilometers in around 8
(20) minutes.

1. Which of the following most closely resembles the first type of shinkansen?
(A)   (B)
(C)   (D)

2. What would be the best title for the passage?
(A) The End of High Speed Trains
(B) Spain, the Future King of High-Speed Trains
(C) The Past, Present, and Future of High-Speed Trains
(D) The Maglev Trains of Today and Tomorrow

> **全訳**

　世界初の高速鉄道サービスである日本の新幹線は，東京オリンピックに間に合わせて1964年に運行を開始した。新幹線は高速鉄道路線という意味を表し，どこか拍子抜けするが，本線を意味している。この列車の最初の形式は0系であり，その短く丸い鼻先は弾丸に似ていた。最高速度は220キロで，2008年に引退するまで40年以上走った。今日では，最速の新幹線は最高速度300キロである。

　ほかの国々も高速鉄道サービスを開発してきた。フランスの TGV (Train a Grande Vitesse, つまり高速鉄道の略) は普段から320キロの速度で走っており，2007年に行われた試験走行で575キロの速度を記録し，在来型鉄道としての最速記録を保持している。スペインが高速鉄道サービスを開始したのは1992年だが，今やヨーロッパでは最長，世界では中国に続いて2番目の長さの距離を運行している。

　最近では，リニアモーターカーがスピードと快適さの点において高速鉄道の限界を押し上げている。リニアモーターカーは磁石を使って列車全体を線路から持ち上げて，それを高速で前方へと進ませる。現在，商業運転をしている最速のリニアモーターカーは，上海マグレブである。上海から上海浦東国際空港までの30キロを最高速度431キロで，約8分で乗客を運んでいる。

1. 次のうちどれが最初の形式の新幹線に最もよく似ているか。
　(A) 鼻先が短くて丸い新幹線
　(B) 鼻先が四角い新幹線
　(C) 鼻先が鋭い新幹線
　(D) 鼻先が細長い新幹線

2. パッセージのタイトルとして最もよいものはどれか。
　(A) 高速鉄道の終わり
　(B) 高速鉄道の未来の王，スペイン
　(C) 高速鉄道の過去，現在，そして未来
　(D) リニアモーターカーの現在とこれから

> **解説**

1. あまりない出題パターンではあるが，これはパッセージで説明されているものの外見を問われる「Illustration問題」である。最初の新幹線については，第1段落第3文に The first type of this train was the 0 Series with a short round nose, which resembled a bullet.「この列車の最初の形式は0系であり，その短く丸い鼻先は弾丸に似ていた」とある。短くて丸い鼻先をした (A) が正解。

2. これは「Title問題」。このパッセージは，第1段落で世界初の高速鉄道サービスを開始した日本について，第2段落ではそれ以外の国について，第3段落では最近の高速鉄道の例としてリニアモーターカーについて説明しており，一貫して高速鉄道について論じている。この内容に最も合うのは (C)。(A)「終わり」と (B)「未来の王」についてはパッセージで言及されていない。(D) はパッセージ全体のタイトルとしては不適切。

Passage 4

Line   The first ballets were lavish spectacles at the courts of 15th century Renaissance Italy to celebrate events such as weddings. Professional dancers would teach the guests the dance moves and then everyone would participate in massive performances. In the 17th century, when this sort of dance became
(5) popular in France, it moved from parties to the stage. Once professionals took to the stage, the focus shifted to technique. Dancers would show off spins, leaps and other difficult moves. By the 19th century, ballets had begun to be choreographed to match the music by classical composers of the time, such as Tchaikovsky, and to tell a story.

(10)   In the 20th century, ballet moved away from telling clear stories to using techniques to express emotions and moods. This movement was called "neoclassical ballet" and it was created by Russian George Balanchine. He wanted to bring advanced Russian techniques to ballet but strip it of any extra storyline or romanticism. Today's ballet follows in the footsteps of neoclassical
(15) ballet, but also draws from the storytelling traditions of earlier ballet. Modern ballet also incorporates elements not found in classical ballet such as floor work and greater use of the upper body.

1. The first paragraph is developed primarily by means of
   (A) the beginnings and development of ballet
   (B) famous 17th century ballet dancers
   (C) the most difficult dance moves in ballet
   (D) the classical composers of ballet music

2. The passage will probably continue with a discussion of
   (A) how to revive the ballet
   (B) the history of Russian ballet
   (C) today's ballet techniques
   (D) the best places to take ballet lessons

CHAPTER 1 Lesson 10 Other Questions

> **全訳**

初期のバレエは，15世紀ルネサンス期のイタリアにおける宮廷の豪華な見世物で，結婚式のような行事を祝うためのものだった。プロのダンサーが来客にダンスの動きを教えた後，全員が壮大なパフォーマンスに参加するのだ。17世紀にはこのようなダンスがフランスで人気となり，それはパーティーから舞台へと移った。いったんプロたちが舞台へと出ると，焦点は技術面へと移向した。ダンサーはスピンや大きなジャンプ，そしてそのほかの難しい動きを披露した。19世紀までには，バレエは，チャイコフスキーのような当時のクラシック音楽の作曲家が作った音楽に合わせるため，またストーリーを伝えるために，振り付けられるようになった。

20世紀には，バレエは明確なストーリーを伝えるものではなくなり，表現手法を用いて感情や雰囲気を表現するものになった。この動きは「新古典主義バレエ」と呼ばれ，ロシア人のジョージ・バランシンによって生み出された。彼は高度なロシアの技法をバレエにもたらしたいと思ったが，一切の余分な物語やロマンチシズムを取り去りたいとも思っていた。今日のバレエは新古典主義バレエの志を受け継いでいるが，初期のバレエの物語を伝えるという伝統も利用している。モダン・バレエはまた，フロアワークや上半身のさらなる活用といった，クラシック・バレエでは見られなかった要素も取り入れている。

1. 第1段落を展開しているのは主に
   (A) バレエの始まりと発展
   (B) 有名な17世紀のバレエダンサーたち
   (C) バレエにおける最も難しいダンスの動き
   (D) バレエ音楽のクラシック作曲家

2. パッセージがおそらく続ける議論は
   (A) バレエを復興させる方法
   (B) ロシアのバレエの歴史
   (C) 今日のバレエの技法
   (D) バレエのレッスンを受ける最適な場所

> **解説**

1. パッセージの構成や展開について問われる「Organization問題」である。第1段落では，第1文でバレエが15世紀に始まったことに触れ，その後の第3文で17世紀，最終文で19世紀のバレエについて説明している。(A) が正解。第1段落では (B) の「17世紀のダンサー」や (C) の「動き」，(D) の「作曲家」にも言及しているが，こうしたことをメインに論じているのではない。

2. これは「After問題」。第1段落で15〜19世紀のバレエについて，第2段落では20世紀の新古典主義バレエについて説明しており，最終文ではモダン・バレエの特徴的な要素に触れている。このことから，続く段落では現代のバレエについてより詳しい説明があると考えられる。(C) が正解。(A) は，バレエが廃れたとは書かれていないのにrevive「〜を復興させる」では不自然。

CHAPTER 2
Practice Tests

■ **Practice Test 1**
問題 ·· 116
解答・解説 ····································· 133

■ **Practice Test 2**
問題 ·· 158
解答・解説 ····································· 173

■ **Practice Test 3**
問題 ·· 197
解答・解説 ····································· 213

Practice Test 1　問題　　Time 55 minutes

Reading Comprehension

Directions: In Section 3, Reading Comprehension, you will read various passages. Each passage will be followed by a number of questions. Please choose the best answer, (A), (B), (C), or (D), to each question. Next, find the number of the question on your answer sheet and fill in the space that corresponds to the letter of the best answer.

Please use only the information given in each passage to answer each question.

Read the following passage:

Line
    The dominant historical narrative of the United States is one of Northern Europeans expanding from the eastern coast of the continent westward into the interior. However, this narrative — even if confined to the 18th and 19th centuries — is substantially incomplete. The traditional narrative overlooks immigrants
(5) from the Spanish Empire and Mexico, with citizens of the latter country becoming Americans when Mexico ceded its northern territories to the United States. The narrative also overlooks immigrants from Asia who were crucial in developing the American West and American Pacific islands. Finally, the traditional narrative downplays the role of Africans, brought forcibly to the United States as slaves, and
(10) Native Americans.

Example

What is the main idea of the passage?

Sample Answer
Ⓐ ● Ⓒ Ⓓ

(A) Scholars have missed important facts about Northern Europeans.
(B) Conventional analyses have minimized some historical facts about America.
(C) Immigrants have been crucial to American economic development.
(D) Historians disagree on the impact of the Spanish Empire on the United States.

The main idea of the passage is that traditional interpretations have not focused on all aspects of American history. Therefore, you should choose (B).

Now begin work on the questions.

116

Questions 1-10

Line   Color blindness affects the lives of around eight percent of the Earth's male population. Less than half of one percent of women share this disorder. The reason for this is simple genetics. Most color blindness is caused by a defect that prevents eyes from growing certain photoreceptor cells called cones. These cones
(5) are all tuned to different wavelengths of light that are perceived as different colors. If an eye lacks the cones tuned to the orange wavelength of light that person cannot see that color. The genes associated with these cones are on the X chromosome, which is why women are mostly resistant to the disorder. If one of their X chromosomes has a faulty gene, they can rely on the same set of genes on
(10) their other X chromosome. Men, who have only one X chromosome, can't rely on this backup chromosome.

   However, there is new research into treating color blindness. Scientists have isolated the genes responsible for these cones and wrapped them in a virus' shell. These modified viruses are then injected into an eye that is missing a particular
(15) type of cone. These genes overwrite the function of the existing cone turning, for example, a cone detecting blue-violet into a cone detecting orange. Studies using monkeys have found that monkeys subjected to this form of gene therapy were able to detect colors that they were not capable of perceiving before.

   While the therapy has been shown to work in animals, there have not
(20) yet been any trials on humans. One concern is safety. The treatment involves injections directly into the eye which could cause infections and pain. This is exacerbated by the fact that the treatment might need to be performed multiple times; in animal trials the effect of the therapy would only last around two years. Since the viruses would have to be administered multiple times, there is a chance
(25) that the body would develop an immunity to them, even if they're not harmful.

117

1. What is the purpose of the first paragraph?
   (A) To discuss a controversial issue
   (B) To define a medical term
   (C) To present a solution to a problem
   (D) To explain the causes of a condition

2. The word "resistant" in line 8 is closest in meaning to
   (A) immune
   (B) difficult
   (C) quarrelsome
   (D) angry

3. According to the passage, the purpose of cones is to
   (A) fight off infections from viruses
   (B) detect certain wavelengths of light
   (C) determine the sex of an individual
   (D) duplicate genes on the X chromosome

4. According to the passage, why are women less likely to have color blindness?
   (A) They have another X chromosome.
   (B) They have more photoreceptor cells in their eyes.
   (C) They are less likely to suffer eye trauma.
   (D) They have better immune systems.

5. The second paragraph is developed primarily by means of
   (A) describing the process of virus infections
   (B) explaining the causes of color blindness in non-human species
   (C) detailing the theory behind a medical procedure
   (D) giving examples of the difficulties of those with color blindness

6. According to the passage, what do manufactured viruses do?
   (A) Ease the pain color blindness causes
   (B) Repair damaged cone cells
   (C) Change the functions of existing photoreceptors
   (D) Destroy defective cells that cause color blindness

7. The word "perceiving" in line 18 is closest in meaning to
   (A) noticing
   (B) using
   (C) enjoying
   (D) training

8. The word "exacerbated" in line 22 is closest in meaning to
   (A) turned around
   (B) made worse
   (C) taken up
   (D) sorted out

9. All of the following are listed as shortcomings of the gene therapy EXCEPT
   (A) price
   (B) multiple treatments
   (C) discomfort
   (D) immune response

10. The paragraph after the passage is most likely about
    (A) other disorders that affect primarily one gender
    (B) ethical concerns about testing on animals
    (C) the history of color blindness
    (D) ways to increase the effectiveness of the treatment

Questions 11-20

Line
In the mid-19th century there was a widespread movement in the United States to create utopian communities. No one knows what triggered such a boom in these communities. It might have been the recent introduction of the Industrial Revolution or a manifestation of Americans developing their own culture distinct
(5) from their European backgrounds. Whatever the case, a huge number of people — usually under the direction of a charismatic leader — decided to leave their old lives behind and live in communes designed to be a paradise on earth.

A majority of these communities were religious. Pastors and other holy men attempted to save their congregations from the corrupting influence of the
(10) outside world by creating settlements based on Biblical teachings. Many of them attempted to return to an "original" form of Christianity unspoiled by modern revisions. However, these societies had wildly differing views on what that meant. Some practiced somber, ascetic lives where there was no dancing, food was strictly regulated, and sexual activity was discouraged. Others practiced free love
(15) and afforded women more opportunities to participate in public life.

Other communities were based on political ideals. Socialism was a newly codified political theory at the time and many communal settlements were created to test out this new form of collective living. There were also anarchist societies that attempted to create communities of self-sufficient members. Sometimes
(20) communities were created based on a single ideal; there were some communes based primarily around vegetarianism.

Very few of these communities survived into the 20th century. A great deal of them lasted less than five years. Many members were more interested in ideals than in tending to the practical needs of farming. Most were ill-prepared for the
(25) realities of creating a self-sufficient village and fell apart once food became scarce. Other communities dissolved over succession disputes. At least one survived in an unexpected form. The Oneida Community was a religious commune under the leadership of John Humphrey Noyes. They made silverware as a means of earning money for the community and when the community fell apart the silverware company
(30) remained. Today the products that carry the Oneida name can still be bought.

11. What is the main purpose of the passage?
    (A) To illustrate the rise of socialism in the United States
    (B) To compare the doctrine of different Christian sects
    (C) To discuss a series of social movements
    (D) To depict the introduction of the Industrial Revolution to America

12. What is suggested as a reason for the sudden boom in utopian communities?
    (A) Poverty and famine in the United States
    (B) Collisions between groups of people from different cultures
    (C) The advancement of women in American society
    (D) Growing industrialization

13. The word "distinct" in line 4 is closest in meaning to
    (A) similar
    (B) particular
    (C) superior
    (D) different

14. The word "practiced" in line 13 is closest in meaning to
    (A) rehearsed
    (B) applied
    (C) lived
    (D) operated

15. According to the passage, a common goal among many religious communes was to
    (A) convert members of other religions
    (B) return to an authentic form of Christianity
    (C) eliminate inequality between the sexes
    (D) fulfill prophecies from the Bible

16. Which of the following is NOT mentioned in the passage as an ideal utopian communities were founded on?
 (A) Manufacturing
 (B) Politics
 (C) Religion
 (D) Vegetarianism

17. The word "collective" in line 18 is closest in meaning to
 (A) shared
 (B) prosperous
 (C) religious
 (D) comfortable

18. What does the passage imply about a large number of these utopian commune members?
 (A) They possessed great farming skills.
 (B) Most of them had some means of earning money.
 (C) Some of them left their commune to join the Oneida Community.
 (D) They were more interested in the principles of their communities than the actual daily work.

19. What is mentioned as a reason utopian communities would fall apart?
 (A) Disputes over how to produce revenue for the commune
 (B) Arguments over who would succeed the original leader
 (C) Confusion over what political system to implement
 (D) Seizures of land by the state and national governments

20. Why does the author mention the Oneida Community?
 (A) To name an important figure that influenced other utopian communities
 (B) To show how far a community can diverge from its original purpose
 (C) To give an illustration of religious views found in a utopian commune
 (D) To provide an example of how little experience communes had at farming

Questions 21-30

Line
Comparative mythology is the study of myths from different cultures. This allows anthropologists to study how cultures evolve and propagate. When multiple cultures share a myth with a similar theme we can surmise that the cultures shared a common ancestor or at least had significant cultural contact. Linguists
(5) can even chart the migration and evolution of language by comparing the names of figures that share the same roles in these parallel stories.

We can use an example to show how cultures on far ends of the earth can trace elements of their heritage back to a common ancestor. There is a myth common across Europe, North Africa, West Asia, and Central Asia of a hero
(10) slaying a dragon. One might think that these dragon myths aren't evidence of a shared mythology, but a shared fear or fascination found inside the minds of all humans. However, these myths share so many traits that it is hard to argue they all developed autonomously.

The dragons are almost always sea serpents of some kind. They are usually
(15) multi-headed and represent chaos in some form. The hero represents order which much must be imposed on chaos. The most strikingly specific aspect of the hero is that he is usually a storm god. Zeus, Thor, and Indra from Greek, Norse, and Indian mythology respectively are all deities of storms and lightening and all took the role of dragon-slayer in their mythologies. Other examples of storm gods in
(20) this same role include Ba'al from Canaan and Marduk from Babylon. Even when the god who slays the dragon isn't a storm god, such as with the Egyptian sun god Ra, he is still associated with the sky in some fashion.

Though this story is associated with societies descending from the ancient Proto Indo-European culture, a nearly identical myth is found far away in Japan.
(25) The myth of the storm god Susano-o fighting the multi-headed sea serpent Orochi fits perfectly into the same archetype. Since this myth isn't ubiquitous in East Asia it suggests a similar origin for early Japanese peoples or a greater level of contact with Indo-Europeans compared to other East Asian cultures.

21. What does the passage mainly discuss?
   (A) The evolution of some specific languages
   (B) The ways dragons have been depicted in art
   (C) The common ancestor of humans
   (D) Common characteristics of myths

22. The word "parallel" in line 6 is closest in meaning to
   (A) excellent
   (B) similar
   (C) bound
   (D) interesting

23. The word "autonomously" in line 13 is closest in meaning to
   (A) accidentally
   (B) independently
   (C) naturally
   (D) slowly

24. The word "imposed" in line 16 is closed in meaning to
   (A) forced
   (B) asked
   (C) moved
   (D) protected

25. What does the passage say is a common attribute of the hero that slays the dragon?
   (A) He creates chaos.
   (B) He appears everywhere.
   (C) He is a storm deity.
   (D) He fails in his first attempt.

26. All of the following are mythologies mentioned in the passage EXCEPT
  (A) Chinese
  (B) Indian
  (C) Greek
  (D) Babylonian

27. Why does the author mention the Egyptian god Ra in paragraph three?
  (A) To show the limits of comparative mythology
  (B) To show the origins of this kind of myth
  (C) To show that exceptions still follow the model
  (D) To show how similar names are preserved between myths

28. The word "ubiquitous" in line 26 is closest in meaning to
  (A) understood
  (B) worrisome
  (C) fraught
  (D) widespread

29. What does the existence of the Orochi myth in Japan imply?
  (A) The myth was based on a historical event.
  (B) Japanese culture has some relationship to Indo-European cultures.
  (C) Similar myths are based on it.
  (D) Similarities with other myths are a coincidence.

30. Which of the following statements does the passage support?
  (A) Most myths are based on some true event that's exaggerated.
  (B) Cultures use myths to teach morals to their children.
  (C) Civilizations create new myths to differentiate themselves.
  (D) Myths remain the same even as cultures diverge.

Questions 31-39

Line When people think of the ancient cultures of the Americas, they might think that all the advanced, monument-building societies were in Central America. The Olmec, Aztec, and Mayan cultures are the first to come to mind with their distinctive tiered pyramids. However, archeologists have uncovered sites in the
(5) Southeast United States that show cultures capable of great feats of construction were present thousands of years ago.

One such site is located in Louisiana, next to the Mississippi River. Since the people that built it disappeared long before European colonists arrived to document it, the site is known as Poverty Point, named after a nearby plantation.
(10) The site is dominated by a series of earthworks in the shape of six concentric crescents. The longest of these C-shaped mounds are over a kilometer long. The crescents all surround a flat plaza in the middle while a series of large mounds surround the perimeter.

Though the construction of the entire site took place over at least a century,
(15) individual elements were completed quickly. The largest mound, which required the movement of 238,000 cubic meters of soil, was completed in around three months. This would have required around 3,000 laborers and used methods as simple as passing baskets full of earth.

Another impressive aspect of the site is the fact that the people who built it
(20) were hunter-gatherers. Since they weren't an agricultural society that could settle down next to the site and build it over time, they had to return to build it between sessions of foraging.

The exact purpose of Poverty Point is a mystery. Since the people of Poverty Point Culture were hunter-gatherers, it wouldn't have been a permanent settlement.
(25) One guess is that it was used for astrological purposes. Some have suggested it is a religious site, but there have not been many religious artifacts found there. A leading hypothesis is that it was used for trade. Artifacts from far-away regions of the continent have been found at the site, suggesting that many peoples came there to exchange and barter.

31. What does the passage mainly discuss?
- (A) The shapes of archeological monuments
- (B) An intriguing archeological site
- (C) Comparison of several Native American cultures
- (D) Construction methods of ancient monuments

32. The passage implies that monuments similar to Poverty Point were
- (A) more usually found in Central America
- (B) mostly built next to rivers
- (C) primarily built after European contact
- (D) used to facilitate farming

33. The word "plantation" in line 9 is closest in meaning to
- (A) farm
- (B) river
- (C) landmark
- (D) town

34. According to the passage, the construction of the entire Poverty Point complex
- (A) was completed in a few months
- (B) was performed by a small group of people
- (C) took 100 years or more
- (D) required a large amount of timber

35. The word "permanent" in line 24 is closest in meaning to
- (A) forgotten
- (B) large
- (C) lasting
- (D) mysterious

36. The word "it" in line 27 refers to
   (A) a leading hypothesis
   (B) the Poverty Point Culture
   (C) Poverty Point
   (D) a mystery

37. The author states that one reason Poverty Point is impressive is because the culture that build it
   (A) had to use swampy earth
   (B) had not invented the wheel
   (C) did not have religion
   (D) were hunter-gatherers

38. All of the following are explanations of Poverty Point's purpose EXCEPT
   (A) religious temple
   (B) performance space
   (C) trading point
   (D) astrological instrument

39. What does the passage imply about the relationship of the Poverty Point Culture to trade?
   (A) It only took place during the summer.
   (B) It was not used by the culture.
   (C) It was very important to them.
   (D) It was developed after agriculture.

Questions 40-50

Line   Before a new drug can be put on the market, it must go through a rigorous process that determines if it is both safe and effective. Most countries follow a similar protocol for these clinical trials, and in the United States the process is done by the United States Food and Drug Administration (FDA).

(5)   Before a drug is submitted for consideration by the FDA, a drug manufacturer will run its own tests. Many of these tests will be conducted in the lab in artificial environments and may include testing on animals. The drug manufacturers will perform these tests by themselves, but may solicit guidance from the FDA.

The manufacturer then files a formal application to the FDA, which oversees
(10) Phase 1 trials. These studies use a small batch of 20 to 80 healthy people to take the drug. Since these volunteers don't have the disease the drug is trying to treat, only safety is being tested here. If the test subjects are not harmed by the drug and the side-effects are minimal the trials proceed to Phase 2.

Phase 2 tests the efficacy of the drug. A collection of around 30 to 300 people
(15) who suffer from the disease the drug is attempting to treat is split into two groups. One receives the new drug while the other receives either a currently accepted drug or a placebo, a medicine that has no actual effect yet psychologically helps improve a patient's medical condition. If the group receiving the new drug fares no better than the other group, the drug is rejected. If the group instead shows
(20) significant improvement, the drug can pass on to Phase 3.

This final phase uses thousands of test subjects to make sure the results from Phase 2 were not a statistical anomaly. These larger populations can also determine if there are differing risks for specific demographics such as a specific age group or gender. Only after these final trials will a drug be eligible for a
(25) final application for the FDA to consider. Even after these trials the drug will be monitored for potential health risks once on the market. If dangers arise that were not uncovered in trials a drug can be pulled from shelves.

40. What does the passage mainly discuss?
 (A) How drugs are sold in the United States
 (B) How animals are used in testing new drugs
 (C) How drugs are approved in the United States
 (D) How drugs are manufactured in the United States

41. The word "protocol" in line 3 is closest in meaning to
 (A) schedule
 (B) appetite
 (C) process
 (D) advice

42. Tests run by the manufacturer are different from FDA tests because they
 (A) use far more test subjects
 (B) are sometimes performed on animals
 (C) test at far larger doses
 (D) run multiple tests simultaneously

43. The word "solicit" in line 8 is closest in meaning to
 (A) ignore
 (B) support
 (C) request
 (D) collect

44. According to the passage, what is unique about Phase 1?
   (A) It is administered by the manufacturer.
   (B) It uses test subjects that are paid.
   (C) It uses the most test subjects.
   (D) It does not test if the drug works.

45. The word "efficacy" in line 14 is closest in meaning to
   (A) expandability
   (B) effectiveness
   (C) expertise
   (D) effort

46. In Phase 2, what is the new drug tested against?
   (A) Another drug undergoing trials
   (B) A placebo or existing drug
   (C) No treatment whatsoever
   (D) A drug treating another disease

47. The word "eligible" in line 24 is closest in meaning to
   (A) hampered
   (B) tried
   (C) barred
   (D) qualified

48. According to the passage, which phase uses the largest number of human test subjects?
  (A) Pre-application tests
  (B) Phase 1
  (C) Phase 2
  (D) Phase 3

49. What most likely is the paragraph following this passage about?
  (A) Who makes up the board at the FDA
  (B) Where most drug manufacturers are based
  (C) How drug manufacturers research diseases
  (D) What would cause a drug to be pulled by the FDA

50. Where does the author give the definition of a placebo?
  (A) Lines 14-15
  (B) Lines 17-18
  (C) Lines 18-19
  (D) Lines 21-22

Practice Test 1 解答・解説

リーディング

指示文：セクション3のReading Comprehensionでは，いくつかのパッセージを読みます。それぞれのパッセージの後には質問がいくつかあります。それぞれの質問について最も適切な答えを (A), (B), (C), (D) の中から選びなさい。そして，解答用紙にある選択肢の番号で，正解に該当するもののマーク欄を塗りつぶしなさい。

それぞれの質問には，パッセージ中で与えられる情報だけを用いて答えなさい。

次のパッセージを読みましょう。

　アメリカについての主要な歴史物語は，北ヨーロッパの人々が大陸の東海岸から西に向かって内陸へと勢力を拡大していったという話だ。しかしながらこの話は，18世紀と19世紀に限ったとしても，かなり不完全なものである。この伝統的な話で見落とされているのは，スペイン帝国やメキシコからの移住者だ。メキシコの人々は，メキシコが北側の領土をアメリカに割譲したのを機にアメリカ人になった。この話はさらに，アメリカの西部や太平洋諸島の発展にとって重要だったアジアからの移住者についても見落としている。最後に，伝統的な話では，奴隷として強制的にアメリカに連れてこられたアフリカ人，そしてアメリカ先住民の役割が軽視されている。

例題
このパッセージの主旨は何か。
(A) 学者たちは北ヨーロッパ人に関する重要な事実を見落としてきた。
(B) 従来の分析ではアメリカに関するいくつかの歴史的事実が見くびられている。
(C) 移住者はアメリカの経済発展にとって重要だった。
(D) スペイン帝国がアメリカに与えた影響について，歴史家たちの意見は一致していない。

このパッセージの主旨は，伝統的な解釈はアメリカの歴史のすべての側面に焦点を合わせてきたわけではなかった，ということです。従って，正解は (B) です。

それでは問題を始めてください。

解答一覧

1 **D**	2 **A**	3 **B**	4 **A**	5 **C**	6 **C**	7 **A**	8 **B**	9 **A**
10 **D**	11 **C**	12 **D**	13 **D**	14 **C**	15 **B**	16 **A**	17 **A**	18 **D**
19 **B**	20 **B**	21 **D**	22 **B**	23 **B**	24 **A**	25 **C**	26 **A**	27 **C**
28 **D**	29 **B**	30 **D**	31 **D**	32 **A**	33 **A**	34 **C**	35 **C**	36 **C**
37 **D**	38 **B**	39 **C**	40 **C**	41 **C**	42 **B**	43 **C**	44 **D**	45 **B**
46 **B**	47 **D**	48 **D**	49 **D**	50 **B**				

Questions 1-10

> **パッセージの訳**
>
> 　地球上の男性の人口の約8％が色覚異常に侵されている。女性でこの障害を患う人は1％の半分にも満たない。その理由は単純な遺伝的特徴によるものである。ほとんどの色覚異常は，目において錐体と呼ばれる特定の視細胞の成長が阻まれる欠陥によって起こる。これらの錐体は全て，異なる色として認識されるさまざまな光の波長に同調する。もしある人の目に，オレンジ色の光の波長に同調する錐体が不足していたら，その色は見えない。そうした錐体に関係のある遺伝子は，X染色体にある。それが，ほとんどの女性がこの障害に耐性がある理由だ。女性は片方のX染色体に欠陥のある遺伝子がある場合，もう一方のX染色体の同じ遺伝子の一式に頼ることができる。男性はX染色体が1つしかないので，この予備の染色体に頼れないのだ。
>
> 　しかし，色覚異常の治療に関する新しい研究がある。科学者たちは，このような錐体の原因となる遺伝子を切り離し，ウイルスの殻で包んだ。これらの修正されたウイルスはその後，特定の錐体が欠けている目に注射される。それらの遺伝子は現存の錐体の機能を上書きする。例えば，青紫を見る錐体をオレンジを見る錐体に変えるのである。サルを使った研究では，この遺伝子治療の対象となったサルたちが，以前は認識できなかった色を見ることができたと分かった。
>
> 　治療は動物には効くことが示されたが，人間にはまだ一度も試されていない。1つには安全上の懸念がある。治療には，目に直接注射を打つことが含まれ，それが感染や痛みを引き起こすかもしれない。さらに悪い事実として，その治療は何度か行う必要があるかもしれない。動物実験では治療効果は約2年間しか持続しなかった。ウイルスは何度も投与されなくてはならないので，たとえ害はないとしても，体がそれに対する免疫をつくる可能性があるのだ。

1. 解答 D Purpose Question

第1段落の目的は何か。

(A) 物議を醸す問題を論じること
(B) ある医学用語を定義すること
(C) ある問題への解決法を提示すること
(D) ある症状の原因を説明すること

解説 第1段落では color blindness「色覚異常」が特に男性に起こる仕組みについて説明している。従って (D) が正解。特定の問題や医学用語，解決法などについては触れられていない。

2. 解答 A Vocabulary Question

8行目の resistant という言葉に最も近い意味は

(A) 免疫のある
(B) 難しい
(C) けんかっぱやい
(D) 怒っている

解説 続く2文で，女性は片方のX染色体に欠陥のある遺伝子があっても，もう一方のX染色体の遺伝子に頼れるが，男性にはX染色体が1つしかないので頼れない，という説明がある。つまり，女性は男性よりもこの病気にかかりにくいはずなので，(A) が正解。resistant は「抵抗力のある」という意味。

3. 解答 B Factual Question

パッセージによると，錐体の目的は

(A) ウイルスからの感染を撃退すること
(B) ある種の光の波長を特定すること
(C) 個体の性を決定すること
(D) X染色体の遺伝子を複製すること

解説 第1段落第5文に These cones are all tuned to different wavelengths of light「これらの錐体は全てさまざまな光の波長に同調する」とある。従って (B) が正解。そのほかの選択肢についてはパッセージで触れられていない。

4. 解答 A Factual Question

パッセージによると，女性はなぜ色覚異常によりなりにくいのか。

(A) 女性はもう1つX染色体を持っている。
(B) 女性は目により多くの視細胞がある。
(C) 女性は目の外傷を負いにくい。
(D) 女性の免疫系はより優れている。

[解説] 第1段落最後から2文目 If one of their X chromosomes has a faulty gene, they can rely on the same set of genes on their other X chromosome.「女性は片方のX染色体に欠陥のある遺伝子がある場合，もう一方のX染色体の同じ遺伝子の一式に頼ることができる」から，(A) が正解。

5. 解答 C Other Question (Organization)

第2段落を展開しているのは主に

(A) ウイルス感染の過程についての描写
(B) 人間以外の種における色覚異常の原因についての説明
(C) 医療処置の背後にある理論についての詳述
(D) 色覚異常の人々の困難についての例の提示

[解説] 第2段落は However, there is new research into treating color blindness.「しかし，色覚異常の治療に関する新しい研究がある」で始まり，動物を使用した研究に関する詳細が述べられている。従って (C) が正解。サルを利用した研究について説明があるが，人間以外の種における色覚異常の原因についての研究をしたわけではないので，(B) は誤り。

6. 解答 C Factual Question

パッセージによると，つくられたウイルスは何をするか。

(A) 色覚異常が引き起こす痛みを和らげる
(B) 傷ついた錐体細胞を治す
(C) 現存の視細胞の機能を変える
(D) 色覚異常を起こす欠陥のある細胞を破壊する

[解説] 第2段落で研究中の治療法の詳細が説明されており，第4文に These genes overwrite the function of the existing cone「(ウイルスの殻で包んだ) それらの遺伝子は現存の錐体の機能を上書きする」とある。従って (C) が正解。機能を変化させるだけで，「傷ついた錐体細胞を治す」わけではないので，(B) は誤り。

7.　解答　A　Vocabulary Question

18行目のperceivingという言葉に最も近い意味は

(A) 気付くこと
(B) 使うこと
(C) 楽しむこと
(D) 訓練すること

解説　治療を受けたサルについて，monkeys ... were able to detect colors that they were not capable of perceiving before「サルたちが，以前は perceiving できなかった色を見ることができたと分かった」とあるので，perceiving は detect colors とほぼ同じ意味だと考えられる。(A) が正解。perceive は「(視覚によって) ～を理解する，～に気付く」という意味。

8.　解答　B　Vocabulary Question

22行目のexacerbatedという言葉に最も近い意味は

(A) 好転させられた
(B) 悪化させられた
(C) 取り込まれた
(D) 片付けられた

解説　研究中の治療は，最終段落第3文にある infections and pain「感染や痛み」が懸念されるだけでなく，治療を複数回する必要があるので，a chance that the body would develop an immunity to them「体がそれに対する免疫をつくる可能性」もある。この流れに合う (B) が正解。exacerbate は「～を悪化させる」という意味。

9. 解答 A　Negative Factual Question

次のうち遺伝子治療の欠点として挙げられていないものは

(A) 費用
(B) 複数回の処置
(C) 不快感
(D) 免疫反応

解説 治療の欠点については最終段落にまとめられている。(B) は第4文，(D) は最終文に言及がある。(C) については第3文の pain から欠点の1つだと分かる。「費用」に関しては言及がないので，(A) が正解。

10. 解答 D　Other Question (After)

パッセージに続くと思われる段落は

(A) 主に片方の性に影響するそのほかの病気について
(B) 動物で実験することに関する倫理的な問題について
(C) 色覚異常の歴史について
(D) 治療の効果を上げる方法について

解説 最終段落では，研究中の治療はまだリスクが高く非効率であることを説明しており，これに続く内容としては (D) が適切。性別による影響の違いについては第1段落でしか触れられておらず，(A) が続くとは考えにくい。(B) が入るとしたら第2段落の後である。(C) は第1段落内か，その後で触れる方が自然。

Questions 11-20

> **パッセージの訳**
>
> 　19世紀半ばのアメリカで，理想郷的な共同体をつくろうという運動が広がった。何がきっかけでそのような共同体のブームが起こったのかは分からない。少し前に産業革命がもたらされたせいか，あるいは，アメリカ人が自身のヨーロッパ的な背景とは別に，自分たちの文化を発展させていたことの表れかもしれない。いずれにせよ，膨大な数の人々が，たいていカリスマ的な指導者の指揮の下，それまでの生活を捨てて，地球上の楽園を目指してつくられたコミューンで生活する決心をした。
>
> 　そうした共同体の大多数は宗教的なものだった。聖職者や信心深い者たちが，聖書の教えに基づいた新開地をつくることで，信徒を外の世界の腐敗した影響から救おうとしたのだ。彼らの多くは，近年の修正によって毒されていないキリスト教の"本来の"姿に回帰しようとした。しかし，これらの社会は，その意味するところに関して大きく異なる見解を有した。ある共同体は，踊りはなく，食べ物は厳しく制限され，性的活動は抑制されるという，重苦しく禁欲的な生活を実行した。また，自由恋愛を習慣とし，女性に対して公の場に参加する機会を増やした共同体もあった。
>
> 　政治的な理想に基づいた共同体もあった。社会主義は当時新たに体系化された政治理論で，多くの共同社会がこの新しい共同生活の形を試すためにつくられた。さらに，自給自足の人たちによる共同体をつくろうとした無政府主義的社会もあった。時には，1つの理想に基づいた共同体もつくられた。主に菜食主義に基づいたコミューンもいくつかあったのだ。
>
> 　それらの共同体のうち，20世紀まで生き延びたものはほとんどない。多くは5年も続かなかった。農業という現実的な必要性に注意を払うことより，理想に大きな関心を持つ人々が多かったのだ。ほとんどが自給自足の村をつくるという現実に向けて準備不足で，食料が乏しくなると崩壊した。後継争いで解散した共同体もあった。少なくとも1つが，意外な形で行き残った。オナイダ・コミュニティーはジョン・ハンフリー・ノイズの指導下の宗教的コミューンだった。彼らは共同体のためにお金を稼ぐ手段として銀器を作り，共同体が崩壊したときには銀器の会社が残った。今日でも，オナイダの名前のついた製品を買うことができる。

11. 解答 C Main Idea Question

パッセージの主な目的は何か。

(A) アメリカにおける社会主義の台頭を説明すること
(B) 異なるキリスト教の宗派の教義を比較すること
(C) 一連の社会運動を論ずること
(D) アメリカへの産業革命の導入を描写すること

解説 第1段落第1文が In the mid-19th century there was a widespread movement in the United States to create utopian communities.「19世紀半ばのアメリカ合衆国で，理想郷的な共同体をつくろうという運動が広がった」で始まっており，以降の各段落でさまざまな共同体についての話題を取り上げている。従って (C) が最も近い。

12. 解答 D Inference Question

理想郷的な共同体が突然ブームとなった理由として示唆されているものは何か。

(A) アメリカにおける貧困と飢餓
(B) 異なる文化出身の人々のグループ間の衝突
(C) アメリカ社会における女性の進出
(D) 工業化の高まり

解説 第1段落第2文に No one knows what triggered such a boom in these communities.「何がきっかけでそのような共同体のブームが起こったのかは分からない」とあるが，続く文で可能性として the recent introduction of the Industrial Revolution「少し前に産業革命がもたらされたこと」について述べられている。従って (D) が正解。

13. 解答 D Vocabulary Question

4行目のdistinctという言葉に最も近い意味は

(A) 似通った
(B) 特別な
(C) 優れた
(D) 異なった

解説 distinct 以下は，Americans developing their own culture「アメリカ人が自分たちの文化を発展させること」について説明している部分。独自の文化を発展させるのだから，それは their European backgrounds「彼ら（=アメリカ人）のヨーロッパ的な背景」とは異なるものであったと考えられる。従って (D) が正解。distinct from ～で「～とは別の」という意味。

14. 解答 C Vocabulary Question

13行目のpracticedという言葉に最も近い意味は

(A) 下稽古した
(B) 応用した
(C) 生活した
(D) 操作した

解説 practice には「〜を練習する」という意味以外に「〜を実行する」という意味もある。ここでは目的語が (somber, ascetic) lives「(重苦しく禁欲的な)生活」で、「〜な生活を実行した」とは「〜な生活を送った」ということだと考えられる。従って (C) が正解。

15. 解答 B Factual Question

パッセージによると，多くの宗教的コミューンに共通した目的は

(A) ほかの宗教の人々を改宗させること
(B) キリスト教の本来の形に戻ること
(C) 男女間の不平等をなくすこと
(D) 聖書の預言を実現すること

解説 第2段落第3文に Many of them attempted to return to an "original" form of Christianity unspoiled by modern revisions.「彼ら (＝聖職者や信心深い者たち) の多くは，近年の修正によって毒されていないキリスト教の"本来の"姿に回帰しようとした」とある。従って (B) が正解。authentic は「本物の，真正の」という意味。

16. 解答 A Negative Factual Question

次のうち理想郷的な共同体が基づいていた理想としてパッセージの中で言及されていないものはどれか。

(A) 製造業
(B) 政治
(C) 宗教
(D) 菜食主義

解説 第2段落に宗教的な共同体の説明があり，第3段落では政治的な共同体と菜食主義に基づく共同体について触れている。manufacturing「製造業」についてはパッセージに言及がないので，(A) が正解。

17. 解答 A　Vocabulary Question

18行目のcollectiveという言葉に最も近い意味は

(A) 共有された
(B) 繁栄した
(C) 宗教的な
(D) 快適な

解説 this new form of collective living「この新しい collective な生活の形」から、その前の部分に手がかりを求めると、Socialism「社会主義」、many communal settlements「多くの共同社会」とある。社会主義に基づく共同社会では、生活は shared「共有された、分かち合った」ものであったはずである。従って (A) が正解。collective は「共同の」という意味。

18. 解答 D　Inference Question

これらの理想郷的なコミューンの大多数の人々についてパッセージは何を示唆しているか。

(A) 彼らは高度な農業の技術を有していた。
(B) 彼らの大部分はお金を稼ぐ何らかの手段を持っていた。
(C) オナイダ・コミュニティーに参加するために自分のコミューンを去った者もいた。
(D) 彼らは自分たちの共同体で実際に日々の労働をするよりも、その原理の方に興味があった。

解説 最終段落第3文に Many members were more interested in ideals than in tending to the practical needs of farming.「農業という現実的な必要性に注意を払うことより、理想に大きな関心を持つ人々が多かったのだ」とある。従って (D) が正解。(A) と (B) は最終段落の内容に矛盾する。(C) について言及がない。

19. 解答 B Factual Question

理想郷的共同体が崩壊した理由として何が言及されているか。

(A) コミューンのための財源をつくる方法についての論争
(B) 最初の指導者の跡を誰が継承するかについての議論
(C) どんな政治制度を実行するかについての混乱
(D) 州やアメリカ政府による土地の没収

解説 崩壊した理由については，最終段落で農業や食料の問題について言及した後，第5文で Other communities dissolved over succession disputes.「後継争いで解散した共同体もあった」というもう1つの理由を挙げている。従って (B) が正解。そのほかの選択肢についてはパッセージに説明がない。

20. 解答 B Purpose Question

著者はなぜオナイダ・コミュニティーに言及しているか。

(A) ほかの理想郷的共同体に影響を与えた重要人物の名前を挙げるため
(B) 共同体が当初の目的からどれほどそれる可能性があるかを示すため
(C) 理想郷的共同体内で見られた宗教的見方の実例を挙げるため
(D) 農業においてコミューンの経験がどれほど少なかったか例を提示するため

解説 the Oneida Community については，最終段落第6文以降に説明がある。宗教的コミューンとして創設されたにもかかわらず，その後コミューンが崩壊すると銀器の製造会社として存続することになった経緯が書かれている。この内容を表すものとして適切なのは (B)。そのほかの選択肢についてはパッセージに言及がない。

Questions 21-30

> **パッセージの訳**

　比較神話学は、さまざまな文化における神話の研究である。これによって人類学者たちは、文化がどのように進化し普及するかを研究できる。複数の文化が同じようなテーマの神話を共有している場合、文化が共通の祖先を共有したか、少なくとも重要な文化的接触があったことを推測できる。言語学者は、これらの類似した物語において同じ役割を担う人物の名前を比較することで、言語の移動や進化を体系化することさえできる。

　地球の端と端にある文化が、その伝統の要素を共通の祖先までいかにさかのぼることができるかについて、ある例を使って示すことができる。ヨーロッパ、北アフリカ、西アジア、さらに中央アジアに共通して、ドラゴンを退治する英雄の神話があるのだ。そうしたドラゴンの神話が、共有された神話の証拠ではなく、全ての人間の心の中にある共通の恐れや憧れの証拠だと考える人もいるかもしれない。しかし、これらの神話では非常に多くの特徴が共通しており、その全てが独立して発展したとは考えにくい。

　ドラゴンはほとんど常に、何らかの種類の大海蛇である。ドラゴンはたいてい複数の頭を持ち、何らかの形で混乱を象徴している。英雄は秩序を表し、その秩序は混乱の上に課されなければならない。英雄の最も著しく特徴的な側面は、それがたいてい嵐の神であるということだ。ギリシャ神話、北欧神話、インド神話におけるゼウスとトールとインドラは、それぞれみな嵐と稲妻の神であり、各神話の中でドラゴン退治の役割を果たした。この同じ役割における嵐の神の例には、カナンのバアルとバビロンのマルドゥクも含まれる。ドラゴンを退治する神が嵐の神でない場合でも、エジプトの太陽神ラーのように、やはり何らかの形で空に関係している。

　この物語は古代インド・ヨーロッパ語族の文化に由来する社会と関連があるが、ほとんどそっくりな神話が、遠く離れた日本に見られる。嵐の神であるスサノオが複数の頭を持った大海蛇であるオロチと闘う神話は、完璧に同じ原型に当てはまる。この神話は東アジアの至る所で見られるものではないので、ほかの東アジア文化に比べると、初期の日本人はインド・ヨーロッパ語族と似た起源を持っているか、あるいは相当なレベルの接触があったことを示唆している。

21. 解答 D Main Idea Question

パッセージは主に何について述べているか。

(A) いくつかの特定の言語の進化
(B) 芸術におけるドラゴンの描かれ方
(C) 人間の共通の祖先
(D) 神話の共通の特徴

[解説] パッセージでは Comparative mythology「比較神話学」について，世界の多くの場所で見られる「ドラゴン」の神話を例に説明しているので，(D) が正解。

22. 解答 B Vocabulary Question

6行目の parallel という言葉に最も近い意味は

(A) 素晴らしい
(B) 似ている
(C) 縛られた
(D) 興味深い

[解説] 問われている parallel は形容詞。その意味は第3文の share a myth with a similar theme「同じようなテーマの神話を共有している」などから，「共通，類似」といった意味だと推測できる。(B) が正解。parallel は形容詞で「類似の」，名詞で「類似点」という意味。

23. 解答 B Vocabulary Question

13行目の autonomously という言葉に最も近い意味は

(A) 偶然に
(B) 独立して
(C) 自然に
(D) ゆっくりと

[解説]「しかし，これらの神話では非常に多くの特徴が共通しており，その全てが autonomously に発展したとは考えにくい」という内容から，「ほかの影響を受けることなく，単独で」といった意味だと推測できる。(B) が正解。autonomously は「自発的に，自主的に」という意味。

24. 解答 A Vocabulary Question

16行目のimposedという言葉に最も近い意味は

(A) 強制された
(B) 頼まれた
(C) 移動させられた
(D) 守られた

[解説] order which much must be imposed on chaos「秩序が混乱に impose されなければならない」とあることから, order「秩序」と chaos「混乱」の関係を考える。「混乱」があるところには「秩序」がもたらされる必要があるので, (A) が正解。impose は「〜を押しつける, (義務など) を課す」という意味。

25. 解答 C Factual Question

パッセージはドラゴンを退治する英雄に共通する特質は何だと述べているか。

(A) 英雄は混乱をつくり出す。
(B) 英雄はどこにでも現れる。
(C) 英雄は嵐の神である。
(D) 英雄は最初の試みで失敗する。

[解説] 第3段落第4文に The most strikingly specific aspect of the hero is that he is usually a storm god.「英雄の最も著しく特徴的な側面は, それがたいてい嵐の神であるということだ」とある。従って (C) が正解。deity「神」が難語だが, 第5文から推測することができる。

26. 解答 A Negative Factual Question

次のうちパッセージで言及されていない神話は

(A) 中国の神話
(B) インドの神話
(C) ギリシャの神話
(D) バビロンの神話

[解説] (A) 以外は第3段落で言及されている。また, 日本とアジア全般に関する記述はあるが, 中国の神話については特に説明がない。従って (A) が正解。

27. 解答 C Purpose Question

著者はなぜ第3段落でエジプトの神ラーに言及しているか。

(A) 比較神話学の限界を示すため
(B) この種の神話の起源を示すため
(C) 例外も依然として型に従っていることを示すため
(D) 同じような名前が神話間でどのように残っているかを示すため

解説 Ra is the god who slays the dragon isn't a storm god「ドラゴンを退治する神が嵐の神でない」例であり，still associated with the sky「やはり空に関係して」いることが分かる。つまり，嵐の神ではないという例外的な神であっても，空に関わりを持ち，ドラゴンを退治する存在という原則は変わらないので，(C) が正解。

28. 解答 D Vocabulary Question

26行目のubiquitousという言葉に最も近い意味は

(A) 理解されている
(B) 心配させる
(C) 危険をはらんだ
(D) 普及している

解説 最終文を読むと，日本とほかの東アジア文化を比較し，日本にはインド・ヨーロッパ語族との類似点または深い関わりがあった可能性を示唆している。つまり，オロチのような神話は東アジアではあまり見られないと考えるのが自然。(D) が正解。ubiquitous は「どこにでもある」という意味。

29. 解答 B Inference Question

日本のオロチ神話の存在は何を示唆しているか。

(A) 神話は歴史的出来事に基づいていた。
(B) 日本文化はインド・ヨーロッパ文化と何か関係がある。
(C) 同じような神話がそれに基づいている。
(D) ほかの神話との類似は偶然である。

解説 最終文に it suggests a similar origin for early Japanese peoples or a greater level of contact with Indo-Europeans compared to other East Asian cultures「初期の日本人はインド・ヨーロッパ語族と似た起源を持っているか，あるいは相当なレベルの接触があったことを示唆している」とある。従って (B) が正解。

30. 解答 D Conclusion Question

次の主張のうちパッセージが立証しているものはどれか。

(A) 大部分の神話は誇張された本当の出来事に基づいている。
(B) 文化は子供たちに道徳を教えるために神話を利用する。
(C) 文明は自分たちを差別化するために新しい神話を作り出す。
(D) 文化が分かれても神話は同じままである。

解説 パッセージでは，Comparative mythology「比較神話学」がどのような学問か説明していて，具体例としてさまざまな文化圏で見られる「ドラゴン」にまつわる神話を紹介している。従って (D) が正解。そのほかの選択肢についてはパッセージで言及されていない。

Questions 31-39

> **パッセージの訳**
>
> 　人々がアメリカの古代文明のことを考えるとき，遺跡を建設していた発達した社会は全て中央アメリカにあったと思うかもしれない。特徴的な階段状のピラミッドがあるオルメカ文明，アステカ文明，マヤ文明がまず頭に浮かぶだろう。しかし考古学者たちは，建築技術に優れた文明が何千年も前に存在したことを示す遺跡を，アメリカ南東部で発掘した。
>
> 　そのような遺跡の1つが，ルイジアナ州のミシシッピ川の河畔にある。それを建設した人々は，ヨーロッパの入植者がやって来て記録を残すだいぶ前に消滅してしまったため，その遺跡は近くの大農園の名を取ってポヴァティ・ポイントとして知られている。遺跡は，6つの同心円状の三日月の形をした一連の土塁が中心となっている。これらのC形土塁の最も長いものは1キロ以上に及ぶ。三日月形は全て中央の平らな広場を取り囲んでおり，外辺部を大きな土塁郡が囲んでいる。
>
> 　遺跡全体の建設には少なくとも100年かかったが，個々の要素は短期間に完成された。最大の土塁は23万8,000立方メートルの土の移動を必要としたが，およそ3カ月で完成された。およそ3,000人の労働者が必要で，土を一杯に入れたバケツを渡していくという単純な方法が使われたのだろう。
>
> 　遺跡のもう1つの印象的な局面は，これを建設した人々が狩猟採集生活者だったという事実である。遺跡のそばに居を構え，時間をかけて建設できるような農耕社会ではなかったので，彼らは食料を獲得する活動の合間に戻ってきて建設しなければならなかった。
>
> 　ポヴァティ・ポイントの正確な目的は謎だ。ポヴァティ・ポイント文化の人々は狩猟採集生活者だったので，そこは永住的住居ではなかっただろう。1つの推測としては，占星術の目的に使われたということだ。宗教的な場所だったと提唱する人もいるが，そこで宗教的な工芸品はあまり多く見つかっていない。ある有力な仮説は，交易の目的で使われていたというものだ。大陸のはるか遠くの地域の工芸品が遺跡で見つかっており，交換や交易のために多くの人々がそこに来たことを示唆している。

31. 解答 B Main Idea Question

パッセージは主に何について述べているか。

(A) 古代遺跡の形状
(B) 興味をそそる古代遺跡
(C) いくつかのアメリカ先住民文化の比較
(D) 古代遺跡の建設方法

解説 第1段落最終文に cultures capable of great feats of construction were present thousands of years ago「建築技術に優れた文明が何千年も前に存在した」とあり，その一例として Poverty Point「ポヴァティ・ポイント」を取り上げている。(B) が正解。(A) の「形状」や (D) の「建設方法」を主に述べているわけではない。

32. 解答 A Inference Question

パッセージが示唆するには，ポヴァティ・ポイントに似た遺跡は

(A) たいてい中央アメリカで多く発見された
(B) 主に川の河畔に築かれた
(C) 主にヨーロッパ人との接触後に築かれた
(D) 農業を促進するために使われた

解説 第1段落第1文で they might think that all the advanced, monument-building societies were in Central America「遺跡を建設していた発達した社会は全て中央アメリカにあったと思うかもしれない」と述べた後，中央アメリカだけでないことを示すために「ポヴァティ・ポイント」の例を挙げている。従って (A) が正解。

33. 解答 A Vocabulary Question

9行目の plantation という言葉に最も近い意味は

(A) 農場
(B) 川
(C) 史跡
(D) 町

解説 plantation は「大規模農園，プランテーション」のこと。従って (A) が正解。

34. 解答 C Factual Question

パッセージによると，複合体であるポヴァティ・ポイント全体の建設は
(A) 2，3カ月で完了した
(B) 少人数で行われた
(C) 100年かそれ以上かかった
(D) 大量の木材を必要とした

解説 　第3段落第1文に the construction of the entire site took place over at least a century「遺跡全体の建設には少なくとも100年かかった」とあるので (C) が正解。(A) は同じ部分と合わない。(B) は第3文に矛盾する。(D) の「木材」について言及がない。

35. 解答 C Vocabulary Question

24行目の permanent という言葉に最も近い意味は
(A) 忘れられた
(B) 大きな
(C) 長続きする
(D) 謎めいている

解説 　「ポヴァティ・ポイント文化の人々は狩猟採集生活者だったので，そこは permanent な住居ではなかっただろう」とある。「狩猟採集生活者」の生活様式から推測すると，ずっと同じ場所にとどまっていなかったはずだと考えられる。(C) が正解。permanent は「永続する」という意味。

36. 解答 C Reference Question

27行目の it という言葉が指すのは
(A) 有力な仮説
(B) ポヴァティ・ポイント文化
(C) ポヴァティ・ポイント
(D) 謎

解説 　この it は前文の suggested に続く節の主語 it と同じものを指している。つまり，Poverty Point のこと。a religious site「宗教的な場所だった」，it was used for trade「交易の目的で使われていた」などから，(B) の「文化」よりも，場所そのものを表している (C) が適切。

37. 解答 D　Factual Question

著者が述べるには，ポヴァティ・ポイントが印象的な1つの理由はそれを築いた文化が

(A) 沼の多い土地を使わなければならなかったから
(B) 車輪を発明していなかったから
(C) 宗教を持たなかったから
(D) 狩猟採集生活者だったから

解説 第4段落第1文に Another impressive aspect of the site is the fact that the people who built it were hunter-gatherers.「遺跡のもう1つの印象的な局面は，これを建設した人々が狩猟採集生活者だったという事実である」とある。従って (D) が正解。(A) や (B) のような内容についてパッセージに言及がない。(C) は最終段落第4文で言及されているが，印象的な理由としてではない。

38. 解答 B　Negative Factual Question

次のうちポヴァティ・ポイントの目的の説明でないものは

(A) 宗教寺院
(B) パーフォーマンス用の場所
(C) 交易の場所
(D) 占星術の道具

解説 最終段落の第3文以降を読むと，(A), (C), (D) については触れているが，(B) に関しては言及がない。従って (B) が正解。

39. 解答 C　Inference Question

ポヴァティ・ポイント文化と交易の関係についてパッセージは何を示唆しているか。

(A) 夏の間だけ行われた。
(B) その文化には使われなかった。
(C) 彼らにとってとても大切だった。
(D) 農耕後に発展した。

解説 最終段落最終文から，大陸各地から品物が送られ，取引されていたことが分かるので，(C)「とても大切だった」と言える。(A) のような説明はパッセージにない。(B) は最終段落第5文に合わない。(D) は第4段落第2文に合わない。

Questions 40-50

> **パッセージの訳**
>
> 　新しい薬は市場に出せるようになる前に，安全かつ効果的かどうかを判断する厳しい手順を踏まなくてはならない。ほとんどの国はこうした臨床試験のために同じような実施要領に従うが，アメリカではこの手順はアメリカ食品医薬品局（FDA）によって行われる。
>
> 　薬品が検討のためにFDAに提出される前に，製薬会社は独自の試験を行う。それらの試験の多くは人工環境内の研究室で行われ，動物実験を含むこともある。製薬会社はそうした試験を独自に行うが，FDAからの指導を求めることもある。
>
> 　製薬会社は，次に正式な出願書類をFDAに提出し，FDAは第1段階の試験を監督する。これらの研究は，20人から80人の健康な人々の小グループを使って，薬を服用させる。これらのボランティアたちは薬が治そうとする病気を持っていないので，ここでは安全性だけがテストされる。もし被験者たちが薬で害を受けず，副作用が最低限度ならば，試験は第2段階に進む。
>
> 　第2段階は薬の効き目をテストする。薬が治そうとしている病気にかかっているおよそ30人から300人の集団が，2つのグループに分けられる。片方は新薬をもらい，もう一方は現在認められている薬または偽薬をもらう。偽薬とは，実際の効果はないが，患者の症状を改善するのに心理的に役立つ薬である。新薬をもらったグループがほかのグループよりも少しもよくならなければ，薬は却下される。代わりにそのグループが著しい改善を示せば，薬は第3段階に進める。
>
> 　この最後の段階は，何千人もの被験者を使い，第2段階の結果が統計上の例外でなかったことを確かめる。こうした大きな集団はまた，特定の年齢層や性といった特定の層の人々にとって，異なるリスクがあるかどうかを見つけることができる。これらの最終試験の後でようやく，薬はFDAが検討するための最終的な出願資格を得る。これらの試験の後でさえ，薬は市場に出てから健康に及ぼし得るリスクを監視される。試験で発見されなかった危険性が生じた場合，薬は棚から回収されることがある。

40. 解答 C　Main Idea Question

パッセージは主に何について述べているか。

(A) アメリカでどのように薬品が売られているか
(B) 新薬の試験にどのように動物が使われているか
(C) アメリカで薬品はどのように認可されるか
(D) アメリカで薬品はどのように製造されるか

解説 第1段落に a rigorous process that determines if it is both safe and effective「それ（＝新しい薬）が安全かつ効果的かどうかを判断する厳しい手順」(第1文) について，in the United States the process is done by the United States Food and Drug Administration (FDA)「アメリカではこの手順はアメリカ食品医薬品局 (FDA) によって行われる」(第2文) とある。(C) が正解。

41. 解答 C　Vocabulary Question

3行目のprotocolという言葉に最も近い意味は

(A) 予定
(B) 食欲
(C) 手順
(D) 忠告

解説 a similar protocol とは，「(第1文の内容と) 同様の protocol」だと考えられる。第1文は process についての話なので，(C) が正解だと推測できる。protocol は「儀礼，実施要領」で，ここでは後者の意味。

42. 解答 B　Factual Question

製薬会社によって行われる試験がFDAの試験と異なる理由は

(A) はるかに多い被験者を使うから
(B) 時々動物に対して行われるから
(C) はるかに多い服用量でテストするから
(D) 同時に複数のテストを行うから

解説 第2段落第2文に製薬会社による試験について … and may include testing on animals「…動物実験を含むこともある」とあるが，第3段落以降で詳述されている FDA の試験に動物利用の話は出てこないので，(B) が正解。

43. 解答 C Vocabulary Question

8行目のsolicitという言葉に最も近い意味は

(A) 無視する
(B) 支持する
(C) 頼む
(D) 集める

解説 The drug manufacturers will perform these tests by themselves, but may solicit guidance from the FDA.「製薬会社はそうした試験を独自に行うが、FDA からの指導を solicit することもある」という文。これまでの内容から (A) は考えにくく、(B) は but の前までの内容とうまくつながらない。残る2つのうち、正解は (C)。solicit は「～を求める、せがむ」という意味。

44. 解答 D Factual Question

パッセージによると、第1段階について独特な点は何か。

(A) 製薬会社によって行われる。
(B) 報酬をもらう被験者を使う。
(C) 最多数の被験者を使う。
(D) 薬が効くかどうかをテストしない。

解説 第3段落第3文に Since these volunteers don't have the disease the drug is trying to treat, only safety is being tested here.「これらのボランティアたちは薬が治そうとする病気を持っていないので、ここでは安全性だけがテストされる」とある。つまり、薬が効くかどうかのテストではないので、(D) が正解。

45. 解答 B Vocabulary Question

14行目のefficacyという言葉に最も近い意味は

(A) 拡張性
(B) 効果
(C) 専門知識
(D) 努力

解説 第4段落の最後に If the group instead shows significant improvement, the drug can pass on to Phase 3.「代わりにそのグループが著しい改善を示せば、薬は第3段階に進める」とあるので、この段階では薬の「効果」が試されると考えられる。(B) が正解。efficacy は「効き目」という意味。

46. 解答 B Factual Question

第2段階において，新薬は何と比べてテストされるか。

(A) 試験中のほかの薬
(B) 偽薬または既存薬
(C) ほかのどの治療とも比べられない
(D) ほかの病気を治療する薬

解説 第4段落第3文に One receives the new drug while the other receives either a currently accepted drug or a placebo, ...「片方は新薬をもらい，もう一方は現在認められている薬または偽薬をもらう」とある。従って (B) が正解。

47. 解答 D Vocabulary Question

24行目の eligible という言葉に最も近い意味は

(A) 妨げられている
(B) 試練を受けた
(C) 禁止された
(D) 資格要件を満たした

解説 eligible を含む文は倒置文で，「これらの最終試験の後でようやく，薬は FDA が検討するための最終的な出願の eligible となる」という意味。(D) を入れると意味上，自然な文になる。eligible は「適格な，資格のある」という意味。

48. 解答 D Factual Question

パッセージによると，どの段階が最も多数の被験者を使うか。

(A) 出願前の試験
(B) 第1段階
(C) 第2段階
(D) 第3段階

解説 出願前の試験については，被験者数の説明はない。第1段階は20〜80人（第3段落第2文），第2段階は30〜300人（第4段落第2文），第3段階は数千人（最終段落第1文）なので，(D) が正解。

49. 解答 D　Other Question (After)

パッセージに続く段落は何についてのものと思われるか。

(A) FDAの委員会を構成するのは誰か
(B) 大部分の製薬会社はどこを拠点としているか
(C) 製薬会社がどのように病気を研究するか
(D) 何が原因で薬はFDAによって除外されるか

解説 最終段落最後の文に If dangers arise that were not uncovered in trials a drug can be pulled from shelves.「試験で発見されなかった危険性が生じた場合，薬は棚から回収されることがある」とあるので，(D) が続くと考えられる。

50. 解答 B　Where Question

著者はどこで偽薬の定義を述べているか。

(A) 14〜15行目
(B) 17〜18行目
(C) 18〜19行目
(D) 21〜22行目

解説 17行目の a medicine 以下が，直前の a placebo の説明になっている。(B) が正解。

Practice Test 2 　問題　　⏱ 55 minutes

Questions 1-10

Line   One of the main problems with rockets as a method to propel spaceships is the weight of the fuel. Spaceships that are made to be heavier need more fuel, which adds even more weight. It's a vicious cycle which makes space travel expensive and results in limited use of rockets once ships have escaped the earth's
(5) gravitational pull. Once out of the atmosphere, rockets mostly coast to their destination. However, a new type of spacecraft could change the way the universe is explored.

   The solar sail is a large, thin, mirrored sheet that a spaceship suspends in front of itself that acts much like a sail on a boat. Instead of capturing the power
(10) of the wind, solar sails use the light and radiation coming off the sun. The force exerted by the sun on objects in space is negligible, but multiplied out over a large surface, it can be enough to power the flight of spaceships through the vacuum of space.

   This need for large sails might seem to present the same problem as the need
(15) for rocket fuel, but solar sails can be built at extremely light weights. The NASA Sunjammer solar sail is 38 meters across but only 5 micrometers thick and weighs less than 35 kilograms. This ability to produce lightweight solar sails is essential, since sails to power manned spacecraft will have to be many kilometers wide.

   Solar sails are an emerging technology, and ships powered by them will still
(20) require the use of rockets to get into orbit. There is also the fact that they require the sun's rays to be effective, making travel outside the solar system unfeasible. However, the last shortcoming may be overcome by putting the energy source on the spacecraft itself. A powerful laser attached to the spaceship could provide the same effect as the sun. The batteries used to power such a laser would still weigh
(25) less than rocket fuel, maintaining the benefits of the solar sail.

1. What does the passage mainly discuss?
   (A) a new technology
   (B) a scientific principle
   (C) the solar system
   (D) the findings of a study

2. The first paragraph is developed primarily by means of
   (A) explaining the physics of solar sails
   (B) introducing a problem to be solved by solar sails
   (C) providing a shortcoming of solar sails
   (D) showing a case where solar sails were used

3. The word "propel" in line 1 is closest in meaning to a
   (A) move
   (B) break
   (C) design
   (D) apply

4. Why are the sails of a boat mentioned in line 9?
   (A) To emphasize the difficulty of moving spaceships
   (B) To describe the power of the wind
   (C) To show how far technology has progressed
   (D) To provide an analogy for how solar sails work

5. The word "negligible" in line 11 is closest in meaning to
   (A) proportional
   (B) effective
   (C) small
   (D) balanced

6. The word "it" in line 12 refers to
   (A) surface
   (B) space
   (C) the sun
   (D) the force

7. What is the main benefit solar sails have over rockets?
   (A) They are faster.
   (B) They are lighter.
   (C) They are easier to build.
   (D) They have fewer moving parts.

8. Why are rockets still required for ships with solar sails?
   (A) They are needed for longer flights.
   (B) They are needed for speed boosts.
   (C) They are needed to make turns in space.
   (D) They are needed to leave the earth's atmosphere.

9. Why does the author mention lasers in the last paragraph?
   (A) To introduce a technology that is considered ineffective
   (B) To provide a workaround for a problem with solar sails
   (C) To mention another propulsion system
   (D) To explain why solar sails can't be used outside the solar system

10. Where does the author explain the importance of the lightness of solar sails?
    (A) Lines 2-3
    (B) Lines 10-13
    (C) Lines 17-18
    (D) Lines 20-21

Questions 11-20

Line

The account of Christopher Columbus sailing for Spain and stumbling upon the American continent in an attempt to find a new route to Asia is a familiar story. However, most people don't consider that Spanish designs for Asia didn't end with Columbus's failure to find a direct passage. In fact, with the
(5) establishment of the Spanish East Indies — what is now known as the Philippines — the need for a trade route to East Asia was more pressing than ever. The passage around the southern tip of Africa was reserved for the Portuguese and the land route over the Asian interior was no longer open to traders. As a result, the Spanish colonies in the Americas weren't just colonial holdings on their own, but
(10) also gateways to Asia.

The most prominent of these Asian gateways was the port of Acapulco on the western coast of Mexico. Goods from Asia were loaded into ships in the Spanish East Indies, which crossed the Pacific Ocean to Acapulco. The goods were then either carried across Central America to be shipped back to Spain across the
(15) Atlantic Ocean or sailed down around the tip of South America to complete the same voyage.

It was a long journey, but still immensely profitable for Spain. China's economy was primarily dependent on silver at the time, and Spain found large quantities of silver in its Mexican colonies. To this day two of the five largest
(20) silver mines in the world are in Mexico. With this silver the Spanish bought luxury goods from Chinese silk and porcelain, to Japanese lacquerware, to spices from across Asia. All of these goods attracted huge prices in Europe and contributed to Spain's coffers.

All these goods had to pass through Acapulco first, and the tiny port grew
(25) in wealth and prominence. It became one of the most cosmopolitan cities in the world with Europeans, Africans, Asians, and Native Americans living in this vibrant trading hub. In fact, Acapulco could be considered one of the first places on earth to feel the effects of globalization.

11. What does the passage mainly discuss?
   (A) The downfall of an empire
   (B) How a country engaged in trade
   (C) The economic system of a country
   (D) The causes of a war

12. The word "designs" in line 3 is closest in meaning to
   (A) intentions
   (B) greetings
   (C) positions
   (D) demands

13. The word "pressing" in line 6 is closest in meaning to
   (A) weak
   (B) questionable
   (C) late
   (D) crucial

14. What can be inferred about Columbus and his arrival on the American continent?
   (A) It eliminated Spain's plans for Asian colonization.
   (B) It aided Spain's colonial empire.
   (C) It started a territorial dispute with Portugal.
   (D) It prompted the need for bigger ships.

15. Spain used a long sea route that spanned two oceans because the other sea route was
   (A) controlled by another country
   (B) no longer open for traders
   (C) in the wrong direction
   (D) too crowded

16. All of the following are mentioned as goods Spain imported from Asia EXCEPT
   (A) lacquerware
   (B) porcelain
   (C) gold
   (D) spices

17. Mexico was Spain's ideal gateway for trade with China because
   (A) China already had a presence in the region
   (B) it was the shortest route between the two countries
   (C) it had a large amount of material China needed
   (D) Spain already had colonies between it and China

18. The word "goods" in line 21 is closest in meaning to
   (A) benefits
   (B) interests
   (C) profits
   (D) products

19. The word "cosmopolitan" in line 25 is closest in meaning to
   (A) new
   (B) multicultural
   (C) critical
   (D) joyous

20. What will the paragraph immediately following this passage likely discuss?
   (A) Sea routes used by the Portuguese
   (B) Chinese silk-making techniques
   (C) Christopher Columbus' early life
   (D) Relations among Acapulco's population

Questions 21-30

Line   In the field of economics there are myriad principles that determine an item's worth and therefore its price. Some are fairly well known such as supply and demand, but there are many more beyond that. However, all of these factors are not perfect. Most are compromised by another economic principle: asymmetric
(5) information. In this case, asymmetric means uneven or favoring one side. In almost all things, someone knows more than the other person. This causes discrepancies between an item's ideal price and its actual price.

The most obvious example of this is when a seller knows more about their wares than a buyer. Someone who sells stereos is more likely to know all about
(10) stereos and their relative worth than a person buying them. The seller would know that the manufacturing costs for two nearly identical models are about the same, but one of them may sell for twice as much if it uses a premium finish on the exterior. With this knowledge a seller would try to push the buyer towards buying the more expensive model since it would result in a much higher profit. This is
(15) where we get the common aphorism "caveat emptor" or "buyer beware." Buyers are usually on the disadvantaged side of asymmetric information.

Still, there are times when the buyer's lack of knowledge harms the seller. Economist George Akerlof demonstrated this principle in his paper "The Market for Lemons," which describes a conundrum in the used car market. Used car
(20) buyers have limited knowledge about the history of a used car; they're not sure if the car is fine or is a "lemon," that is, a dud car. Therefore even though a used car might be in excellent shape, most buyers are still hesitant to pay a high price for it. This causes sellers to not stock cars in excellent shape since they won't receive a good price for them, further degrading the actual and perceived value of a used
(25) car in the minds of buyers.

21. What does the passage mainly discuss?
   (A) Advice for buying certain goods
   (B) The history of a specific market
   (C) An economic principle
   (D) The argument of an economist

22. The word "myriad" in line 1 is closest in meaning to
   (A) unknown
   (B) many
   (C) complicated
   (D) expensive

23. The word "discrepancies" in line 7 is closest in meaning to
   (A) conflicts
   (B) differences
   (C) characteristics
   (D) shortcuts

24. Why does the author mention supply and demand in the first paragraph?
   (A) To give an example of a discredited economic principle
   (B) To introduce the topic underpinning the rest of the passage
   (C) To bring up a term that will be explained later in more detail
   (D) To start off the passage with a familiar concept

25. According to the passage, why are stereo sellers at an advantage against a potential buyer?
   (A) They are good at guessing a buyer's preferences.
   (B) They are in a position of higher authority.
   (C) They know more about their product.
   (D) They serve a lot of customers in one day.

26. Why does the author mention the phrase "caveat emptor" in the second paragraph?
   (A) To introduce a concept to be explained later
   (B) To reveal the economics behind the phrase
   (C) To provide another definition of the main topic
   (D) To demonstrate the cultural background of economics

27. The word "conundrum" in line 19 is closest in meaning to
   (A) problem
   (B) explanation
   (C) mechanic
   (D) apology

28. The passage implies that used car buyers
   (A) tend not to trust a seller's appraisal of a car
   (B) thoroughly research the value of used cars
   (C) know more about used cars than sellers
   (D) only buy cars with excellent facilities

29. Which of the following statements does the passage support?
   (A) Information asymmetry does not affect the used car market.
   (B) Used car sellers only stock cars that are in good shape.
   (C) Small cars make up the majority of the used car market.
   (D) Buyers' fears may lower the quality of the cars that are sold.

30. Which of the following words does the author gives an explanation?
   (A) discrepancy
   (B) caveat
   (C) conundrum
   (D) lemon

Questions 31-40

Line

The figure of the modern music star with legions of ardent fans is a familiar one. Stories of the devotion of adulating fans are part of the contemporary music scene. It's easy to imagine this is a recent development and is a result of the proliferation of mass media. However, even in what we think of as the staid
(5) world of European court music of the 1800's we find an example that matches the archetype of the modern rock star.

Franz Liszt was a Hungarian musician born in 1811. He was a musical prodigy from a young age and traveled around Europe learning from and meeting great composers like Shubert and Beethoven. Liszt was particularly renowned
(10) for his skill as a piano virtuoso. While an accomplished composer it was his flamboyant piano playing that attracted the most attention.

Liszt's performances were unique in several ways. First, he did not play using sheet music, the written notation of a song that instructs musicians what notes to play. Doing so was considered uncouth and displayed an arrogant assurance in
(15) one's abilities. Second, he played so that the audience could see his face in profile. Usually pianists' faces were turned away from the audience, but Liszt put his on display. It didn't hurt that Liszt was considered particularly attractive.

Performances by Liszt were filled with adoring fans, particularly female admirers. Women would cheer and swoon at his concerts and fights would break
(20) out when Liszt threw a glove into the crowd. Devotees would wear necklaces and brooches with his image and some went as far as collecting mementos such as locks of his hair. One woman recovered a used cigar butt from his trash and kept it in a locket engraved with his initials.

The collective fervor was even given its own name: Lisztomania. Today the
(25) word mania might be used for any craze or fad, but back in the 1800's it was used exclusively for psychological conditions. Indeed, physicians at the time thought it was an actual medical condition. They were worried of the "disease" spreading and affecting more people. Instead, like all trends, enthusiasm eventually died out and Liszt took his place in history as one of the first musical superstars.

31. Which of the following is the best title for this passage?
   (A) An Exploration of the Music Fan
   (B) Great Figures from Hungarian Music
   (C) The Precursor to the Modern Rock Star
   (D) The Early Life and Education of Franz Liszt

32. It can be inferred from the passage that ardent fans
   (A) were non-existent until the 20th century
   (B) were the creation of mass media
   (C) existed before the advent of mass media
   (D) are rarely found in Europe

33. The word "proliferation" in line 4 is closest in meaning to
   (A) production
   (B) decrease
   (C) spread
   (D) revolution

34. The word "renowned" in line 9 is closest in meaning to
   (A) considered
   (B) well-known
   (C) great
   (D) notorious

35. According to the passage, all of the following contributed to Liszt's charm EXCEPT
   (A) his flair for composition
   (B) his performance style
   (C) his face
   (D) his acquaintance with great composers

36. The author implies that pianists of Liszt's time
(A) didn't show their faces
(B) didn't write their own music
(C) had lots of fans
(D) didn't perform in public

37. The word "recovered" in line 22 is closest in meaning to
(A) saw
(B) created
(C) took
(D) explained

38. The author states that audience reaction to Liszt's performances was
(A) typical of European audiences
(B) mostly limited to male listeners
(C) unusually passionate for the time
(D) most enthusiastic in his home country

39. The author's attitude towards the physicians mentioned in the final paragraph is
(A) amicable
(B) dismissive
(C) reverent
(D) intrigued

40. Where does the author give the definition of sheet music?
(A) Lines 2-3
(B) Lines 4-6
(C) Lines 10-11
(D) Lines 13-14

Questions 41-50

Line   Since their discovery in the late 19th century one of the defining features of viruses has been their small size. In fact, they were discovered by straining infected liquids through filters too fine to let bacteria through. Viruses are usually a hundred times smaller than bacteria and it wasn't until the invention of electron
(5) microscopes that they could be seen. However, in the past 15 years a streak of discoveries have upended our understanding of viruses and even the tree of life.

In 2003 French scientists took a closer look at a strange bacteria called Bradfordcoccus collected more than 10 years ago by an English researcher. Bradfordcoccus was odd in that it did not seem to feed and grow on nutrients
(10) but still didn't die off. The "bacteria" turned out to be a colossal virus which they named Mimivirus. It was impressive not just in size but in complexity. While most viruses only had 10 genes this new virus had over a thousand. This increased genetic complexity allowed it to behave in a unique way. Most viruses inject their DNA into a host cell and hijack the cell's nucleus to produce copies.
(15) Mimiviruses insert themselves into a cell and then make copies of themselves on their own using the raw materials found in the cell.

This discovery radically changed the perception of what viruses could look like. Before long even larger viruses with even more genes were discovered. The largest of these viruses, Pithovirus, can even be seen with a normal microscope.
(20) Since these giant viruses had an established precedent, previously inexplicable microbes were now looked at in a new light.

The existence of these giant viruses has created considerable debate as to their origin. They could be viruses that somehow grew larger. They could be an entirely new branch on the tree of life, something different from viruses and
(25) bacteria altogether. An especially intriguing theory is that they were a bacteria that evolved into a virus. People usually think of things evolving into more advanced, complex beings, but this would be a living organism evolving into a less complex, non-living entity.

41. What does the passage mainly discuss?
   (A) Tracing the discovery of viruses
   (B) Exploring an unusual type of virus
   (C) Explaining research methods of biologists
   (D) Hypothesizing on the origins of life on earth

42. Why does the author mention electron microscopes in the first paragraph?
   (A) To explain the methods of scientists
   (B) To disprove the smallness of viruses
   (C) To emphasize the size of viruses
   (D) To indicate the importance of technology

43. The word "hijack" in line 14 is closest in meaning to
   (A) bring over
   (B) turn around
   (C) put in
   (D) take over

44. According to the passage, scientists first thought that Mimivirus was
   (A) a smaller virus
   (B) a bacteria
   (C) inorganic matter
   (D) multiple viruses

45. The passage implies that the extra genes found in giant viruses are
   (A) more like multicellular organisms
   (B) junk DNA that doesn't do anything
   (C) needed to maintain their larger size
   (D) used in their unique duplication process

46. The word "perception" in line 17 is closest in meaning to
   (A) meaning
   (B) view
   (C) lesson
   (D) session

47. The word "precedent" in line 20 is closest in meaning to
   (A) meeting
   (B) purpose
   (C) example
   (D) relationship

48. All of the following are listed as differences between regular viruses and giant viruses EXCEPT
   (A) shape
   (B) size
   (C) number of genes
   (D) reproduction methods

49. The passage suggests that scientists found new giant viruses after the first was discovered because
   (A) more money was directed to research
   (B) the location of the discovery was searched
   (C) they now knew what to look for
   (D) it inspired more people to become scientists

50. All of the following are suggested origins for giant viruses EXCEPT
   (A) life that came to earth from an asteroid
   (B) a distinct origin apart from viruses and bacteria
   (C) viruses that grew to become larger
   (D) bacteria that evolved into viruses

Practice Test 2 解答・解説

解答一覧

1 **A**	2 **B**	3 **A**	4 **D**	5 **C**	6 **D**	7 **B**	8 **D**	9 **B**
10 **C**	11 **B**	12 **A**	13 **D**	14 **B**	15 **A**	16 **C**	17 **C**	18 **D**
19 **B**	20 **D**	21 **C**	22 **B**	23 **B**	24 **D**	25 **C**	26 **B**	27 **A**
28 **A**	29 **D**	30 **D**	31 **C**	32 **C**	33 **C**	34 **B**	35 **D**	36 **B**
37 **C**	38 **C**	39 **B**	40 **D**	41 **B**	42 **C**	43 **D**	44 **B**	45 **D**
46 **B**	47 **C**	48 **A**	49 **C**	50 **A**				

Questions 1-10

パッセージの訳

　宇宙船を進ませる方法としてのロケットの主な問題の1つは，燃料の重さである。より重く作られた宇宙船はより多くの燃料を必要とし，またその燃料さえも重さを加える。この悪循環のために，宇宙旅行の費用は高価になり，地球の引力から脱出した後のロケットの使用が限定されるという結果になる。いったん大気圏を出れば，ロケットはたいてい惰力で目的地へと進む。しかし，新しいタイプの宇宙船は，宇宙探検の方法を変えられるかもしれない。

　ソーラーセイル（太陽帆）は大きく薄い鏡になった板で，宇宙船の前にぶら下げると，ちょうど船の帆のような役割を果たす。風の力を捉える代わりに，ソーラーセイルは太陽が発する光と放射エネルギーを利用する。太陽が宇宙にある物体に及ぼす力は取るに足らないが，大きな面積の上でそれを増加させれば，宇宙の真空状態の中を飛ぶ力を宇宙船に十分与えることができる。

　このような大きな帆の必要性は，ロケット燃料の必要性と同じ問題を呈するように思えるが，ソーラーセイルは非常に軽量に作ることができる。NASAのサンジャマー・ソーラーセイルは直径38メートルだが，厚さはたったの5マイクロメーターで，重さは35キロ未満だ。軽量のソーラーセイルを作るこの能力は必要不可欠である。なぜなら，有人の宇宙船を動かすための帆は，幅が何キロもなければならないからだ。

　ソーラーセイルは新たな技術であり，ソーラーセイルで進む宇宙船も，軌道に入るためにはまだロケットを使う必要がある。さらに，ソーラーセイルが効果を発揮するには太陽の光線を必要とするので，太陽系外での飛行が実行困難だという事実もある。しかし，最後の欠点も，宇宙船そのものにエネルギー源を搭載することで克服できるかもしれない。宇宙船に装着した強力なレーザー装置は，太陽と同じ効果を生むはずだ。そのようなレーザーを起動するのに使われるバッテリーは，それでもロケット燃料よりは軽く，ソーラーセイルの利点を保てるだろう。

1. 解答 A　Main Idea Question

パッセージは主に何について述べているか。

(A) 新しい技術
(B) 科学原理
(C) 太陽系
(D) 研究によって発見された事柄

解説　第1段落でロケットの問題点を挙げた後，However で始まる最終文で「新しいタイプの宇宙船は，宇宙探検の方法を変えられるかもしれない」と言い，以降の段落で新技術である「ソーラーセイル」の説明をしている。従って (A) が正解。何かの研究結果が明らかになったという内容ではないので，(D) は誤り。

2. 解答 B　Other Question (Organization)

第1段落を展開しているのは主に

(A) ソーラーセイルの物理を説明すること
(B) ソーラーセイルが解決する問題を紹介すること
(C) ソーラーセイルの欠点を述べること
(D) ソーラーセイルが使われたある事例を示すこと

解説　第1段落ではまず「燃料」，「重量」，「費用」にかかわるロケットの問題点を指摘し，その解決法として a new type of spacecraft「新しいタイプの宇宙船」（ソーラーセイルを備えた宇宙船）に触れている。従って (B) が正解。

3. 解答 A　Vocabulary Question

1行目のpropelという言葉に最も近い意味は

(A) 動かす
(B) 壊す
(C) 設計する
(D) 適用する

解説　rockets as a method to propel spaceships「宇宙船を propel する方法としてのロケット」から，ロケットの役割を考えると，(A) が正解だと分かる。propel は「〜を進ませる」という意味。-er が付いた形の名詞 propeller「プロペラ，推進器」からも推測可能。

4. 解答 D　Purpose Question

9行目で船の帆が言及されているのはなぜか。

(A) 宇宙船を動かす難しさを強調するため
(B) 風の力を表現するため
(C) 技術がどれほど進歩したかを示すため
(D) ソーラーセイルの働きに対して類比を提供するため

解説　第2段落第1文ではソーラーセイルについて，like a sail on a boat「船の帆のような」役割を果たすと説明している。つまり船の帆にたとえることでソーラーセイルの働きを説明しているので，(D) が正解。analogy は「類比，類似点」という意味。

5. 解答 C　Vocabulary Question

11行目のnegligibleという言葉に最も近い意味は

(A) 比例した
(B) 効果的な
(C) 小さな
(D) 安定した

解説　直後の but multiplied out over a large surface は分詞構文で，「しかし大きな面積の上でそれを増加させれば」という意味。なぜ増加させる必要があるのかを考えると，太陽の及ぼす力が「小さい」からだと推測できる。negligible は「取るに足らない」という意味。(C) が正解。

6. 解答 D　Reference Question

12行目のitという言葉が指すのは

(A) 表面
(B) 宇宙
(C) 太陽
(D) 力

解説　it は multiplied out over a large surface の意味上の主語でもある。「増加させれば，それは飛ぶ力を宇宙船に十分与えることができる」から，it は文前半の主語 The force exerted by the sun on objects in space「太陽によって宇宙にある物体に及ぼされる力」を指していると分かる。(D) が正解。

175

7. 解答 B　Factual Question

ソーラーセイルがロケットに及ぼす主な利点は何か。

(A) より速い。
(B) より軽い。
(C) より簡単に作れる。
(D) 可動部分が少ない。

解説　第1段落で宇宙船の「重量」の問題を取り上げたのを受けて，第3段落では solar sails can be built at extremely light weights「ソーラーセイルは非常に軽量に作ることができる」（第1文）など，ソーラーセイルがとても軽量であることを説明している。従って (B) が正解。

8. 解答 D　Factual Question

ソーラーセイルのある宇宙船になぜまだロケットが必要なのか。

(A) より長く飛行するために必要である。
(B) 速度を上げるために必要である。
(C) 宇宙で方向転換するために必要である。
(D) 地球の大気圏を出るために必要である。

解説　最終段落第1文に ships powered by them (= solar sails) will still require the use of rockets to get into orbit「それら（=ソーラーセイル）で進む宇宙船も，軌道に入るためにはまだロケットを使う必要がある」とある。get into orbit を leave the earth's atmosphere と言い換えている (D) が正解。

9. 解答 B Purpose Question

最終段落で著者がレーザーに言及するのはなぜか。

(A) 効果がないと考えられている技術を紹介するため
(B) ソーラーセイルにおける問題の回避策を提供するため
(C) 別の推進システムに言及するため
(D) ソーラーセイルがなぜ太陽系の外で使うことができないかを説明するため

解説 最終段落から，ソーラーセイルには shortcoming「欠点」があり，それを克服するためには putting the energy source on the spacecraft itself「宇宙船そのものにエネルギー源を搭載すること」が必要であり，レーザーがその「エネルギー源」の役割を果たすと分かる。従って (B) が正解。

10. 解答 C Where Question

著者はどこでソーラーセイルの軽さの重要性を説明しているか。

(A) 2～3行目
(B) 10～13行目
(C) 17～18行目
(D) 20～21行目

解説 第3段落第3文に，This ability to produce lightweight solar sails is essential「軽量のソーラーセイルを作るこの能力は必要不可欠である」とあり，その直後の since 以降でその理由が述べられている。(C) が正解。

Questions 11-20

> **パッセージの訳**

　クリストファー・コロンブスがスペインのために航海し、アジアへの新しいルートを見つけようとしてアメリカ大陸に行き当たったという記述は、よく知られている話だ。しかしほとんどの人は、スペインのアジアへの計画は、コロンブスが直行海路を発見しそこなったことで終わらなかったとは考えない。実際は、現在はフィリピンとして知られているスペイン領東インドの設立とともに、東アジアへの貿易ルートの必要性はそれまでにも増して差し迫ったものになっていたのだ。アフリカ南端周辺の航路はポルトガル人が保有しており、アジアの内陸を通る陸路はもはや商人たちに開かれてはいなかった。結果として、アメリカにあるスペインの植民地は、自分たちの植民地としての保有地というだけでなく、アジアへの玄関口でもあったのだ。

　そうしたアジアへの玄関口の中で最も有名なのが、メキシコ西部海岸にあるアカプルコの港だった。アジアからの商品はスペイン領東インドで船に積み込まれ、太平洋を渡ってアカプルコへと運ばれた。商品はその後、中央アメリカを通って運ばれてから大西洋を通ってスペインに船で運ばれるか、あるいは南アメリカの先端を回って同じ航海を完了した。

　航海には長い時間がかかったが、それでもスペインにとっては非常に利益をもたらすものだった。当時、中国の経済は主に銀に依存しており、スペインは自分たちのメキシコの植民地で大量の銀を発見した。今日に至るまで、世界の5大銀鉱のうちの2つはメキシコにある。この銀で、スペインは中国の絹や磁器から日本の漆器、アジア中の香辛料に至るまでのぜいたく品を買った。これらの商品は全てヨーロッパで高値を呼び、スペインの財源に寄与した。

　それらの品物は全てまずアカプルコを通らなければならなかったので、この小さな港は富を増し、有名になった。ヨーロッパ人、アフリカ人、アジア人、アメリカ先住民などが住んでいたこの活気あふれる貿易中心地は、世界で最も国際的な都市の1つになった。それどころか、アカプルコはグローバル化の影響を感じられる、地球で最初の場所の1つと考えてもいいだろう。

11. 解答 B Main Idea Question

パッセージは主に何について述べているか。

(A) ある帝国の没落
(B) ある国がどのように貿易に関わったか
(C) ある国の経済制度
(D) ある戦争の原因

[解説] 第1段落の最終文に the Spanish colonies in the Americas weren't just colonial holdings on their own, but also gateways to Asia「アメリカにあるスペインの植民地は, 自分たちの植民地としての保有地というだけでなく, アジアへの玄関口でもあったのだ」とあり, 第2段落以降ではアカプルコを拠点とした交易について説明している。従って (B) が正解。

12. 解答 A Vocabulary Question

3行目の designs という言葉に最も近い意味は

(A) 意図
(B) 挨拶
(C) 位置
(D) 要求

[解説] 第1段落第1文に in an attempt to find a new route to Asia「アジアへの新しいルートを見つけようとして」とあり, Spanish designs for Asia とは「スペインのアジアに対する計画(構想)」といった意味だと推測できる。(A) が正解。design には「計画(≒ plan), 意図(≒intention)」という意味がある。

13. 解答 D Vocabulary Question

6行目の pressing という言葉に最も近い意味は

(A) 弱い
(B) 疑わしい
(C) 遅い
(D) 極めて重要な

[解説] 直後の文以降を読むと, アフリカ南端やアジア内陸を通れないことから, 東アジアへの貿易ルートの必要性は非常に高まっていたはずである。正解は (D)。pressing は「急を要する」という意味。

14. 解答 B　Inference Question

コロンブスと彼のアメリカ大陸への到達について何が推測できるか。

(A) スペインのアジア植民地化計画をつぶした。
(B) スペインの植民地帝国の助けとなった。
(C) ポルトガルとの領土争いを生じさせた。
(D) より大きな船の必要性を誘発した。

解説 コロンブスがアメリカ大陸にたどり着き，アジアとの重要な交易拠点ができた結果が第3段落で述べられている。第1文の immensely profitable for Spain「スペインにとっては非常に利益をもたらすもの」や最終文の contributed to Spain's coffers「スペインの財源に寄与した」などから，(B) が正解。

15. 解答 A　Factual Question

スペインが2つの大洋に及ぶ長い海路を使った理由は，ほかの海路は

(A) 別の国に支配されていたから
(B) もう商人には開かれていなかったから
(C) 異なる方角だったから
(D) 混みすぎていたから

解説 第1段落にスペインがアメリカにある植民地をアジアへの玄関口にした経緯が書かれている。第4文の The passage around the southern tip of Africa was reserved for the Portuguese「アフリカ南端周辺の航路はポルトガル人が保有していた」から (A) が正解。(B) は第4文からアジア内陸を通る陸路のことなので，誤り。

16. 解答 C　Negative Factual Question

次のうちスペインがアジアから輸入した品物として挙げられていないものは

(A) 漆器
(B) 磁器
(C) 金
(D) 香辛料

解説 第3段落最後から2つ目の文に具体的な交易品目が挙げられている。the Spanish bought luxury goods from Chinese silk and porcelain, to Japanese lacquerware, to spices from across Asia「スペインは中国の絹や磁器から日本の漆器，アジア中の香辛料に至るまでのぜいたく品を買った」とあるので，言及されていない (C) が正解。

17. 解答 C Factual Question

メキシコが中国との貿易のためにスペインの理想的な玄関口だった理由は

(A) 中国はその地域ですでに存在感を示していたから
(B) 2つの国の間の最短ルートだったから
(C) 中国が必要としていた原料がそこには大量にあったから
(D) スペインはすでにそこと中国の間に植民地を有していたから

解説 中国との交易の状況は第3段落で説明されている。第2文の China's economy was primarily dependent on silver at the time, and Spain found large quantities of silver in its Mexican colonies.「当時、中国の経済は主に銀に依存しており、スペインは自分たちのメキシコの植民地で大量の銀を発見した」から (C) が正解。silver が選択肢では material と言い換えられている。

18. 解答 D Vocabulary Question

21行目の goods という言葉に最も近い意味は

(A) 恩恵
(B) 興味
(C) 利益
(D) 製品

解説 続く内容から goods は具体的には Chinese silk and porcelain「中国の絹や磁器」、Japanese lacquerware「日本の漆器」、spices from across Asia「アジア中の香辛料」のことだと分かる。従って (D) が正解。

19. 解答 B　Vocabulary Question

25行目の cosmopolitan という言葉に最も近い意味は

(A) 新しい
(B) 多文化の
(C) 危機的な
(D) 楽しげな

解説 one of the most cosmopolitan cities in the world に続く with 以下でその様子が説明されている。with Europeans, Africans, Asians, and Native Americans living in this vibrant trading hub「ヨーロッパ人、アフリカ人、アジア人、アメリカ先住民などが住んでいたこの活気あふれる貿易中心地」とあるので、正解は (B) だと推測できる。cosmopolitan は「国際色豊かな」という意味。

20. 解答 D　Other Question (After)

パッセージの直後に続く段落は何について論じると思われるか。

(A) ポルトガル人によって使われた海路
(B) 中国の絹を作る技術
(C) クリストファー・コロンブスの幼少期
(D) アカプルコ住民間の関係

解説 (A) については第1段落に説明があり、(B) については第3段落で補足すべき内容なので、いずれも1つの段落としてこのパッセージに続けるのはおかしい。(C) のコロンブスについては第1段落で本文への導入として触れているだけで、このパッセージに続けるのは不自然。最終段落からさらに具体的な話へと展開する (D) が正解。

Questions 21-30

> **パッセージの訳**
>
> 　経済学の分野では，ある商品の価値と，その価値ゆえの価格を決める無数の原則がある。需要と供給のようにかなり知られたものもあるが，それ以外にも数多くある。しかし，それらのどの要素も完璧ではない。大部分は別の経済原則によって弱体化する。情報の非対称性である。この場合の非対称とは，公平でない，あるいは一方に好都合だという意味だ。ほとんど全てのものにおいて，誰かがほかの人よりもよく知っている。これが，ある品物の理想的な価格と実際の価格の食い違いを生む。
>
> 　これの最も明らかな例は，買い手よりも売り手の方が製品についてよく知っている場合だ。ステレオを売る人は，買う人よりもステレオとその相対価値についてよく知っているはずだ。売り手は，2つのほとんど同じに見える型の製造費用はあまり変わらなくても，一方が外装に高級な仕上げを使っていれば，2倍の値段で売れるだろうということを知っているだろう。売り手はこの知識を使って，より高価な型を買うよう，買い手に勧めようとするだろう。その方が利益もずっと大きくなるからだ。これが，よく聞く「買い手の危険持ち」すなわち「買い手は用心せよ」という格言の由来である。買い手はたいてい，非対称情報の不利な側にいる。
>
> 　ただ，買い手側の知識不足が売り手に害をなすこともある。経済学者のジョージ・アカロフは，中古車市場における難問について述べた自身の論文『レモン市場』の中で，この原則を説明した。中古車の買い手は，中古車の来歴について限られた知識しかない。その車が良質であるか，あるいは「レモン」すなわち不良車であるかが分からないのだ。従って，たとえ中古車の状態が非常に優れていても，ほとんどの買い手はそれに対して高額を支払うことをためらう。その結果，良い値段がつかないため，売り手は良質な車を在庫に置かなくなり，中古車の実際の価値と買い手の心の中で認識される価値がさらに下がるのだ。

21. **解答** **C** Main Idea Question

パッセージは主に何について述べているか。

(A) 特定の品物を買うための助言
(B) 特定の市場の歴史
(C) 経済原則
(D) ある経済学者の論議

解説 第1段落で経済の principles「原則」が無数にあることと，それらの食い違いが引き起こす結果について説明しており，第2段落以降では seller と buyer の立場からさらに具体的な話を展開している。従って (C) が正解。第2，3段落は商品の購入に関する助言についてではないので，(A) は誤り。また，(B) と (D) は主要な話題ではない。

183

22. 解答 B Vocabulary Question

1行目の myriad という言葉に最も近い意味は

(A) 知られていない
(B) 多くの
(C) 複雑な
(D) 高くつく

解説 直後の文の Some are fairly well known …, but there are many more beyond that.「…かなり知られたものもあるが，それ以外にも数多くある」から (B) が正解だと推測できる。(A) や (C) ではこの文の内容に合わなくなる。(D) だと第2文以降の内容に全くつながらない。

23. 解答 B Vocabulary Question

7行目の discrepancies という言葉に最も近い意味は

(A) 争い
(B) 違い
(C) 特徴
(D) 近道

解説 続く between an item's ideal price and its actual price「ある品物の理想的な価格と実際の価格の間で」から，両者の間で何が生じるのかを考える。正解は (B)。discrepancy は「差異，相違」という意味。

24. 解答 D Purpose Question

著者はなぜ第1段落で需要と供給に言及しているか。

(A) 信用を落とした経済原則の例を挙げるため
(B) 残りのパッセージを支える話題を紹介するため
(C) 後にさらに詳しく説明される用語を話題にするため
(D) よく知られた概念でパッセージを始めるため

解説 Some (= Some principles) are fairly well known such as supply and demand「需要と供給のようにかなり知られたもの（＝原則）もある」とあり，supply and demand はよく知られた経済原則の具体例であることが分かる。(D) が正解。需要と供給については後のパッセージ内では触れられないので，(B) と (C) は誤り。

25. 解答 C Factual Question

パッセージによると，ステレオの売り手はなぜ見込み客に対して有利なのか。

(A) 彼らは買い手の好みを察するのがうまい。
(B) 彼らはより高い権限のある地位にいる。
(C) 彼らは自分たちの製品についてもっと知っている。
(D) 彼らは1日にたくさんの顧客と接する。

[解説] 第2段落第2文に「ステレオを売る人は，買う人よりもステレオとその相対価値についてよく知っているはずだ」とあり，その状況を最終文で「買い手はたいてい，非対称情報の不利な側にいる」とまとめている。買い手は製品に関する詳しい知識によって有利な立場に立っているので，(C) が正解。

26. 解答 B Purpose Question

著者はなぜ第2段落で caveat emptor という言い回しに言及しているか。

(A) 後に説明される概念を紹介するため
(B) 言い回しの背景にある経済学を明らかにするため
(C) 主題の別の定義を提供するため
(D) 経済学の文化的背景を説明するため

[解説] "caveat emptor" をその後で "buyer beware" と言い換え，さらに最終文で買い手が不利な立場に置かれる経済原則に言及している。従って (B) が正解。beware は「気を付ける」という意味。

27. 解答 A Vocabulary Question

19行目の conundrum という言葉に最も近い意味は

(A) 問題
(B) 説明
(C) 機械工
(D) 謝罪

[解説] "The Market for Lemons" とは which describes a conundrum in the used car market「中古車市場における conundrum について述べている」ものだとあり，以降で "The Market for Lemons" について詳しく説明している。その内容は悪化する一方の売り手の状況を述べたものなので，(A) が正解だと判断できる。

185

28. 解答 A Inference Question

パッセージが示唆するには，中古車の買い手は

(A) 売り手の車の評価を信用しない傾向がある
(B) 中古車の価値を徹底的に調べる
(C) 売り手よりも中古車についてよく知っている
(D) 非常に優れた設備が備わった車だけを買う

解説 最終段落で，中古車の買い手は，買い手の知識不足が売り手に損をさせる例として取り上げられている。従って (B) と (C) は不適切。車の設備については言及がないので (D) も誤り。正解は (A)。第3，4文に，車の価値を信じられずに高額を支払えない買い手について述べられている。

29. 解答 D Conclusion Question

次の主張のうちパッセージが立証しているものはどれか。

(A) 情報の非対称性は中古車市場に影響しない。
(B) 中古車の売り手は状態の良い車のみを在庫に置く。
(C) 小型車が中古車市場の大多数を占める。
(D) 買い手の恐れが売りに出される車の品質を下げるかもしれない。

解説 (A) は最終段落の内容に矛盾する。(B) は最終段落の最終文に矛盾する。(C) については言及がない。正解は (D)。最終段落の後半部分から，買い手が高額の支払いをためらうことで，売り手が良質な商品を売らなくなるということが分かる。

30. 解答 D Where Question

次の言葉のうち著者が説明しているものはどれか。

(A) 不一致
(B) 警告
(C) 難題
(D) レモン

解説 最終落第3文に a "lemon," that is, a dud car「『レモン』すなわち不良車」とある。従って (D) が正解。(B) は "caveat emptor" というフレーズの説明はあるが，caveat だけの説明はないので不適切。

Questions 31-40

> **パッセージの訳**

　熱狂的なファンを大勢抱える現代の音楽スターはよくいる。こびへつらうファンの献身の話も，今日の音楽シーンの一部となっている。これが最近成り立ったものであり，マスメディアのまん延の結果だと想像するのはたやすい。ところが，1800年代のヨーロッパ宮廷音楽という，堅苦しい世界と思えるところにも，現代のロックスターの典型に一致する例があるのだ。

　フランツ・リストは1811年生まれのハンガリー人の音楽家だ。彼は幼いころから音楽の天才児で，ヨーロッパ中を旅しながらシューベルトやベートーヴェンなどの偉大な作曲家たちに会って学んだ。リストは特にピアノの名手としての技術で有名だった。優れた作曲家である一方，最も関心を引いたのは彼の華やかなピアノ演奏だった。

　リストの演奏はいくつかの点で独特だった。1つ目に，彼は楽譜を使った演奏はしなかった。楽譜は，音楽家にどの音符を弾くかを指示する曲の表記である。楽譜を使わない演奏は礼儀知らずと見なされ，自分の能力に対する横柄な自信の表れであった。2つ目に，彼は聴衆に自分の横顔が見えるようにして演奏した。ピアニストの顔はたいてい聴衆から背けられていたのだが，リストは自分の顔を見せびらかしたのだ。リストは特に魅力的だと思われていたので，そうしても差し障りはなかった。

　リストによる演奏会は，崇拝するファン，特に女性の賞賛者であふれた。女性たちは彼の演奏会で歓声を上げ，卒倒し，リストが手袋を観客の中に投げ入れると，争いが起こった。熱愛者たちは彼が描かれたネックレスやブローチを身に着け，中には彼の髪の房といった記念品を集める人までいた。ある女性は彼のごみ箱から葉巻の吸い殻を拾い，彼のイニシャルを彫ったロケットに入れていた。

　この集団的熱狂には独自の名称まで与えられた。リストマニアだ。今日，マニアという言葉はあらゆる熱狂や流行などに用いられるが，1800年代には心理的状況に限って用いられていた。実は，当時の医者たちはこれを実際の内科的疾患だと考えていたのだ。医者たちは「病気」が広がり，多くの人々がかかることを心配していた。ところが，あらゆる風潮と同じように，熱狂はやがて消え，リストは最初の音楽のスーパースターの1人として歴史上にその地位を確立したのである。

31. 解答 C Other Question (Title)

次のうちパッセージのタイトルとして最もよいものはどれか。

(A) 音楽ファンの探検
(B) ハンガリー音楽の偉人たち
(C) 現代ロックスターの先駆者
(D) フランツ・リストの幼少期と教育

解説 このパッセージは，フランツ・リストという音楽のスーパースターについて述べたものなので (A) は不適切。ハンガリー音楽については説明がないので (B) も不適切。幼少期のリストと教育については第2段落で簡単に触れているだけなので (D) も不適切。正解はリストという人そのものを表している (C)。precursor は「先駆者」という意味。

32. 解答 C Inference Question

パッセージから推測できるのは，熱狂的なファンは

(A) 20世紀まで存在しなかった
(B) マスメディアの創作である
(C) マスメディアの出現以前から存在した
(D) ヨーロッパではめったに見られない

解説 (A) はパッセージ全体の内容に矛盾する。(B) のような記述はない。(D) について直接的な言及はないが，第1段落の内容からは不適切だと判断できる。正解は (C)。マスコミの具体的な出現時期に関する説明はないが，第1段落後半の内容から，1800年代はマスコミの影響力とは無縁の時代だったと分かるので，妥当だと判断できる。

33. 解答 C Vocabulary Question

4行目の proliferation という言葉に最も近い意味は

(A) 生産
(B) 減少
(C) 拡散
(D) 革命

解説 第1段落第3文では，熱狂的なファンについて「これが最近成り立ったものであり，マスメディアの proliferation の結果だと想像するのはたやすい」と述べているので，(C) が正解だと判断できる。proliferation は「まん延，急増」という意味。

34. 解答 B Vocabulary Question

9行目の renowned という言葉に最も近い意味は

(A) よく考えられた
(B) よく知られた
(C) 偉大な
(D) 悪名高い

[解説] 第2段落全体の内容から renowned は良いイメージの単語だと推測できるので，(B) か (C) に絞ることができる。正解は (B)。renowned は形容詞で「有名な，著名な」という意味。

35. 解答 D Negative Factual Question

パッセージによると，次のうちリストの魅力を助長しなかったものは

(A) 彼の作曲の才能
(B) 彼の演奏スタイル
(C) 彼の顔
(D) 彼の偉大な作曲家たちとの交際

[解説] (A) については第2段落最終文，(B) については第3段落第1，2文，(C) については第3段落第4文以降に説明がある。(D) については，交際があったことは第2段落から分かるが，それがリストの魅力を助長したのかどうかは分からない。従って，これが正解。

36. 解答 A Inference Question

著者が示唆するには，リストの時代のピアニストたちは

(A) 顔を見せなかった
(B) 自分の曲を書かなかった
(C) ファンが大勢いた
(D) 人前で演奏しなかった

[解説] 第3段落の最後から2文目に Usually pianists' faces were turned away from the audience「ピアニストの顔はたいてい聴衆から背けられていた」とある。従って (A) が正解。(C) についてはリストについては当てはまるが，リストの時代のピアニストたち全般に言えることだとは判断できない。

37. 解答 C　Vocabulary Question

22行目の recovered という言葉に最も近い意味は

(A) 見た
(B) 創作した
(C) 取った
(D) 説明した

解説 第4段落では熱狂するファンの様子が描写されており，最終文は「吸い殻をごみ箱から『取り出して』，ロケットにしまった」といった内容になると推測できる。正解は (C)。recover には他動詞で「～を回収する，取り戻す」という意味がある。

38. 解答 C　Factual Question

著者が述べるには，リストの演奏への聴衆の反応は

(A) ヨーロッパの聴衆の典型だった
(B) ほとんど男性の聴衆に限られた
(C) 当時にしては珍しく情熱的だった
(D) 彼の祖国では最も熱狂的だった

解説 マニアと呼ばれるほどファンが熱狂した状況について，最終段落第2文では Today the word mania might be used for any craze or fad, but back in the 1800's it was used exclusively for psychological conditions.「今日，マニアという言葉はあらゆる熱狂や流行などに用いられるが，1800年代には心理的状況に限って用いられていた」と説明している。この状況を端的に述べている (C) が正解。

39. 解答 B　Other Question (Attitude)

最終段落で言及された医者たちに対する著者の態度は

(A) 友好的である
(B) 否定的である
(C) うやうやしい
(D) 好奇心をそそられている

解説 医者たちは人がマニアの状態になる病気がまん延することを心配していたが，著者は，Instead 以降でそれが杞憂だったことを説明している。この流れに最も近い態度は (B)。amicable は friendly「友好的な」，reverent は respectful「敬意を表す」，intrigued は fascinated「夢中になって」の類義語。

40. 解答 D　Where Question

著者はどこで sheet music の定義を述べているか。

(A) 2〜3行目
(B) 4〜6行目
(C) 10〜11行目
(D) 13〜14行目

解説 sheet music が出てくるのは第3段落第2文（パッセージ13行目）で，カンマに続いて the written notation of a song that instructs musicians what notes to play「音楽家にどの音符を弾くかを指示する曲の表記である」という説明がある。(D) が正解。

Questions 41-50

> **パッセージの訳**
>
> 　19世紀後半の発見以来，ウイルスを決定づける特徴の1つは，その小さなサイズだった。実際，ウイルスは，バクテリアが通り抜けられないほどの細かいフィルターで，汚染された液体をこしたことによって発見された。ウイルスは通常，バクテリアよりも100倍小さく，電子顕微鏡の発明以前に見られることはなかった。しかし，ここ15年間の一連の発見によって，ウイルス，さらには系統樹への我々の理解がひっくり返された。
>
> 　2003年，フランス人科学者たちは，10年以上前にイギリス人研究者たちによって集められたブラッドフォード球菌という変わったバクテリアをより綿密に調べた。ブラッドフォード球菌は奇妙だった。栄養物を食べて成長しているようではないのに，それでも全滅しないのだ。その「バクテリア」は巨大なウイルスであることが分かり，彼らはそれをミミウイルスと名付けた。それはサイズだけではなく複雑さにおいても印象的だった。大部分のウイルスはたった10しか遺伝子を持たないのに，この新しいウイルスには1,000以上もあった。この多大なる遺伝子的な複雑さのおかげで，ウイルスは独自の振る舞いができたのだ。ほとんどのウイルスは自分たちのDNAを寄生動物の細胞に注入し，細胞核を乗っ取って複製を作る。ミミウイルスは自分たち自身を細胞に入れ，その後，細胞内で見つかる原料を使って，自分たちの複製をつくる。
>
> 　この発見は，ウイルスがどのような姿に見え得るかという認識を根本的に変えた。間もなく，さらに大きくさらにたくさんの遺伝子を持つウイルスが発見された。これらのウイルスのうち最大のピソウイルスは，普通の顕微鏡でも見えるほどだ。これらの巨大ウイルスには確立した前例があったので，それまでは説明のつかなかった微生物たちが，今では新たな観点から見られるようになった。
>
> 　これらの巨大ウイルスの存在は，その起源に関して相当な議論を呼んだ。彼らは何らかの方法で大きくなったウイルスかもしれない。系統樹の全く新しい枝であり，ウイルスとバクテリアを全て合わせたものとも異なる何かかもしれない。特に興味をそそる学説は，それらがウイルスに進化したバクテリアだったというものだ。人々はたいてい，物体がより発達した複雑な生物へ進化すると考えるが，これについては，生きている有機体がより単純な非生物へ進化したということかもしれないのである。

41. 解答 B Main Idea Question

パッセージは主に何について述べているか。

(A) ウイルスの発見の跡をたどること
(B) 珍しいタイプのウイルスを探ること
(C) 生物学者の研究方法を説明すること
(D) 地球上の生命の起源についての仮説を立てること

解説 第1段落最終文 However 以降に「ここ15年間の一連の発見によって，ウイルス，さらには系統樹への我々の理解がひっくり返された」とあり，第2段落以降が常識を覆す大型のウイルスの具体的な説明となっている。従って (B) が正解。

42. 解答 C Purpose Question

著者はなぜ第1段落で電子顕微鏡に言及しているか。

(A) 科学者の方法を説明するため
(B) ウイルスの小ささが誤りであることを証明するため
(C) ウイルスのサイズを強調するため
(D) 技術の重要性を示すため

解説 第1段落第3文に Viruses are usually a hundred times smaller than bacteria and it wasn't until the invention of electron microscopes that they could be seen.「ウイルスは通常，バクテリアよりも100倍小さく，電子顕微鏡の発明以前に見られることはなかった」とある。つまり，電子顕微鏡に言及することでいかにウイルスが小さいかを説明しているので，(C) が正解。

43. 解答 D Vocabulary Question

14行目の hijack という言葉に最も近い意味は

(A) 呼び寄せる
(B) 方向転換する
(C) 中に入れる
(D) 乗っ取る

解説 hijack には「(飛行機) をハイジャックする」という意味のほかに，「(荷物) を奪う」や「(場や組織) を乗っ取る」という意味がある。(D) が正解。

44. 解答 B Factual Question

パッセージによると，科学者たちは初め，ミミウイルスは

(A) より小さなウイルスだと思った
(B) バクテリアだと思った
(C) 無生物の成分だと思った
(D) 複合のウイルスだと思った

解説 第2段落前半の流れをつかむ。第1，2文に出てくる Bradfordcoccus は，実際にはバクテリアではなく巨大なウイルスで，Mimivirus と名付けられたことが第3文から分かる。従って (B) が正解。第3文の主語に The "bacteria" とダブルクォーテーションがついているのは，実際にはバクテリアではないことを示唆するため。

45. 解答 D Inference Question

パッセージが示唆するには，巨大ウイルス中に見つかった余分にある遺伝子は

(A) 多細胞生物のようである
(B) 何もしないジャンク DNA である
(C) その大きなサイズを維持するために必要とされている
(D) その独特の複製過程に使われている

解説 第2段落第5文に，巨大ウイルスには通常よりもかなり多くの遺伝子があり，その結果が第6文の This increased genetic complexity allowed it to behave in a unique way.「この多大なる遺伝子的な複雑さのおかげで，ウイルスは独自の振る舞いができたのだ」だと分かる。続く2文で具体的な行動の例として複製過程の説明があるので，(D) が正解。

46. 解答 B Vocabulary Question

17行目の perception という言葉に最も近い意味は

(A) 意味
(B) 見方
(C) 教訓
(D) 期間

解説 This discovery radically changed the perception of what viruses could look like.「この発見は，ウイルスがどのような姿に見え得るかという perception を根本的に変えた」という流れに合うのは (B)。perception は「認識，理解」という意味。

47. 解答 C Vocabulary Question

20行目の precedent という言葉に最も近い意味は

(A) 会合
(B) 目的
(C) 例
(D) 関係

解説 Since these giant viruses had an established precedent, previously inexplicable microbes were now looked at in a new light. 「これらの巨大ウイルスには確立した precedent があったので，それまでは説明のつかなかった微生物たちが，今では新たな観点から見られるようになった」という流れに合うのは (C)。precedent は「先例，前例」という意味。

48. 解答 A Negative Factual Question

次のうち通常のウイルスと巨大ウイルスの違いとして挙げられていないものは

(A) 形
(B) サイズ
(C) 遺伝子の数
(D) 生殖方法

解説 (B), (C), (D) の違いについては第2段落で明示されているが，(A) について特に言及はない。従って (A) が正解。

49. 解答 C　Inference Question

パッセージが示唆するには，科学者たちが最初のウイルスが発見された後に新しい巨大ウイルスを発見した理由は

(A) 研究のためにより多くの資金が当てられたから
(B) 発見場所が捜索されたから
(C) 何を探せばいいかが今では分かったから
(D) それがより多くの人々を科学者になるよう促したから

[解説] 第3段落から，巨大ウイルスの発見がウイルスに関する見方を変え，そうしたウイルスが先例となったことで，新たな巨大ウイルスの発見につながったことが分かる。つまり，(C) が正解。

50. 解答 A　Negative Factual Question

次のうち巨大ウイルスの起源だと示唆されていないものは

(A) 小惑星から地球にやってきた生命
(B) ウイルスやバクテリアとはっきりと異なる起源
(C) 成長してより大きくなったウイルス
(D) ウイルスへと進化したバクテリア

[解説] 起源に関する説明は最終段落にある。(B) は第3文，(C) は第2文，(D) は第4文の内容に一致する。地球外の生命について本文に説明がないので，(A) が正解。

Practice Test 3   問題   Time 55 minutes

Questions 1-10

Line   As global demand for fresh water increases, many are turning to the sea to alleviate the ever-growing need. Desalination — removing salt from water — is the most prevalent method for utilizing sea water to meet a country's fresh water requirements. Desert countries with access to the ocean can augment their fresh
(5)   water supply using this technology. Israel currently obtains a quarter of its fresh water supply from desalination. The process is expensive and energy-intensive and only suitable where it is absolutely necessary. However, a newer technology has invented a use for ocean water that's less complex and reinforces a region's existing water supply.

(10)   Saltwater greenhouses are built to aid agriculture in the hottest deserts on earth. Current installations are in the Sahara, the Arabian Peninsula, and Australia. Unlike normal greenhouses that are meant to be warm, saltwater greenhouses are intended to keep their interiors cool. They do this by pumping untreated ocean water into the greenhouse and then into honeycomb-shaped
(15)   cardboard filters. The water then evaporates, leaving the salt in the filters. This evaporation cools the air up to 15 degrees Celsius. This allows crops that wouldn't stand up to the desert's harsh conditions to be grown.

   The evaporation also increases the humidity inside the greenhouse. This means that less water is lost by plants through transpiration. The less arid the
(20)   atmosphere, the less it sucks moisture out of the leaves of crops. This means the crops require less watering. Even though the untreated salt water being pumped in isn't being used to water the crops, the benefits provided by it mean that less fresh water is required for agriculture.

   The increased humidity can even provide a small amount of water for
(25)   irrigation. If the humidity stays high enough some of it will condense into liquid water on ceilings and walls and can be collected. However, the amount that condenses is irregular and will never be enough for all watering needs. At most it can be an added benefit to lighten the load on the fresh water supply.

1. What does the passage mainly discuss?
   (A) Methods for using solar power to generate electricity
   (B) What types of plants grow best in hot, dry conditions
   (C) Methods for turning saltwater into fresh water
   (D) A new type of technology for growing crops in the desert

2. The word "alleviate" in line 2 is closest in meaning to
   (A) lighten
   (B) mask
   (C) increase
   (D) explore

3. The word "augment" in line 4 is closest in meaning to
   (A) increase
   (B) store
   (C) irrigate
   (D) provide

4. The words "They" in line 13 refers to
   (A) the hottest deserts
   (B) saltwater greenhouses
   (C) current installations
   (D) the Sahara, the Arabian Peninsula, and Australia

5. The passage mentions all the following are locations with saltwater greenhouses EXCEPT
   (A) Israel
   (B) Australia
   (C) the Sahara
   (D) the Arabian Peninsula

6. Why does the author mention the honeycomb-shaped cardboard filters?
   (A) To explain how plants inside saltwater greenhouses are pollinated
   (B) To describe a theoretical improvement to the technology
   (C) To give details on a mechanism used by saltwater greenhouses
   (D) To compare saltwater greenhouses to traditional greenhouses

7. The word "arid" in line 19 is closest in meaning to
   (A) old
   (B) fresh
   (C) abundant
   (D) dry

8. According to the passage, saltwater greenhouses reduce the need for fresh water by
   (A) providing the minerals plants need to grow
   (B) reducing the amount of water for construction
   (C) making plants require less water to survive
   (D) promoting crops that survive in desert conditions

9. All of the following are benefits provided by saltwater greenhouses EXCEPT
   (A) temperature control
   (B) improved yields
   (C) humidity regulation
   (D) auxiliary irrigation

10. Which of the following statements does the passage support?
    (A) Saltwater greenhouses work best in deserts next to the ocean.
    (B) Saltwater greenhouses completely eliminate the need for fresh water.
    (C) Saltwater greenhouses have not yet been proven to be useful.
    (D) Saltwater greenhouses are only appropriate for growing flowering plants.

Questions 11-20

Line   In the early 1700's the newly formed Kingdom of Great Britain was severely in debt. The debt was so large in fact that portions of it were still being paid as late as 2013. The nation was at war with adversaries all over Europe and those wars needed to be paid for. Parliament was too gridlocked to pass laws to raise taxes,
(5) and foreign creditors were in short supply. What's more, the Bank of England was controlled by a different political party than the Treasury. In desperation, the head of the Treasury founded the South Sea Company (SSC), a corporation that took on and consolidated the country's debt.

A company that did nothing but hold debt wasn't an attractive proposition, so
(10) the SSC convinced the government to give it the exclusive rights to facilitate trade in the South Seas, or Central and South America. This seemed like a lucrative monopoly. After all, the British East India Company was producing massive wealth with a similar charter. However, Central and South America was still ruled by Spain, which had recently concluded a war with Britain. Spain placed onerous
(15) limits on the SSC, limits that would prevent it from ever making a profit.

This, however, did not deter investors. Citizens were enchanted by the promises of riches from the South Seas. The SSC also bribed members of parliament into buying shares of the company. At one point, the King himself was installed as the head of the board. The prestige and profile of the company was
(20) so great that it was considered too big to fail. From an initial stock price of £100 per share, the price rocketed to an astronomical £1,000 per share. At one point the estimated value of the SSC was greater than all the money that existed in Great Britain.

The hyper-inflated value of a company that did not produce a profit could not
(25) stand. In the space of three weeks the price plummeted from £1,000 per share to £150 per share. Fortunes were destroyed and the ruling government collapsed. The disaster caused by the collapse was so severe Parliament passed the Bubble Act to prevent another calamity.

11. What does the passage mainly discuss?
   (A) The history of a financial disaster
   (B) The wars fought by Great Britain
   (C) The financial aspect of war
   (D) The role of corporations in banking

12. The passage implies the head of the Treasury founded the South Sea Company because
   (A) Spain had invited him to help colonize South America
   (B) he needed a way to organize all of the nation's debt
   (C) settlers needed a way to move from England to the New World
   (D) the British Army needed naval support to aid it in wartime

13. The word "consolidated" in line 8 is closest in meaning to
   (A) solved
   (B) prevented
   (C) closed
   (D) merged

14. The word "lucrative" in line 11 is closest in meaning to
   (A) superficial
   (B) studious
   (C) profitable
   (D) lengthy

15. What was the main obstacle the South Sea Company had in making a profit?
   (A) The restraints put on it by Spain
   (B) Not enough people buying stock
   (C) The lack of support from the government
   (D) The British East India Company's monopoly

16. The word "deter" in line 16 is closest in meaning to
   (A) deceive
   (B) stop
   (C) induce
   (D) convince

17. All of the following are reasons the South Sea Company was perceived to be valuable EXCEPT
   (A) it had direct involvement from the royal family
   (B) members of Parliament were among its investors
   (C) it was already bringing back gold from America
   (D) the similar East India Company was profitable

18. What was the fate of the South Sea Company?
   (A) It was bought by the Spanish government.
   (B) It was broken up into smaller companies.
   (C) Its stock price collapsed.
   (D) It remained profitable for centuries.

19. The word "plummeted" in line 25 is closest in meaning to
   (A) maintained
   (B) fell
   (C) invited
   (D) exploded

20. The next paragraph following the passage is most likely about
   (A) Spanish colonialism in Central and South America
   (B) the biographies of the founders of the South Sea Company
   (C) similar financial disasters throughout history
   (D) how the Bubble Act intended to prevent similar disasters

Questions 21-30

Line   There are thousands of venomous and poisonous animal species on nearly every continent on earth, many of whom use their toxicity not to hunt for food, but as a defense mechanism. These animals can inject potential predators with venom from barbs and fangs or they can simply have poison in their skin such that
(5)   any animal that eats them will become violently sick or even die.

However, such adaptations are a last resort and of no use to the individual animal if it needs to be eaten in order to make a predator sick. That's why many poisonous animals are brightly colored or have distinctive patterns. This is a concept known as aposematism. If many poisonous animals are aposematic, then
(10)   predators will come to instinctively avoid such animals.

The phenomenon is widespread among the animal kingdom from the brilliant colors of poison dart frogs to the dazzling patterns of the blue ringed octopus. Some of the most stunning colors found on animals is the result of animals showcasing their own toxicity. Even when colors are muted the markings on an
(15)   animal advertise its danger. The skunk may be a comparatively drab black and white, but its characteristic stripes let everyone know not to trifle with it.

Aposematism is so prevalent that other animals take advantage of it. Animals that are not poisonous themselves have evolved to resemble the flashy appearance of poisonous animals. The hoverfly is a harmless insect that evades predators by
(20)   resembling wasps and bees. The milk snake is a non-venomous snake whose red, black, and yellow striping closely imitates the patterns of the deadly coral snake. The imitation isn't perfect; on milk snakes long red bands touch short black bands while on the coral snake long red bands border short yellow bands.

Aposematism isn't a universally shared trait among poisonous animals.
(25)   The stonefish gets its name by resembling a non-descript rock but is the most poisonous fish in the world. Stonefish rely on both camouflage and poison to avoid predators. Still, it's a good rule of thumb to assume that any vividly colored animal is poisonous in the wild.

21. What does the passage mainly discuss?
   (A) A common attribute shared by many poisonous animals
   (B) The way animals use camouflage to protect themselves
   (C) Methods for hunting used by venomous animals
   (D) The coloration of several species of snakes

22. The word "distinctive" in line 8 is closest in meaning to
   (A) worthy
   (B) proposed
   (C) distant
   (D) unique

23. The word "brilliant" in line 11 is closest in meaning to
   (A) intense
   (B) smart
   (C) venerated
   (D) unknown

24. The word "trifle" in line 16 is closest in meaning to
   (A) race
   (B) play
   (C) create
   (D) evolve

25. The word "imitates" in line 21 is closest in meaning to
   (A) invents
   (B) mimics
   (C) captures
   (D) regulates

26. According to the passage, aposematism is
    (A) only used in vertebrate animals
    (B) found in predators as well as prey
    (C) mostly found in aquatic animals
    (D) used by non-poisonous animals as well

27. The author implies that
    (A) bright colors are only seen in certain continents
    (B) venomous animals tend to live in tropical climates
    (C) poisonous skin itself isn't useful to individual animals
    (D) smaller animals are more likely to be poisonous

28. All of the following are mentioned as animals that display aposematism EXCEPT
    (A) stonefish
    (B) blue ringed octopuses
    (C) poison dart frogs
    (D) skunks

29. The passage states that
    (A) the brighter the color, the more poisonous an animal is
    (B) researchers are still finding new aposematic animals
    (C) not all poisonous animals are aposematic
    (D) aposematism is a recent evolutionary feature

30. Which of the following most closely represents the pattern of the milk snake described in lines 20-23?

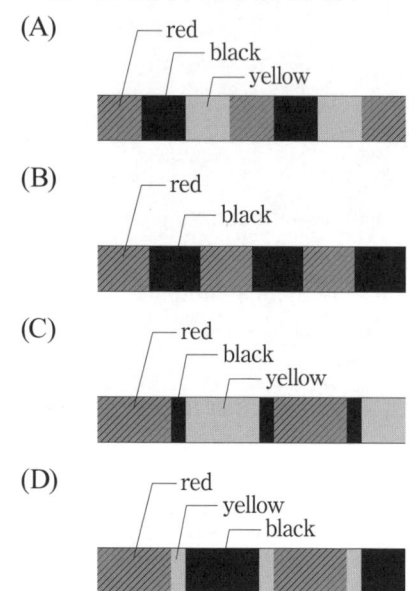

(A) red, black, yellow

(B) red, black

(C) red, black, yellow

(D) red, yellow, black

Questions 31-40

Line The invention of photography in the 19th century had profound effects on the development of painting. No longer was a master painter needed to accurately depict a portrait or landscape. The camera took over the role of faithfully reproducing the real world from the artist. Consequently, painters began to
(5) produce more and more abstract and subjective works. Freed from the constraints of representational art, painters were permitted to explore techniques and styles that eschewed realism and embraced the expressive.

Of course, all art movements are reactionary and eventually the pendulum swung the other way. In 1960's America, an era where abstract expressionism was
(10) the dominant artistic paradigm, a group of artists called the Photorealists took up the mantle of realism. The movement didn't just pick up where painting masters of the 19th century left off, though. After all, the old realists didn't have to compete with the accuracy of cameras. If the Photorealists were going to be taken seriously, they would have to match or even exceed the verisimilitude that photography offered.

(15) Photorealistic paintings were painstakingly drafted and formed from meticulous brushstrokes in sharp contrast to the impulsive and improvisational techniques used by abstract painters. Paintings not only attempted to faithfully present the living world, but specifically chose subjects that were difficult to portray. Diners were a common subject since the setting provided many
(20) opportunities to depict reflective surfaces such as chrome and glass. They were also used frequently since Photorealists tended to choose settings and subjects that were mundane. Landscapes favored commonplace urban and suburban settings while portraits were of unattractive people.

The movement survives today in an altered state, where it is more usually
(25) called Hyperrealism. Sculpture is a much larger part of the movement, with artists like John DeAndrea and Duane Hanson producing human sculptures that are almost unnerving in their accuracy. Ron Mueck has gained particular notoriety through his larger-than-life statues which depict photo-realistic humans that are ten times the size of real people. All of the subjects' flaws and imperfections are blown up to a
(30) massive scale, confronting the viewer with an unvarnished view of humanity.

31. Why does the author mention 1960's America?
   (A) To describe the artistic background of the Photorealists
   (B) To mention the new technological innovations that changed art
   (C) To show what factors contributed to the decline of the Photorealist movement
   (D) To downplay the influence Europe had on this new artistic endeavor

32. According to the passage, the camera
   (A) changed the priorities of artists
   (B) helped painters sophisticate their art
   (C) helped increase demand for representational art
   (D) made abstract art out-of-date

33. It can be inferred from the passage that art movements
   (A) are usually in opposition to the movements that precede them
   (B) usually shift from realism to abstractionism
   (C) tend to ignore tradition established by masters
   (D) are reluctant to take advantage of new technologies

34. According to the passage, Photorealistic paintings tended to
   (A) take a short time to complete
   (B) fetch extraordinary prices
   (C) portray everyday scenes
   (D) take teams of artists to paint

35. The words "they" in line 14 refers to
   (A) painting masters of the 19th century
   (B) the old realists
   (C) Photorealists
   (D) cameras

36. The word "mundane" in line 22 is closest in meaning to
    (A) beautiful
    (B) rare
    (C) modern
    (D) ordinary

37. The word "unnerving" in line 27 is closest in meaning to
    (A) relatable
    (B) frightening
    (C) majestic
    (D) boring

38. The passage implies that the current incarnation of the Photorealistic movement
    (A) is more prevalent in Europe
    (B) has dwindled to a very small size
    (C) primarily uses a different medium
    (D) depicts wildly divergent subjects

39. Where in the passage does the author mention the standard that Photorealists had to compete with?
    (A) Lines 5-7
    (B) Lines 9-11
    (C) Lines 13-14
    (D) Lines 15-17

40. Which of the following words does the author give an explanation?
    (A) Photorealistic paintings
    (B) brushstrokes
    (C) unattractive people
    (D) Expressionism

Questions 41-50

Line	In phone gaming, the market is dominated by free-to-play games, games which cost nothing to download but provide opportunities for players to spend money to enhance their experience. Money can be spent on in-game items that speed up play or provide bonuses. In some multiplayer games, these items can be
(5) bequeathed to other teammates, thereby helping their chances against opponents. In theory, the free-to-play model lets players try out a game before spending any money, allowing them to decide if they like it before paying.

In practice, many players end up not paying at all. Either they trudge through the game's obstacles without the benefits paid items would afford them, or they
(10) simply abandon the game in favor of another free game. Most of those who do pay only spend a small amount, about on par with a game that asks you to pay up front. Yet these free-to-play games top the top-grossing charts. Where does all the money come from?

These games primarily make their money from "whales": players who spend
(15) much more money than the average player. To be on the threshold for being a whale, one should spend over a hundred dollars a month on a game, though some spend thousands a month. Even though these players make up a miniscule amount of a game's player base — often less than one percent — they account for more than half of a game's revenue.

(20)	Whales are a profitable resource for game makers, but a tenuous one. One reason whales spend is the effect they can have on other players. They can both dominate opponents in combat and provide massive amounts of aid to teammates. In some sense, other players are "content" for the whales. Whales enjoy occupying this place of power over other players. However, since whales are so much more
(25) powerful, regular players can become disenfranchised. Who wants to play if you're just going to be beaten by whales who have paid their way to success? If non-paying players abandon the game, then the whales won't have anyone to show off against. This causes the whales to abandon the game and the whole enterprise collapses.

41. What is the main purpose of the first paragraph?
 (A) To compare classic games to modern games
 (B) To show common pitfalls of making phone games
 (C) To provide the biography of a typical whale
 (D) To set out the parameters of free-to-play games

42. The word "enhance" in line 3 is closest in meaning to
 (A) trivialize
 (B) attach
 (C) lengthen
 (D) improve

43. According to the passage, phone games make most of their money from
 (A) very small transactions
 (B) cosmetic changes to games
 (C) a small fraction of players
 (D) in-game advertisements

44. According to the passage, the majority of players of free-to-play games
 (A) finish the game
 (B) don't pay anything
 (C) play multiple games
 (D) are younger players

45. Why does the author mention the top-grossing charts?
 (A) To prove there isn't much money to be made in mobile games
 (B) To demonstrate how games based on cartoons are the most popular
 (C) To show how hard it is to measure success with mobile games
 (D) To establish how much money free-to-play games make

211

46. The phrase "on the threshold" in line 15 is closest in meaning to
   (A) at the starting point
   (B) over the top
   (C) in the direction
   (D) on the side

47. The passage implies that the players who don't pay are important for making money because they
   (A) look at in-game advertisements
   (B) tell their friends about the game
   (C) serve as opponents for whales
   (D) buy merchandise based on the game

48. The word "occupying" in line 23 is closest in meaning to
   (A) betraying
   (B) inhabiting
   (C) discovering
   (D) shortening

49. It can be inferred from the passage that the current method for making money in phone games is
   (A) uncertain
   (B) old fashioned
   (C) promising
   (D) expensive

50. Which of the following best describes the organization of the passage?
   (A) The author states a hypothesis, gives evidence supporting it, and then ends with arguments against it.
   (B) The author introduces a case study, details how events transpired, and then makes conclusions.
   (C) The author presents a model, explains how it works, and then presents problems with the model.
   (D) The author asks a questions, lists possible answers from multiple sources, and then chooses the best one.

Practice Test 3　解答・解説

解答一覧

1 **D**	2 **A**	3 **A**	4 **B**	5 **A**	6 **C**	7 **D**	8 **C**	9 **B**
10 **A**	11 **A**	12 **B**	13 **D**	14 **C**	15 **A**	16 **B**	17 **C**	18 **C**
19 **B**	20 **D**	21 **A**	22 **D**	23 **A**	24 **B**	25 **B**	26 **D**	27 **C**
28 **A**	29 **C**	30 **C**	31 **B**	32 **A**	33 **A**	34 **C**	35 **C**	36 **B**
37 **B**	38 **C**	39 **C**	40 **A**	41 **D**	42 **D**	43 **C**	44 **B**	45 **D**
46 **A**	47 **C**	48 **B**	49 **A**	50 **C**				

Questions 1-10

> **パッセージの訳**
>
> 　淡水の世界的需要が増すにつれ，増える一方の需要を軽減するために，多くが海に関心を向けている。脱塩，つまり海水から塩を取り除くことは，国の淡水の要求に応えるために海水を利用する最も普及している方法である。海を利用できる砂漠の国々は，この技術を使って淡水の供給を増やすことができる。イスラエルは現在，淡水の供給の4分の1を脱塩から得ている。この処理は費用が高く，しかもエネルギーを大量に消費するので，絶対に必要な場所にしか適していない。しかし，さらに新しい技術が，海水を使用する方法をつくり出した。あまり複雑ではなく，その地域に現存する水の供給を補強するやり方である。
>
> 　塩水温室は，地球上で最も暑い砂漠における農業を補助するために建てられる。現在，施設はサハラ砂漠，アラビア半島，オーストラリアに存在する。温かくするために作られる普通の温室と異なり，塩水温室は室内を涼しく保つことを目的とする。未処理の海水を温室にポンプで引き込み，蜂の巣状の厚紙製のフィルターに通すことでそれを行う。すると水は蒸発し，フィルターの中に塩を残す。この蒸発が，摂氏15度まで気温を下げる。こうして，砂漠の厳しい環境に耐えられない作物を育てることができるのだ。
>
> 　また，蒸発によって温室内の湿度も増す。これで，蒸散によって植物が失う水分が少なくなる。大気の乾きが少ないほど，作物の葉の湿気も吸い取られなくなる。すなわち，作物がそれほど水やりを必要としなくなる。たとえ汲み入れられる未処理の海水が作物の水やりに使われないとしても，農業に必要な淡水が減るという恩恵がもたらされるのだ。
>
> 　増えた湿気は，かんがい用の水を少量提供してくれさえする。湿気が十分に高いと，そのいくらかは天井や壁に凝縮されて水滴となってたまり，集めることができる。しかし，凝縮される量は一定ではないので，水やりの必要量を全てまかなうほどまでにはならないだろう。せいぜい，淡水供給の負担を軽くするという付加利益にしかならない。

1.　解答　D　　Main Idea Question

パッセージは主に何について述べているか。

(A) 発電するために太陽エネルギーを使う方法
(B) 暑く乾燥した環境の中で最もよく育つ植物はどのような種類か
(C) 塩水を淡水に変える方法
(D) 砂漠で穀物を育てる新しいタイプの技術

解説 パッセージでは，脱塩の技術を用いた塩水温室について説明している。(C) か (D) で迷うが，(C) の methods「方法，方法論」については，第2段落でフィルターを使うという簡単な説明があるのみ。パッセージ全体の内容を表している (D) の方が適切。

2.　解答　A　　Vocabulary Question

2行目の alleviate という言葉に最も近い意味は

(A) 軽くする
(B) 隠す
(C) 増やす
(D) 探検する

解説 As global demand for fresh water increases, many are turning to the sea to alleviate the ever-growing need.「淡水の世界的需要が増すにつれ，増える一方の需要を alleviate するために，多くが海に関心を向けている」という文。需給がさし迫っているのだから，需要を「減らす，軽減する」と考えるのが自然。(A) が正解。alleviate は「〜を軽減する」という意味。

3.　解答　A　　Vocabulary Question

4行目の augment という言葉に最も近い意味は

(A) 増やす
(B) 貯める
(C) かんがいする
(D) 提供する

解説 Desert countries with access to the ocean can augment their fresh water supply using this technology.「海を利用できる砂漠の国々は，この技術（＝脱塩）を使って淡水の供給を augment できる」という文。脱塩は淡水を得るための技術なので，(A) が正解だと判断できる。augment は「〜を増大させる」という意味。

4. 解答 B Reference Question

13行目の They という言葉が指すのは

(A) 最も暑い砂漠
(B) 塩水温室
(C) 現在の設備
(D) サハラ砂漠，アラビア半島，オーストラリア

解説 They do this の this は直前の to keep their interiors cool「室内を涼しく保つこと」を指しているので，They はその主語にあたる saltwater greenhouses を受けているとわかる。(B) が正解。

5. 解答 A Negative Factual Question

次のうち塩水温室のある場所としてパッセージが言及していないものは

(A) イスラエル
(B) オーストラリア
(C) サハラ砂漠
(D) アラビア半島

解説 (B), (C), (D) については第2段落第2文に言及がある。(A) Israel については，第1段落第4文に「淡水の供給の4分の1を脱塩から得ている」という説明はあるが，それ以降の文章と第2段落第1文から, saltwater greenhouse はそれよりも新しい技術だとわかる。従って (A) が正解。

6. 解答 C Purpose Question

著者はなぜ蜂の巣状の厚紙製のフィルターに言及しているか。

(A) 塩水温室内の植物がどのように受粉されるかを説明するため
(B) 技術の理論的改良を説明するため
(C) 塩水温室で使われるメカニズムに関して詳細を伝えるため
(D) 塩水温室と伝統的な温室を比べるため

解説 蜂の巣状の厚紙製のフィルターについては，塩水温室の仕組みを説明している第2段落に説明があり，「未処理の海水を…蜂の巣状の厚紙製のフィルターに通す」（第4文），「すると水は蒸発し，フィルターの中に塩を残す」（第5文）とある。従って (C) が正解。

7. 解答 D　Vocabulary Question

19行目の arid という言葉に最も近い意味は

(A) 古い
(B) 新鮮な
(C) 豊富な
(D) 乾燥した

解説　The less arid the atmosphere, the less it sucks moisture out of the leaves of crops. は〈the ＋比較級～, the ＋比較級 …〉「～すればするほどますます…する」の構文で、「大気が arid でなければないほど、ますますそれは作物の葉から湿気を吸い取らなくなる」が直訳。大気が乾いていなければ、葉から奪われる水分も少ないはず。正解は (D)。arid は「湿気のない」という意味。

8. 解答 C　Factual Question

パッセージによると、塩水温室は淡水の需要を減らすために

(A) 植物が育つために必要なミネラルを提供する
(B) 建設のための水量を減らす
(C) 植物が生き残るために必要な水の量を減らす
(D) 砂漠の環境でも生きられる穀物を奨励する

解説　第3段落最後の2文に塩水温室が農業における淡水需要に与える影響について説明がある。「作物がそれほど水やりを必要としなくなる」、「農業に必要な淡水が減る」という内容に一致する (C) が正解。

9. 解答 B　Negative Factual Question

次のうち塩水温室が提供する恩恵でないものは

(A) 温度管理
(B) 改善された収穫高
(C) 湿度調節
(D) 補助かんがい装置

解説　(A) については第2段落，(C) については第3段落，(D) については第4段落に説明がある。(B) については，直接的な言及がないので，これが正解。

10. 解答 A　Conclusion Question

次の主張のうちパッセージが立証しているものはどれか。

(A) 塩水温室は海の隣にある砂漠で最もうまく機能する。
(B) 塩水温室は淡水の需要を完全に排除する。
(C) 塩水温室はまだ役立つことが立証されていない。
(D) 塩水温室は花の咲く植物を育てることにのみ適している。

解説　塩水温室は，第2段落第1文から暑い砂漠地帯に向いていることが分かる。また，第1段落第2文に説明がある脱塩と同様，海水を使うため，海から近い場所に建てる必要があると推測できる。従って (A) が正解。(B) は，最終段落から淡水需要を完全にまかなうものではないことがわかるので，不適切。

Questions 11-20

> **パッセージの訳**
>
> 　1700年代初頭，新たに生まれた大英帝国は，深刻な借金を抱えていた。実際，借金は相当多額だったので，その一部は2013年まで払い続けられていたほどだった。イギリスはヨーロッパ中の敵対国と戦争をしており，そうした戦争の費用も支払わなければならなかった。議会は行き詰まり，増税のための法案を通すことができず，外国の債権者たちも不足していた。さらに，イングランド銀行は大蔵省ではなく別の政党に支配されていた。大蔵卿は苦し紛れに南海会社（SSC）を設立した。国の債務を引き受け，1つにまとめる会社である。
>
> 　何もせず負債だけを抱える会社というのは魅力的な事業ではなかったので，南海会社は南海，つまり中南米での貿易を促進する独占権を与えてくれるよう政府を説得した。これはもうけを独占するように思えた。何しろ，イギリス東インド会社は同じような特権で巨大な富を築いていたからだ。しかし，中南米は，イギリスとの戦争を終えたばかりのスペインによっていまだに支配されていた。スペインは南海会社に厄介な制限をかけた。とても利益を生み出せないような制限である。
>
> 　しかし，投資者たちはそれでも思いとどまらなかった。市民は南海からの富の約束に魅せられた。南海会社はさらに議員たちに賄賂を贈り，会社の株を買わせた。一時は国王自身も社長に就任させられた。会社の威信と評判はとても大きかったので，この大きな会社が倒産するとは考えられていなかった。株価は当初の1株100ポンドから，天文学的な1株1,000ポンドまで急上昇した。ある時点で，南海会社の評価額は，イギリスに存在するお金の全額より多かった。
>
> 　利益を生まない会社の過度に膨らみすぎた価値は，持ちこたえられなかった。3週間の間に，株価は1株1,000ポンドから150ポンドにまで急落した。財産は失われ，政府は崩壊した。崩壊によって起こった大惨事は非常に深刻だったので，新たな災難を防ぐために，議会は泡沫会社禁止法を通した。

11.　解答　A　Main Idea Question

パッセージは主に何について述べているか。

(A) 財政破綻の歴史
(B) 大英帝国が戦った戦争
(C) 戦争の経済的側面
(D) 銀行業における企業の役割

解説　パッセージは南海会社の設立から破綻までを説明しており，最終段落では南海会社の最後の状態を disaster「大惨事」と呼んでいる。従って (A) が正解。

12. 解答 B Inference Question

パッセージが示唆するには，大蔵卿が南海会社を設立した理由は

(A) スペインが南アメリカを植民地化する手助けをしてもらうために彼を招いたから
(B) 彼は国の借金を全額整理する方法を必要としていたから
(C) 開拓者たちはイギリスから新世界へと移動する方法を必要としていたから
(D) イギリス陸軍は戦争時には海軍の支援を必要としていたから

解説 第1段落最終文に the head of the Treasury founded the South Sea Company (SSC), a corporation that took on and consolidated the country's debt「大蔵卿は国の債務を引き受け，1つにまとめる会社である南海会社 (SSC) を設立した」とある。これを organize を使って言い換えている (B) が正解。

13. 解答 D Vocabulary Question

8行目の consolidated という言葉に最も近い意味は

(A) 解決した
(B) 防いだ
(C) 閉めた
(D) 統合した

解説 consolidate は「個体の」という意味の solid に，「一緒に」という意味の接頭辞 con- と，動詞を作る接尾辞 -ate が付いた形。「一緒に固める」から「1つにまとめる」という意味を表す。この意味に最も近いのは (D)。

14. 解答 C Vocabulary Question

11行目の lucrative という言葉に最も近い意味は

(A) 表面的な
(B) 学問的な
(C) もうかる
(D) 長期にわたる

解説 前文の，負債だけを抱える会社は魅力的ではなかったので，政府に中南米での貿易を促進する独占権を求めた，という内容から，南海会社は利益を出したいと考えていたことがわかる。つまり「『利益を生むための』独占」を求めていたはず。正解は (C) で，lucrative は「もうかる」という意味。

15. 解答 A Factual Question

南海会社が利益を上げる際の主な障害は何であったか。

(A) スペインによって課された規制
(B) 株を買う人が十分ではなかったこと
(C) 政府からの援助の欠如
(D) イギリス東インド会社の独占

解説 第2段落最後の2文に南海会社が中南米で活動する上での課題について述べられており，中南米を支配していたスペインがとても利益を生み出せないような制限を南海会社にかけていたことが分かる。limits を restraints で言い換えている (A) が正解。

16. 解答 B Vocabulary Question

16行目の deter という言葉に最も近い意味は

(A) だます
(B) 止める
(C) 誘導する
(D) 納得させる

解説 第3段落第1文は，「（スペインによる制限はあったが）しかしこれは投資者たちを deter しなかった」という内容。その後，株価が上がっていく状況が述べられているので，「投資者たちを『止め』なかった」といった意味になるはず。正解は (B) で，deter は「〜を思いとどまらせる」という意味。

17. 解答 C Negative Factual Question

次のうち南海会社に価値があると認められた理由でないものは

(A) 王室が直接関与していた
(B) 投資者の中に国会議員がいた
(C) すでにアメリカから金を持ち帰ってきていた
(D) 同じような東インド会社がもうかっていた

解説 (A) については第3段落第4文，(B) については第3段落第3文，(D) については第2段落第3文に説明がある。従って (C) が正解。

18. 解答 C Factual Question

南海会社の運命はどのようなものであったか。

(A) スペイン政府に買い取られた。
(B) 小さな会社に分割された。
(C) 株価が暴落した。
(D) 何世紀も利益を上げ続けた。

[解説] 質問文の fate は「運命」という意味。最終段落から，南海会社は最終的に株価が大暴落したことが分かるので，(C) が正解。

19. 解答 B Vocabulary Question

25行目の plummeted という言葉に最も近い意味は

(A) 維持した
(B) 落ちた
(C) 招いた
(D) 爆発した

[解説] 最終段落は，南海会社は持ちこたえられず，財産は失われ，政府は崩壊し，大惨事になったという内容。従って，「株価は1株1,000ポンドから150ポンドにまで『暴落した』」といった意味になるはず。正解は (B) で，plummet は「急に下がる」という意味。

20. 解答 D Other Question (After)

パッセージに続く次の段落はおそらく

(A) 中南米におけるスペインの植民地政策について
(B) 南海会社の創始者たちの経歴について
(C) 歴史における似たような財政破綻について
(D) 泡沫会社禁止法がどのように同じような破綻を防ごうとしていたかについて

[解説] 最終段落では，南海会社の失敗を受けて the Bubble Act を制定したとあり，その目的について to prevent another calamity「新たな災難を防ぐため」と説明している。その後の段落ではその具体的な内容が続くと考えるのが自然。(D) が正解。

Questions 21-30

> **パッセージの訳**

　地球上のほぼ全大陸に，有毒で有害な動物種が何千も存在している。その多くは餌を狩るためにその毒性を使うのではなく，防御機制として使う。そうした有毒動物たちは，捕食者になりそうな相手にとげや牙から毒を注入するか，あるいは単純に，食べた動物が猛烈に苦しむか死んでしまうくらいの毒を肌に持っていることもある。

　しかし，そのような適応は最後の手段であり，捕食者の具合を悪くするために食われるべきであるとしたら，その動物にとっては何の役にも立たない。だから，毒を持つ動物たちの多くは，派手な色をしているか，目立つ模様をまとっている。これは警戒色として知られる概念である。もし多くの有毒な動物が警戒色をしていたら，捕食者たちは本能的にそんな動物を避けるようになるだろう。

　ヤドクガエルの派手な色から，ヒョウモンダコの非常に明るい模様まで，この現象は動物界ではよく見られる。動物に見られるこの上なく驚くべき色の中には，動物たちが自らの毒性を見せている結果としてそうなっている場合もある。たとえ抑えた色調でも，動物は模様で危険性を告げている。スカンクは比較的くすんだ黒と白ではあるが，その特徴的なしまが，もてあそばないようにとみんなに知らせているのだ。

　警戒色はとてもよく見られるので，ほかの動物がそれを利用するほどである。自らに毒がない動物たちは，有毒な動物の派手な外見に似るように進化した。ハナアブは害のない昆虫で，スズメバチやミツバチに似ることで捕食者たちから巧みに逃げる。ミルクヘビは無毒のヘビで，その赤と黒と黄色のしまは，致命的なサンゴヘビの模様をよくまねている。模倣は完璧ではなく，ミルクヘビの長くて赤いしまは短くて黒いしまに接しているが，サンゴヘビの長くて赤いしまは短くて黄色いしまに接している。

　警戒色は，有毒な動物において普遍的に共通する特徴ではない。オニダルマオコゼはどこにでもあるような岩に似ているのでその名が付いているが，世界で最も有毒な魚だ。オニダルマオコゼはカモフラージュと毒の両方に頼って捕食者を避けているのだ。それでも，鮮やかな色をした動物は野生では有毒だと見なすのが，正しい経験則である。

21. 解答 A　Main Idea Question

パッセージは主に何について述べているか。

(A) 多くの毒のある動物に共通する一般的な特性
(B) 動物が身を守るためにカモフラージュを使うやり方
(C) 有毒の動物が使う狩りの方法
(D) ヘビのいくつかの種の彩色

解説　パッセージでは有毒な動物の色や模様について説明し，最終段落最終文では，Still, it's a good rule of thumb to assume that any vividly colored animal is poisonous in the wild.「それでも，鮮やかな色をした動物は野生では有毒だと見なすのが，正しい経験則である」とまとめている。(A) が正解。(B) のカモフラージュは一部の動物の例。

22. 解答 D　Vocabulary Question

8行目の distinctive という言葉に最も近い意味は

(A) 価値がある
(B) 提案されている
(C) 遠い
(D) 独特の

解説　有毒な動物たちは，最後の手段をとらなくてもよいように，many poisonous animals are brightly colored or have distinctive patterns「毒を持つ動物たちの多くは，派手な色をしているか，distinctive な模様をまとっている」という内容。つまり，目立つ色や模様でその存在を知らせる必要があると考えられるので，(D) が正解。distinctive は「独特の」という意味。

23. 解答 A　Vocabulary Question

11行目の brilliant という言葉に最も近い意味は

(A) 強烈な
(B) 賢い
(C) あがめられた
(D) 未知の

解説　brilliant は colors「(ヤドクガエルの) 色」を修飾している。「色」を修飾する形容詞として適切なのは (A)。brilliant は「きらきらと輝く」という意味。intense には「(色が) 濃い」という意味もある。

223

24. 解答 B　Vocabulary Question

16行目の trifle という言葉に最も近い意味は

(A) 競争する
(B) 遊ぶ
(C) つくる
(D) 進化する

解説 第3段落では，有毒な動物が敵を寄せ付けないために，独特の色や模様を身にまとっていることが説明されており，スカンクのしま模様もその一例だと考えられることから，trifle は「近づく，関わる」といった意味だと推測できる。正解は (B)。trifle with 〜 は「〜をもてあそぶ」という意味で，ここでは play に意味が最も近い。

25. 解答 B　Vocabulary Question

21行目の imitates という言葉に最も近い意味は

(A) 発明する
(B) まねる
(C) 捕える
(D) 制御する

解説 前の2文で，無毒な動物が有毒な動物に見た目を似せることで敵から身を守る例が挙げられている。従って imitate は「〜に似せる」といった意味になると推測できる。正解は (B)。imitate は「まねる，似せて作る」という意味。

26. 解答 D　Factual Question

パッセージによると，警告色は

(A) 脊椎動物だけが使う
(B) 獲物と同じく捕食動物にも見られる
(C) 主に水生動物に見られる
(D) 無毒の動物も使う

解説 aposematism は難しい単語だが，第1〜3段落の内容から，独特の色や模様で敵を寄せ付けないことを表す語だと推測できる。第4段落第1，2文を読むと，毒のない動物もこうした aposematism を利用していることが分かるので，(D) が正解。

27. 解答 C Inference Question

著者が示唆するには，

(A) 派手な色は特定の大陸でしか見られない
(B) 有毒な動物は熱帯性気候に住む傾向がある
(C) 毒のある皮膚そのものは個々の動物にとって役に立たない
(D) 小さい動物はより毒性があると思われる

解説 (A)，(B)，(D) については本文に言及がない。(C) については第2段落第1文に … of no use to the individual animal if it needs to be eaten in order to make a predator sick「…捕食者の具合を悪くするために食われるべきであるとしたら，その動物にとっては何の役にも立たない」とあり，この内容に一致する。

28. 解答 A Negative Factual Question

次のうち警戒色を示す動物として挙げられていないものは

(A) オニダルマオコゼ
(B) ヒョウモンダコ
(C) ヤドクガエル
(D) スカンク

解説 (B) と (C) については第3段落第1文，(D) については同じ段落の最終文で取り上げられている。(A) は第4段落に出てくるが，すべての有毒な動物が aposematism を備えているとは限らないことを示すために，例外的な存在として紹介されている。従って (A) が正解。

29. 解答 C Factual Question

パッセージが述べるには,
(A) 色が鮮やかなほど動物は毒性が強い
(B) 研究者たちは今でも新しい有毒な動物を発見している
(C) 毒性のある動物が全て警戒色をしているわけではない
(D) 警戒色は最近の進化の特色である

[解説] 最終段落第1文に Aposematism isn't a universally shared trait among poisonous animals.「警戒色は,有毒な動物において普遍的に共通する特徴ではない」とある。従って (C) が正解。

30. 解答 C Other Question (Illustration)

次のうちどれが 20～23 行目で述べられるミルクヘビの模様を最もよく表しているか。
(A) 赤・黒・黄色の順番でしまになっている模様
(B) 赤・黒のしま模様
(C) 赤・黒・黄色のしまで,長くて赤いしまが短くて黒いしまに接している模様
(D) 赤・黒・黄色のしまで,長くて赤いしまが短くて黄色いしまに接している模様

[解説] パッセージでは,ミルクヘビの色と模様については,「赤と黒と黄色のしまであること」と,「長くて赤いしまが短くて黒いしまに接していること」の2点を挙げている。これに合うイラストは (C)。

Questions 31-40

> **パッセージの訳**
>
> 　19世紀の写真の発明は，絵画の発展に甚大な影響を与えた。もはや絵画の巨匠は肖像画や風景を正確に描く必要がなくなった。カメラは，芸術家から現実世界を忠実に再現する役割を引き継いだ。その結果，画家たちはどんどん抽象的で主観的な作品を作り始めた。描写主義の芸術という抑制から解放され，画家たちはリアリズムを控えて，表現性を利用するテクニックやスタイルを探ることを許された。
>
> 　もちろん，全ての芸術活動は反動的であり，やがて振り子は反対側に振れた。抽象表現主義が優勢な芸術パラダイムであった1960年代のアメリカにおいて，スーパーリアリストと呼ばれる芸術家たちのグループが，リアリズムの役割を引き継いだ。だが，その運動は19世紀の絵画の巨匠たちが終わらせたものを再び始めただけではなかった。何しろ，昔のリアリストたちはカメラの正確さと競う必要がなかったのだ。スーパーリアリストたちが真剣に受け止められるとしたら，写真が提供する迫真性に匹敵するか，さらにそれを越えなくてはならないだろう。
>
> 　スーパーリアリズムの絵画は，抽象画家たちが使った衝動的で即興的なテクニックとは全く対照的に，細部まで行き届いた筆の運びで丹念に描かれ，形づくられた。絵画は現実世界を忠実に提示しようとしたばかりでなく，特に表現するのが難しい対象を選んだ。ダイナー（軽食レストラン）は，その状況がクロムメッキやガラスといった反射面を描く多くの機会を提供してくれたため，一般的な題材だった。それらがよく使われたのは，スーパーリアリストたちが日常的な状況や題材を選ぶ傾向があったからだ。風景画は都会や郊外のありふれた状況が好まれ，肖像画では魅力のない人々が描かれた。
>
> 　その運動は今日，形を変えて生き残っており，ハイパーリアリズムと呼ばれることが多い。彫刻がその運動の大部分で，ジョン・デ・アンドレアやドゥエイン・ハンソンのような芸術家たちが，動揺させるほど正確な人体彫刻を製作している。ロン・ミュエクは実際の人々のサイズより10倍大きい写実的な人間を描写した桁外れな彫像で，特に悪評を得た。対象の欠点や不完全さが全て大規模に引き延ばされ，人間のありのままの姿を見る者に突きつけるのだ。

31. 解答 A　Purpose Question

著者はなぜ1960年代のアメリカに言及しているか。

(A) スーパーリアリストたちの芸術的背景を説明するため
(B) 芸術を変えた新しい技術革新について述べるため
(C) スーパーリアリスト運動の落ちこみの要因を示すため
(D) この新しい芸術の試みに対するヨーロッパの影響を軽く扱うため

解説 1960年代のアメリカについては，第2段落第2文に「抽象表現主義が優勢な芸術パラダイムであった1960年代のアメリカにおいて，スーパーリアリストと呼ばれる芸術家たちのグループが，リアリズムの役割を引き継いだ」とある。この内容に合う (A) が正解。

32. 解答 A　Factual Question

パッセージによると，カメラは

(A) 芸術家たちの優先事項を変えた
(B) 画家たちが芸術を洗練させるのを助けた
(C) 描写主義の芸術に対する需要が増すのを促した
(D) 抽象芸術を時代遅れにした

解説 カメラが登場した結果については，Consequently で始まる第1段落第4文で説明されている。「その結果，画家たちはどんどん抽象的で主観的な作品を作り始めた」とあり，(A) がこの内容に一致する。

33. 解答 A　Inference Question

パッセージから推測できるのは，芸術運動は

(A) たいてい先立つ運動とは対照的である
(B) たいてい写実主義から抽象主義へと変化する
(C) 巨匠たちが確立した伝統を無視する傾向にある
(D) 新しいテクノロジーを利用したがらない

解説 第2段落第1文に Of course, all art movements are reactionary and eventually the pendulum swung the other way.「もちろん，全ての芸術活動は反動的であり，やがて振り子は反対側に振れた」とある。(A) が正解。第1段落で写実主義から抽象主義への変化に言及しているが，現代にも当てはまる一般論ではないので，(B) は不適切。

34. 解答 C Factual Question

パッセージによると，スーパーリアリズムの絵画は傾向として

(A) 短時間で完成した
(B) 法外な値が付いた
(C) 日常的な場面を表現した
(D) 絵を描くために芸術家のチームを要した

[解説] 第3段落第4文に They were also used frequently since Photorealists tended to choose settings and subjects that were mundane.「それらがよく使われたのは，スーパーリアリストたちが日常的な状況や題材を選ぶ傾向があったからだ」とある。これに合う (C) が正解。

35. 解答 C Reference Question

14行目の they という言葉が指すのは

(A) 19世紀の絵画の巨匠たち
(B) 古いリアリストたち
(C) スーパーリアリストたち
(D) カメラ

[解説] they would have to match or even exceed the verisimilitude that photography offered「写真が提供する迫真性に匹敵するか，さらにそれを越えなくてはならないだろう」とある。写真の迫真性に挑むのは If 節の主語である Photorealists「スーパーリアリストたち」のはず。(C) が正解。

36. 解答 D Vocabulary Question

22行目の mundane という言葉に最も近い意味は

(A) 美しい
(B) 珍しい
(C) 現代的な
(D) 日常的な

[解説] 次の文に，風景画は commonplace「ありふれた」状況が好まれ，肖像画は unattractive「魅力のない」人々が描かれた，とある。この内容に合う (D) が正解。mundane は「平凡な，ありきたりの」という意味。

37.　解答　B　　Vocabulary Question

27行目の unnerving という言葉に最も近い意味は

(A) 関連づけられる
(B) ぎょっとさせる
(C) 壮大な
(D) 退屈な

解説　unnerving は，動詞 nerve「〜を勇気づける」に否定や反対の意味を表す接頭辞 un- が付いて -ing 形になったもので，「動揺させるような」という意味。これに最も意味が近いのは (B)。

38.　解答　C　　Inference Question

パッセージが示唆するには，現代のスーパーリアリズム運動の形は

(A) ヨーロッパではより広く普及している
(B) とても小さな規模へと縮小している
(C) 主として異なる材料を使っている
(D) 大きく異なる題材を描いている

解説　incarnation は「ある時期の姿（形）」という意味。この意味がわからなくても current という語から，スーパーリアリズムの現状を表す選択肢を選ぶ。その説明があるのは最終段落で The movement survives today in an altered state「その運動は今日，形を変えて生き残っている」，Sculpture is a much larger part of the movement「彫刻がその運動の大部分である」とある。この内容に合う (C) が正解。

39. 解答 C Where Question

著者はパッセージのどこでスーパーリアリストたちが対抗しなければならなかった基準に言及しているか。

(A) 5～7行目
(B) 9～11行目
(C) 13～14行目
(D) 15～17行目

[解説] 第2段落最終文にスーパーリアリストたちが対抗しなければならなかったものについて説明があり，具体的には the verisimilitude that photography offered「写真が提供する迫真性」である。正解は (C)。

40. 解答 A Where Question

次の語句のうち著者が説明をしているものはどれか。

(A) スーパーリアリスティックな絵画
(B) 筆遣い
(C) 魅力のない人々
(D) 表現主義

[解説] (B) は第3段落第1文，(C) は第3段落最終文に出てくるが，その説明はない。(D) については，第2段落第2文の abstract expressionism に関する説明が第1段落にあるが，expressionism「表現主義」そのものの説明はない。第3段落で詳しく説明されている (A) が正解。

Questions 41-50

> **パッセージの訳**

　携帯電話ゲーム市場は，プレー無料のゲームで占められている。ダウンロードするのにはお金がかからないが，体験内容をよりよくするためにお金を費やす機会がプレーヤーに与えられるゲームである。プレーをスピードアップさせたり，特典をもらえたりするゲーム内のアイテムにお金を費やすことができるのだ。多人数参加型ゲームの中には，そうしたアイテムをほかのチームメイトに贈って，敵に勝つチャンスを助けたりできるものもある。理論的には，無料でプレーできるゲームモデルは，お金を費やす前にプレーヤーにゲームを試させていて，それによって彼らは気に入ったかどうかを支払い前に決めることができるわけだ。

　実際のところ，多くのプレーヤーは結局お金を一切払わない。有料アイテムが与えてくれる特典なしでゲームの障害物をとぼとぼと進むか，ゲームをやめてほかの無料ゲームに移るかする。お金を払う人も，ほとんどが少額でしかなく，1つのゲームが支払いを求める前金と同じぐらいの料金だ。しかし，それらの無料ゲームが，最高売上げチャートの首位を占めるのだ。そのお金はどこから来るのだろうか。

　そうしたゲームは，主に「クジラ」たちからお金を得ている。平均的プレーヤーよりもはるかに多くのお金を費やすプレーヤーたちだ。クジラであるための出発点に立つには，1つのゲームに1カ月100ドル以上費やすべきなのだが，1カ月に数千ドル費やす者もいる。そうしたプレーヤーたちがゲームプレーヤー層に占める部分は，しばしば1%にも満たず極めて小さいが，ゲームの収益の半分以上を占める。

　ゲームメーカーにとって，クジラはもうかるが不安定な資金源だ。クジラがお金を費やす1つの理由は，彼らがほかのプレーヤーたちに及ぼす影響のためだ。彼らは戦いにおいて敵を支配できるし，チームメイトに多大な援助も与えられる。ある意味，ほかのプレーヤーたちはクジラにとって「コンテンツ」なのだ。クジラは，ほかのプレーヤーに対する権力の座を占めていることを楽しむ。しかし，クジラたちはあまりにも強く，普通のプレーヤーたちの特権が奪われかねない。成功するためにお金を払ったクジラたちに叩きのめされるだけだとしたら，誰が遊びたがるだろうか。もしお金を払わないプレーヤーたちがゲームをやめたら，クジラたちには力を誇示する相手がいなくなる。するとクジラたちもゲームをやめてしまい，事業全体が崩壊することになるのだ。

41. 解答 D Purpose Question

第1段落の主な目的は何か。

(A) 古典的なゲームと現代のゲームを比較すること
(B) 携帯電話ゲームを作ることでよく陥る落とし穴を示すこと
(C) 典型的なクジラの経歴を提供すること
(D) 無料ゲームの範囲を提示すること

[解説] 第1段落は，パッセージの導入として無料ゲームがどういうものかを説明している。正解は (D) で，the parameters of 〜 で「〜の範囲」という意味。(A) と (B) について説明がない。(C) は第3, 4段落に出てくる内容。

42. 解答 D Vocabulary Question

3行目の enhance という言葉に最も近い意味は

(A) つまらなくする
(B) 添付する
(C) 長くする
(D) 改善する

[解説] 冒頭で，無料ゲームについて … but provide opportunities for players to spend money to enhance their experience「体験を enhance するためにお金を費やす機会がプレーヤーに与えられる」と説明しており，お金を払う目的は，経験を「楽しいものにする，よりよいものにする」ためだと推測できる。正解は (D) で，enhance は「〜を高める，よりよくする」という意味。

43. 解答 C Factual Question

パッセージによると，携帯電話ゲームが得るお金の大半は

(A) 非常に少額の取引からである
(B) ゲームのデザイン変更からである
(C) プレーヤーたちのごく一部からである
(D) ゲーム内の広告からである

[解説] 第2段落の最後に「そのお金はどこから来るのだろうか」とあるので第3段落を注意して読むと，第1文でゲームに多くのお金を費やす「クジラ」に言及している。そして最終文には，these players make up a miniscule amount of a game's player base「そうしたプレーヤーたち (＝クジラ) がゲームプレーヤー層に占める部分は極めて小さい」とあるので，(C) が正解。

44. 解答 **B**　Factual Question

パッセージによると，無料ゲームのプレーヤーの大部分は

(A) ゲームを終える
(B) お金を全く払わない
(C) 複数のゲームをする
(D) 若いプレーヤーである

解説　第2段落第1文に In practice, many players end up not paying at all.「実際のところ，多くのプレーヤーは結局お金を一切払わない」とある。従って (B) が正解。(A) は第2段落第2文後半の内容に合わない。(C) と (D) について本文で言及されていない。

45. 解答 **D**　Purpose Question

著者はなぜ最高売上げチャートに言及しているか。

(A) 携帯電話ゲームではあまりお金がもうからないということを証明するため
(B) マンガが元になったゲームがどのように一番人気になったかを示すため
(C) 携帯電話ゲームでの成功を測るのがどれほど難しいかを示すため
(D) 無料のゲームがどれほどお金になるかを証明するため

解説　the top-grossing charts に言及しているのは第2段落の最後から2つ目の文。お金を一切払わない，あるいは払っても少額のプレーヤーばかりであるという状況を説明した上で，「しかし，それらの無料ゲームが，最高売上げチャートの首位を占めるのだ」と言っている。つまり，(D) のためだと考えられる。(A) は反対の内容。(B) と (C) については言及されていない。

46. 解答 **A**　Vocabulary Question

15行目の on the threshold という言い回しに最も近い意味は

(A) 出発点に
(B) 限度を超えて
(C) 方向に
(D) 味方に

解説　「クジラであるための on the threshold になるには，1つのゲームに1カ月100ドル以上費やすべきなのだが…」という内容。(C), (D) はこの内容に合わず，不自然。(B) はその後の「数千ドル費やすものもいる」の内容につながらないので，誤り。正解は (A)。threshold は「出発点，入り口」という意味。

47. 解答 C Inference Question

パッセージが示唆するには，お金を払わないプレーヤーたちが重要である理由は彼らが

(A) ゲーム内の広告を見るからである
(B) 彼らの友だちにゲームについて話すからである
(C) クジラの敵の役割を果たすからである
(D) ゲームに基づいた商品を買うからである

解説　お金を払わないプレーヤーの重要性については最終段落に「クジラ」との関係から説明があり，「クジラ」にとっては力を見せつける相手としてお金を払わないプレーヤーが必要であることが分かる。従って (C) が正解。

48. 解答 B Vocabulary Question

23行目の occupying という言葉に最も近い意味は

(A) 裏切ること
(B) 住むこと
(C) 発見すること
(D) 短縮すること

解説　occupy は「～を占有する，～に居住する」という意味。「(ある場所) に住む」という意味の (B) が正解。(A) と (D) は目的語の this place of power と合わない。occupy に「～を見つける」といった意味はないので，(C) も誤り。

49. 解答 A　Inference Question

パッセージから示唆できるのは，携帯電話ゲームでもうける現在の方法は

(A) 不安定だ
(B) 旧式だ
(C) 前途有望だ
(D) 費用がかかる

[解説] the current method for making money in phone games とは「クジラ」に頼った事業運営のこと。最終段落最後の2文から，こうした事業はお金を払わないプレーヤーがいなくなれば収入源である「クジラ」もいなくなり，事業全体が崩壊してしまうことが分かる。また，同段落第1文では「クジラ」を tenuous「不安定な，もろい」と形容している。(A) が正解。

50. 解答 C　Other Question (Organization)

次のうちパッセージの構成を最もよく表しているものはどれか。

(A) 著者は仮説を述べ，それを立証する証拠を上げ，それに対する議論で締めくくっている。
(B) 著者は事例研究を紹介し，出来事がどのように起こるかを詳述し，結論を述べている。
(C) 著者は典型を提示し，その機能を説明し，次にその典型の問題を提示している。
(D) 著者は質問をし，複数の情報源からの考えられる答えを並べ，最もよい答えを選んでいる。

[解説] このパッセージは，第1段落で無料ゲームの概略を説明し，第2〜3段落でその収益構造について詳しく述べ，最後の段落では「クジラ」に頼る無料ゲーム事業の危うさに言及している。つまり (C) が正解。

CHAPTER 3
重要語彙リスト

パッセージに出てきた重要語彙

【Lesson 1】

☐	float	動	浮く
☐	static	形	静的な
☐	backlash	名	反動；反感
☐	overrun	動	はびこる，群がる
☐	platform	名	(政党・候補者の) 政綱，綱領
☐	notably	副	著しく，とりわけ
☐	slavery	名	奴隷制度
☐	bootleg	名	密造；密売
☐	law enforcement		警察，法執行機関
☐	distill	動	蒸留する
☐	testament	名	証拠，証明
☐	bygone	形	過ぎ去った，過去の
☐	incentive	名	動機づけ，誘因
☐	exploit	動	利用する；開発する
☐	grant	動	与える，許可する
☐	stifle	動	抑える；窒息させる
☐	molten	形	溶けた，溶解した
☐	realm	名	領域，範囲
☐	axis	名	地軸；軸
☐	amass	動	集める，蓄積する

【Lesson 2】

- [ ] traction 　　　　　　　名 支持；牽引力
- [ ] demolish 　　　　　　　動 取り壊す，破壊する
- [ ] specimen 　　　　　　　名 見本
- [ ] consumption 　　　　　 名 消費
- [ ] miniscule 　　　　　　 形 非常に小さい
- [ ] appraise 　　　　　　　動 評価する，鑑定する，査定する
- [ ] attribute 　　　　　　　名 特性
- [ ] gemstone 　　　　　　　名 宝石の原石
- [ ] innate 　　　　　　　　形 本来の；持って生まれた
- [ ] ubiquitous 　　　　　　形 至る所にある，偏在する
- [ ] ridge 　　　　　　　　　名 隆起；山の背
- [ ] stuff 　　　　　　　　　動 詰め物をする
- [ ] ingredient 　　　　　　名 食材；原料
- [ ] geographic 　　　　　　形 地理学的な
- [ ] address 　　　　　　　　動 （問題などに）取り組む，対処する
- [ ] boundary 　　　　　　　名 境界
- [ ] electoral 　　　　　　　形 選挙の
- [ ] demographics 　　　　　名 人口統計，特定の人口集団
- [ ] ethnicity 　　　　　　　名 民族性
- [ ] wedge 　　　　　　　　　名 くさび，くさび形のもの

CHAPTER 3　重要語彙リスト

239

【Lesson 3】

☐	long-haul	形 長距離（長期）に渡る
☐	arguably	副 議論の余地はあるかもしれないが
☐	definitely	副 確かに，明確に
☐	perilous	形 危険な
☐	challenging	形 困難な，能力が試される
☐	summit	動 登頂する
☐	treacherous	形 油断ならない，危険な
☐	prize	名 称号；賞
☐	lethal	形 死を招く，致死的な
☐	claim	動 （人命を）奪う；主張する
☐	ascent	名 登山；上昇
☐	shatter	名 粉砕　動 粉砕する
☐	significant	形 重要な
☐	mass-produced	形 大量生産された
☐	quartz	名 石英，クォーツ
☐	accurately	副 正確に
☐	notification	名 通知，告知
☐	owl	名 フクロウ
☐	burst	名 爆発，破裂
☐	metaphor	名 隠喩，比喩

【Lesson 4】

- [ ] oath　　　　　　　　名 誓い
- [ ] uphold　　　　　　　動 維持する；支持する
- [ ] empathy　　　　　　名 感情移入，共感
- [ ] astounding　　　　　形 びっくり仰天させるような
- [ ] bill　　　　　　　　名 (鳥の)くちばし
- [ ] nectar　　　　　　　名 (花の)蜜
- [ ] streak　　　　　　　名 筋，しま
- [ ] meteor　　　　　　　名 流星
- [ ] friction　　　　　　名 摩擦
- [ ] debris　　　　　　　名 破片，残骸
- [ ] orbit　　　　　　　名 軌道
- [ ] meteorite　　　　　名 (地球に落下した)隕石
- [ ] helix　　　　　　　名 らせん
- [ ] physiology　　　　　名 生理学
- [ ] supervision　　　　名 監督，管理
- [ ] downplay　　　　　　動 軽く扱う
- [ ] restrain　　　　　　動 抑える，抑止する
- [ ] insane　　　　　　　形 正気でない，心神喪失の
- [ ] institutionalize　　動 施設に収容する
- [ ] renovation　　　　　名 改修，修復

241

【Lesson 5】

- [ ] condemn — 動 有罪判決を下す；非難する
- [ ] augment — 動 増加させる，増強させる
- [ ] embed — 動 埋め込む
- [ ] advocate — 名 主張者，擁護者　動 主張する
- [ ] inept — 形 不器用な，適性に欠ける
- [ ] excel — 動 優れる
- [ ] prompt — 動 促す，きっかけを与える
- [ ] transmissible — 形 伝染性の
- [ ] radiation — 名 放射線，放射能
- [ ] agent — 名 媒介者，仲介者
- [ ] devastating — 形 破壊的な，衝撃的な
- [ ] tumor — 名 腫瘍
- [ ] eventually — 副 結局，最後には
- [ ] integral — 形 不可欠の
- [ ] ingest — 動 摂取する
- [ ] infect — 動 感染させる
- [ ] endangered — 形 絶滅の危機に瀕した
- [ ] tribe — 名 部族
- [ ] persecution — 名 迫害
- [ ] affiliation — 名 (政治的な)所属，友好関係

【Lesson 6】

- [ ] layer　　　　　　動 層にする　　名 層
- [ ] carve　　　　　　動 彫る，彫刻する
- [ ] fragility　　　　　名 もろさ，壊れやすさ
- [ ] intact　　　　　　形 手を触れていない，無傷の
- [ ] alternative　　　名 代替となるもの
- [ ] prevalent　　　　形 広まっている
- [ ] chariot　　　　　名 二輪馬車
- [ ] implement　　　　動 実用化する；実行する
- [ ] diverse　　　　　形 多様な
- [ ] sync　　　　　　動 同調する
- [ ] dynasty　　　　　名 王朝
- [ ] populace　　　　名 大衆，(地域の)全民衆
- [ ] fabric　　　　　　名 構造；織物
- [ ] ethical　　　　　形 倫理的な
- [ ] quandary　　　　名 困難，難局
- [ ] emergency　　　　名 非常事態，緊急事態
- [ ] injury　　　　　名 傷害，けが
- [ ] pedestrian　　　名 歩行者
- [ ] swerve　　　　　動 急に向きを変える
- [ ] culpable　　　　　形 過失のある，咎められるべき

【Lesson 7】

- [ ] knot — 名 結び目
- [ ] symmetrical — 形 左右対称の
- [ ] prestigious — 形 名声のある
- [ ] expertise — 名 専門的技術, 専門知識
- [ ] refuel — 動 燃料を補給する
- [ ] entire — 形 全体の
- [ ] disallow — 動 許さない, 禁ずる
- [ ] elongate — 動 伸ばす
- [ ] properly — 副 適切に
- [ ] diabetes — 名 糖尿病
- [ ] artificial — 形 人工の
- [ ] downside — 名 否定的側面
- [ ] substitute — 名 代用物
- [ ] abandon — 動 捨てる, やめる
- [ ] ban — 動 禁じる
- [ ] commonplace — 形 ごく普通の
- [ ] designate — 動 指定する

【Lesson 8】

- [ ] mass — 名 (the masses) 大衆
- [ ] lead — 名 鉛
- [ ] graphite — 名 黒鉛

☐ brittle	形 もろい	
☐ encase	動 ～を入れ物に入れる，包む	
☐ experimentation	名 実験	
☐ methodology	名 方法論，手順	
☐ inventor	名 発明家	
☐ botanist	名 植物学者	
☐ reject	動 拒否する	
☐ numerous	形 多数の	
☐ combustion	名 燃焼	
☐ make strides	大きく飛躍する	
☐ hydrogen	名 水素	
☐ surpass	動 勝る，超える	
☐ solution	名 解決策	

【Lesson 9】

☐ monastery	名 修道院，僧院	
☐ brew	動 (ビールなどを)醸造する	
☐ predominant	形 支配的な，有力な	
☐ herd	動 群れを先導する　名 群れ	
☐ retrieve	動 (獲物を)捜して持ってくる	
☐ institution	名 団体，組織；施設	
☐ breed	名 品種，種　動 品種改良する	
☐ exaggerate	動 強調する	

☐	preoccupation	名	関心，没頭
☐	aesthetics	名	美学
☐	chronic	形	慢性の
☐	ailment	名	病気
☐	compound	名	化合物，混合物
☐	render	動	…を〜にする
☐	digestive	形	消化の
☐	propagate	動	繁殖させる
☐	on the fly		急いで；準備なしに
☐	superstition	名	迷信
☐	synonym	名	同意語
☐	prohibition	名	禁止

【Lesson 10】

☐	oat	名	(oats) えん麦，オート
☐	overall	形	全体の
☐	joust	動	馬上やり合戦をする
☐	wizard	名	魔法使い；天才
☐	mythical	形	神話の，架空の
☐	creature	名	生き物
☐	reenactment	名	再演，再現
☐	landmark	名	(陸上の) 目印となるもの
☐	lean	動	傾く

☐	clay	名	粘土
☐	halt	動	停止させる
☐	stabilize	動	安定させる
☐	resident	名	住人
☐	anticlimactically	副	盛り上がらないことに，面白くないことに
☐	bullet	名	弾丸
☐	lavish	形	ぜいたくな，豪華な
☐	spectacle	名	見世物
☐	choreograph	動	振り付けをする
☐	neoclassical	形	新古典主義の
☐	incorporate	動	組み込む，合体させる

【Practice Test 1 (1-10)】

☐	disorder	名	障害，不調
☐	genetics	名	遺伝学
☐	defect	名	欠陥
☐	perceive	動	気付く，知覚する
☐	chromosome	名	染色体
☐	faulty	形	欠点のある，不完全な
☐	inject	動	注入する，注射する
☐	infection	名	感染
☐	exacerbate	動	悪化させる
☐	immunity	名	免疫

【Practice Test 1 (11-20)】

☐	manifestation	名 現れ；表明
☐	distinct	形 まったく異なる
☐	settlement	名 入植地
☐	somber	形 地味な
☐	anarchist	名 無政府主義者
☐	self-sufficient	形 自給自足の
☐	scarce	形 不足して
☐	dissolve	動 解散する；分解する
☐	succession	名 継承；連続
☐	dispute	名 論争　動 論争する

【Practice Test 1 (21-30)】

☐	mythology	名 神話学；神話
☐	anthropologist	名 人類学者
☐	propagate	動 広まる；繁殖させる
☐	surmise	動 推測する
☐	ancestor	名 祖先
☐	heritage	名 遺産
☐	fascination	名 魅せられた状態；魅力
☐	trait	名 特徴
☐	impose	動 課する，押し付ける
☐	archetype	名 原型，典型例

【Practice Test 1 (31-39)】

- [ ] tier　　　　　　　動 段々に積む　名 段
- [ ] archaeologist　　名 考古学者
- [ ] capable　　　　　形 能力のある
- [ ] feat　　　　　　　名 功績，偉業
- [ ] dominate　　　　動 大部分を占める；支配する
- [ ] crescent　　　　　名 三日月
- [ ] perimeter　　　　名 周囲，周辺
- [ ] forage　　　　　動 食糧を探す；探し回る
- [ ] astrological　　　形 占星術の
- [ ] artifact　　　　　名 工芸品；遺物

【Practice Test 1 (40-50)】

- [ ] rigorous　　　　　形 厳密な
- [ ] protocol　　　　　名 儀礼；実施要領
- [ ] solicit　　　　　動 強く求める，要請する
- [ ] batch　　　　　　名 一群
- [ ] subject　　　　　名 被験者
- [ ] minimal　　　　　形 最小限の
- [ ] efficacy　　　　　名 効果
- [ ] placebo　　　　　名 偽薬（効果）
- [ ] anomaly　　　　　名 異常，異例
- [ ] eligible　　　　　形 資格のある

【Practice Test 2 (1-10)】

- ☐ propel — 動 推進する
- ☐ vicious — 形 悪い
- ☐ destination — 名 目的地
- ☐ radiation — 名 放射線, 放射能
- ☐ exert — 動 (力などを) 用いる, 行使する
- ☐ negligible — 形 取るに足らない, ささいな
- ☐ vacuum — 名 真空
- ☐ manned — 形 人を乗せた, 有人の
- ☐ emerging — 形 新興の
- ☐ shortcoming — 名 欠点

【Practice Test 2 (11-20)】

- ☐ colony — 名 植民地
- ☐ prominent — 形 有名な; 卓越した
- ☐ load — 動 (荷を) 積む
- ☐ immensely — 副 とても, 大いに
- ☐ mine — 名 鉱山
- ☐ porcelain — 名 磁器
- ☐ attract — 動 引きつける
- ☐ prominence — 名 目立つこと; 卓越
- ☐ vibrant — 形 活気に満ちた
- ☐ hub — 名 中心

【Practice Test 2 (21-30)】

☐ myriad	形	無数の
☐ fairly	副	かなり
☐ compromise	動	折衷する；妥協する
☐ asymmetric	形	非対称の
☐ discrepancy	名	相違，差異
☐ ware	名	売り物，商品
☐ identical	形	まったく同じ，そっくりの
☐ aphorism	名	格言，警句
☐ conundrum	名	難問，謎
☐ degrade	動	下げる，落とす

【Practice Test 2 (31-40)】

☐ legion	名	一群；軍団
☐ ardent	形	熱烈な
☐ devotion	名	深い愛情，献身
☐ proliferation	名	急増；拡散
☐ prodigy	名	神童，天才児
☐ renowned	形	著名な
☐ accomplished	形	優れた，熟練の
☐ arrogant	形	傲慢な
☐ adore	動	熱愛する
☐ engrave	動	彫る，刻む

CHAPTER 3 重要語彙リスト

【Practice Test 2 (41-50)】

- ☐ strain — 動 ろ過する；痛める
- ☐ nutrient — 名 栄養物
- ☐ colossal — 形 巨大な
- ☐ perception — 名 認知
- ☐ precedent — 名 先例
- ☐ inexplicable — 形 説明できない
- ☐ microbe — 名 微生物
- ☐ intriguing — 形 興味深い，おもしろい
- ☐ evolve — 動 進化する
- ☐ entity — 名 存在，実体

【Practice Test 3 (1-10)】

- ☐ alleviate — 動 軽減する，緩和する
- ☐ prevalent — 形 広く行き渡った，普及している
- ☐ utilize — 動 利用する，役立たせる
- ☐ augment — 動 増加させる，増強させる
- ☐ reinforce — 動 補強する
- ☐ evaporate — 動 蒸発する
- ☐ humidity — 名 湿気
- ☐ arid — 形 乾燥した，不毛の
- ☐ irrigation — 名 かんがい
- ☐ condense — 動 凝縮する

【Practice Test 3 (11-20)】

☐	adversary	名 敵
☐	gridlock	名 停滞, 行き詰まりの状態
☐	consolidate	動 合併整理する
☐	lucrative	形 もうかる, 金になる
☐	deter	動 やめさせる, 阻止する
☐	enchant	動 うっとりさせる
☐	bribe	動 賄賂を送る
☐	prestige	名 威信；名声
☐	astronomical	形 天文学的な
☐	plummet	動 急落する

【Practice Test 3 (21-30)】

☐	venomous	形 有毒な
☐	predator	名 捕食者
☐	dazzle	動 目をくらませる, 幻惑させる
☐	stun	動 気絶させる；ぼうっとさせる
☐	mute	動 色調を弱める；音を消す　形 無言の
☐	comparatively	副 比較的に
☐	flashy	形 派手な, けばけばしい
☐	evade	動 避ける, 逃げる
☐	imitate	動 まねる, 似せて作る
☐	deadly	形 致命的な

【Practice Test 3 (31-40)】

- ☐ profound — 形 深い；重大な
- ☐ constraint — 名 制約
- ☐ pendulum — 名 振り子
- ☐ painstakingly — 副 入念に，労を惜しまずに
- ☐ meticulous — 形 細かな
- ☐ portray — 動 表現する，描く
- ☐ reflective — 形 反射する；思慮深い
- ☐ mundane — 形 平凡な，ありふれた
- ☐ massive — 形 大きな
- ☐ confront — 動 直面する，向かい合う

【Practice Test 3 (41-50)】

- ☐ enhance — 動 (質を)高める
- ☐ opponent — 名 敵
- ☐ obstacle — 名 障害
- ☐ top-grossing — 形 興行収入(売上げ)トップの
- ☐ threshold — 名 出発点，境界，閾値
- ☐ miniscule — 形 非常に小さい
- ☐ revenue — 名 収益
- ☐ tenuous — 形 もろい，薄い；乏しい
- ☐ enterprise — 名 事業，企て
- ☐ collapse — 動 崩壊する

Answer Sheet

	EXAMPLE				
	CORRECT	INCORRECT	INCORRECT	INCORRECT	INCORRECT
	Ⓐ Ⓑ ● Ⓓ	Ⓐ Ⓑ ✓ Ⓓ	Ⓐ Ⓑ ✗ Ⓓ	Ⓐ Ⓑ • Ⓓ	Ⓐ Ⓑ Ⓒ Ⓓ

Practice Test 1

1 Ⓐ Ⓑ Ⓒ Ⓓ	16 Ⓐ Ⓑ Ⓒ Ⓓ	31 Ⓐ Ⓑ Ⓒ Ⓓ	46 Ⓐ Ⓑ Ⓒ Ⓓ
2 Ⓐ Ⓑ Ⓒ Ⓓ	17 Ⓐ Ⓑ Ⓒ Ⓓ	32 Ⓐ Ⓑ Ⓒ Ⓓ	47 Ⓐ Ⓑ Ⓒ Ⓓ
3 Ⓐ Ⓑ Ⓒ Ⓓ	18 Ⓐ Ⓑ Ⓒ Ⓓ	33 Ⓐ Ⓑ Ⓒ Ⓓ	48 Ⓐ Ⓑ Ⓒ Ⓓ
4 Ⓐ Ⓑ Ⓒ Ⓓ	19 Ⓐ Ⓑ Ⓒ Ⓓ	34 Ⓐ Ⓑ Ⓒ Ⓓ	49 Ⓐ Ⓑ Ⓒ Ⓓ
5 Ⓐ Ⓑ Ⓒ Ⓓ	20 Ⓐ Ⓑ Ⓒ Ⓓ	35 Ⓐ Ⓑ Ⓒ Ⓓ	50 Ⓐ Ⓑ Ⓒ Ⓓ
6 Ⓐ Ⓑ Ⓒ Ⓓ	21 Ⓐ Ⓑ Ⓒ Ⓓ	36 Ⓐ Ⓑ Ⓒ Ⓓ	
7 Ⓐ Ⓑ Ⓒ Ⓓ	22 Ⓐ Ⓑ Ⓒ Ⓓ	37 Ⓐ Ⓑ Ⓒ Ⓓ	
8 Ⓐ Ⓑ Ⓒ Ⓓ	23 Ⓐ Ⓑ Ⓒ Ⓓ	38 Ⓐ Ⓑ Ⓒ Ⓓ	
9 Ⓐ Ⓑ Ⓒ Ⓓ	24 Ⓐ Ⓑ Ⓒ Ⓓ	39 Ⓐ Ⓑ Ⓒ Ⓓ	
10 Ⓐ Ⓑ Ⓒ Ⓓ	25 Ⓐ Ⓑ Ⓒ Ⓓ	40 Ⓐ Ⓑ Ⓒ Ⓓ	
11 Ⓐ Ⓑ Ⓒ Ⓓ	26 Ⓐ Ⓑ Ⓒ Ⓓ	41 Ⓐ Ⓑ Ⓒ Ⓓ	
12 Ⓐ Ⓑ Ⓒ Ⓓ	27 Ⓐ Ⓑ Ⓒ Ⓓ	42 Ⓐ Ⓑ Ⓒ Ⓓ	
13 Ⓐ Ⓑ Ⓒ Ⓓ	28 Ⓐ Ⓑ Ⓒ Ⓓ	43 Ⓐ Ⓑ Ⓒ Ⓓ	
14 Ⓐ Ⓑ Ⓒ Ⓓ	29 Ⓐ Ⓑ Ⓒ Ⓓ	44 Ⓐ Ⓑ Ⓒ Ⓓ	
15 Ⓐ Ⓑ Ⓒ Ⓓ	30 Ⓐ Ⓑ Ⓒ Ⓓ	45 Ⓐ Ⓑ Ⓒ Ⓓ	

キリトリ線

Practice Test 2

1 Ⓐ Ⓑ Ⓒ Ⓓ	16 Ⓐ Ⓑ Ⓒ Ⓓ	31 Ⓐ Ⓑ Ⓒ Ⓓ	46 Ⓐ Ⓑ Ⓒ Ⓓ
2 Ⓐ Ⓑ Ⓒ Ⓓ	17 Ⓐ Ⓑ Ⓒ Ⓓ	32 Ⓐ Ⓑ Ⓒ Ⓓ	47 Ⓐ Ⓑ Ⓒ Ⓓ
3 Ⓐ Ⓑ Ⓒ Ⓓ	18 Ⓐ Ⓑ Ⓒ Ⓓ	33 Ⓐ Ⓑ Ⓒ Ⓓ	48 Ⓐ Ⓑ Ⓒ Ⓓ
4 Ⓐ Ⓑ Ⓒ Ⓓ	19 Ⓐ Ⓑ Ⓒ Ⓓ	34 Ⓐ Ⓑ Ⓒ Ⓓ	49 Ⓐ Ⓑ Ⓒ Ⓓ
5 Ⓐ Ⓑ Ⓒ Ⓓ	20 Ⓐ Ⓑ Ⓒ Ⓓ	35 Ⓐ Ⓑ Ⓒ Ⓓ	50 Ⓐ Ⓑ Ⓒ Ⓓ
6 Ⓐ Ⓑ Ⓒ Ⓓ	21 Ⓐ Ⓑ Ⓒ Ⓓ	36 Ⓐ Ⓑ Ⓒ Ⓓ	
7 Ⓐ Ⓑ Ⓒ Ⓓ	22 Ⓐ Ⓑ Ⓒ Ⓓ	37 Ⓐ Ⓑ Ⓒ Ⓓ	
8 Ⓐ Ⓑ Ⓒ Ⓓ	23 Ⓐ Ⓑ Ⓒ Ⓓ	38 Ⓐ Ⓑ Ⓒ Ⓓ	
9 Ⓐ Ⓑ Ⓒ Ⓓ	24 Ⓐ Ⓑ Ⓒ Ⓓ	39 Ⓐ Ⓑ Ⓒ Ⓓ	
10 Ⓐ Ⓑ Ⓒ Ⓓ	25 Ⓐ Ⓑ Ⓒ Ⓓ	40 Ⓐ Ⓑ Ⓒ Ⓓ	
11 Ⓐ Ⓑ Ⓒ Ⓓ	26 Ⓐ Ⓑ Ⓒ Ⓓ	41 Ⓐ Ⓑ Ⓒ Ⓓ	
12 Ⓐ Ⓑ Ⓒ Ⓓ	27 Ⓐ Ⓑ Ⓒ Ⓓ	42 Ⓐ Ⓑ Ⓒ Ⓓ	
13 Ⓐ Ⓑ Ⓒ Ⓓ	28 Ⓐ Ⓑ Ⓒ Ⓓ	43 Ⓐ Ⓑ Ⓒ Ⓓ	
14 Ⓐ Ⓑ Ⓒ Ⓓ	29 Ⓐ Ⓑ Ⓒ Ⓓ	44 Ⓐ Ⓑ Ⓒ Ⓓ	
15 Ⓐ Ⓑ Ⓒ Ⓓ	30 Ⓐ Ⓑ Ⓒ Ⓓ	45 Ⓐ Ⓑ Ⓒ Ⓓ	

Practice Test 3

1 Ⓐ Ⓑ Ⓒ Ⓓ	16 Ⓐ Ⓑ Ⓒ Ⓓ	31 Ⓐ Ⓑ Ⓒ Ⓓ	46 Ⓐ Ⓑ Ⓒ Ⓓ
2 Ⓐ Ⓑ Ⓒ Ⓓ	17 Ⓐ Ⓑ Ⓒ Ⓓ	32 Ⓐ Ⓑ Ⓒ Ⓓ	47 Ⓐ Ⓑ Ⓒ Ⓓ
3 Ⓐ Ⓑ Ⓒ Ⓓ	18 Ⓐ Ⓑ Ⓒ Ⓓ	33 Ⓐ Ⓑ Ⓒ Ⓓ	48 Ⓐ Ⓑ Ⓒ Ⓓ
4 Ⓐ Ⓑ Ⓒ Ⓓ	19 Ⓐ Ⓑ Ⓒ Ⓓ	34 Ⓐ Ⓑ Ⓒ Ⓓ	49 Ⓐ Ⓑ Ⓒ Ⓓ
5 Ⓐ Ⓑ Ⓒ Ⓓ	20 Ⓐ Ⓑ Ⓒ Ⓓ	35 Ⓐ Ⓑ Ⓒ Ⓓ	50 Ⓐ Ⓑ Ⓒ Ⓓ
6 Ⓐ Ⓑ Ⓒ Ⓓ	21 Ⓐ Ⓑ Ⓒ Ⓓ	36 Ⓐ Ⓑ Ⓒ Ⓓ	
7 Ⓐ Ⓑ Ⓒ Ⓓ	22 Ⓐ Ⓑ Ⓒ Ⓓ	37 Ⓐ Ⓑ Ⓒ Ⓓ	
8 Ⓐ Ⓑ Ⓒ Ⓓ	23 Ⓐ Ⓑ Ⓒ Ⓓ	38 Ⓐ Ⓑ Ⓒ Ⓓ	
9 Ⓐ Ⓑ Ⓒ Ⓓ	24 Ⓐ Ⓑ Ⓒ Ⓓ	39 Ⓐ Ⓑ Ⓒ Ⓓ	
10 Ⓐ Ⓑ Ⓒ Ⓓ	25 Ⓐ Ⓑ Ⓒ Ⓓ	40 Ⓐ Ⓑ Ⓒ Ⓓ	
11 Ⓐ Ⓑ Ⓒ Ⓓ	26 Ⓐ Ⓑ Ⓒ Ⓓ	41 Ⓐ Ⓑ Ⓒ Ⓓ	
12 Ⓐ Ⓑ Ⓒ Ⓓ	27 Ⓐ Ⓑ Ⓒ Ⓓ	42 Ⓐ Ⓑ Ⓒ Ⓓ	
13 Ⓐ Ⓑ Ⓒ Ⓓ	28 Ⓐ Ⓑ Ⓒ Ⓓ	43 Ⓐ Ⓑ Ⓒ Ⓓ	
14 Ⓐ Ⓑ Ⓒ Ⓓ	29 Ⓐ Ⓑ Ⓒ Ⓓ	44 Ⓐ Ⓑ Ⓒ Ⓓ	
15 Ⓐ Ⓑ Ⓒ Ⓓ	30 Ⓐ Ⓑ Ⓒ Ⓓ	45 Ⓐ Ⓑ Ⓒ Ⓓ	